EVER YOURS AFFLY

Acknowledgements

This book owes much to the Fathers of the Birmingham Oratory who gave me access to papers, pictures and photographs. The Archivist there, Gerard Tracey, has been described as 'immensely knowledgeable' and I gratefully endorse this and would add that he is unfailingly helpful to others. Other Archivists have been generous with time and trouble and I thank the National Trust and the volunteer Archivist at Baddesley Clinton, John Jarman, for information and for the portrait of Lady Chatterton. Also the Dominican Sisters at Stone, especially Sister Mary Hugh O.P. Meriol Trevor, the author of a great Newman biography, has been both helpful and encouraging and I thank her, too.

Acknowledgements are due to the Warden and Fellows of Keble College, Oxford and to the descendants of Newman's sister, Jemima Mozley (Eleanor and Margaret Miller and Geoffrey Thomas) for permission to include some of the illustrations. I should also like to thank Jo Ratcliffe, Gracewing Production Co-ordinator, and Carole Essex, typist. They helped me in the making of this book with singular cheerfulness.

EVER YOURS AFFLY

John Henry Newman
and His Female Circle

Gracewing.

First published in 1996

Gracewing
Fowler Wright Books
2 Southern Ave, Leominster
Herefordshire HR6 0QF

ISBN 0 85244 315 3

Typesetting by Action Typesetting Ltd,
Gloucester, GL1 1SP

Printed by Redwood Books,
Trowbridge, Wiltshire, BA14 8RN

Contents

Index to Illustrations

Preface

Newman has recently been called a misogynist, by academics who can't have read his letters written over many years to women friends, and theirs to him. Everyone knows the difficulties intelligent women faced in the nineteenth century in making their own lives, and these were exacerbated for those who became Catholics, often against the wishes of husbands or relations.

Joyce Sugg has searched out much information about these mostly forgotten women and their lives make fascinating reading. They called on Newman for sympathetic advice and assistance, often practical, as when he advised the indomitable and artistic Maria Giberne, when she was an old nun in France lacking teeth, not to swallow unmasticated meat – 'You are not an ostrich'. Such was the human and humorous nature of his friendship, but perhaps it was because they were women that he sometimes 'let out' to them his feelings on the trials and controversies among Catholics over, for instance, the Temporal Power of the Papacy and Papal Infallibility. Although he did not promote the movement for the emancipation of women, he encouraged his friends to sharpen and inform their minds, especially necessary in an age when they would have to meet the increasing influence of rationalists who denied the existence of God.

So Joyce Sugg, as well as exploring the lives of these Victorian women and presenting a lively narrative, opens up our understanding of Newman's personal character, aspects of which often go unnoticed by those who concentrate on his ideas and public actions.

Meriol Trevor

Introduction

Sometimes a book generates another book. This one grew from an anthology of Newman's letters that I put together, published by the Oxford University Press in 1983 as *A Packet of Letters*. The anthology was then translated into French, given a new introduction by André Bordeaux and published in Paris by Tequi, under the title *Choix de Lettres*. André Bordeaux said at one point that as a woman I had had a partiality for the letters Newman wrote to women. No woman likes to think that scholarly choice is dictated by gender! – but this comment set me thinking further. Yes, I had been deeply interested in this part of Newman's correspondence and I wanted to know more about this group of Victorian women.

Anyone, man or woman, would be conscious, when looking through the great tomes of the published *Letters and Diaries of John Henry Newman* that these letters are very numerous. They touch on the stories, the problems and the characters of a most assorted group. There are letters to his mother and sisters; to single women like Maria Rosina Giberne and Emily Bowles whom he had known since his tractarian days, when he was a clergyman of the Church of England, an Oxford don and one of the leaders of the Oxford Movement; letters to married women, the wives of his friends; to nuns and to a whole host of converts who wanted his help and advice when they were considering a change to the Roman Church or when they were trying to live as earnest Catholics.

They were all so different in character and in the circumstances of their lives but the similarities and the links were there too. They were nearly all converts to Rome, often experiencing a first conversion to the tenets of the Tractarians and then, after prolonged thought and study, asking to be received into the Church of Rome. It took courage to do this in an age when Catholics were still regarded with deep suspicion and it was particularly difficult for women who found it hard to break from their families or to oppose their husbands' ideas and beliefs. They were protected by the strong insistence on family ties but they were essentially dependant and found it hard to rebel. They were not all of the same social rank: Newman's friends range from the aristocratic Lady Georgiana Fullerton and the Duchess of Norfolk to Mary Holmes the governess, Eleanor Bretherton the daughter of a Birmingham business man and the wife of a struggling clerk, Margaret Hallahan who started life as a servant girl and Jane Todd who was a seamstress. In the main, however, they were 'ladies', women from the middle class and generally intelligent people who read seriously, followed sermons closely and studied ecclesiastical developments and debates. They were often highly literate although their education had been narrow and home-produced: they usually worked with a governess while their brothers went away to school and to university. It is surprising that not one of this group joined the movement for the emancipation of women and for their higher education. Probably part of the reason was that, as middle class ladies, they did not think in terms of the necessity for earning a living. Of course, their religious concerns (for they were all religiously minded) also kept them apart from what could be seen as a dangerous breaking away from social and church structures.

They inhabited a little world within Victorian England. The Catholics, particularly the converts, had very strong links with one another: they married people within the same circle, made friends with other converts, knew the same churches and the same priests. As I investigated these lives, I saw them more and more not as individual stories

but as pieces that make up a curious whole, a picture of
one section of the society of the mid-nineteenth century.
They shared the same concerns and they were all
admirable in their zeal, their prayerfulness and their
charity. Though they were not in general concerned with
politics and could not be called reformers, they laboured
mightily to improve the conditions of the underprivileged
in London, Birmingham, the industrial Midlands. The
theme of work for charitable relief is a constant thread in
the fabric: nuns, married women and spinsters all gave
themselves to it generously. The other constant in the
activities of these women was their passion for writing,
usually some kind of religious writing – poems, translations, saints' lives, memoirs and particularly novels. The
number of their publications is astonishing.

And of course they wrote letters. Because they wrote to
Newman who was both a great keeper of his own correspondence and such an intellectual and ecclesiastical giant
that every word he wrote is of abiding interest, many of
their letters have survived and a great many more of his to
them. These documents tell us much about him.
Newman's complex character is as many-faceted as a great
cut diamond and I have made no attempt to analyse the
different aspects of his nature, nor have I examined his
thought, though inevitably every piece of advice he gave or
even light comments on life and events bear the imprint of
his thinking. I have deemed it enough simply to present
him as a wise spiritual guide and a very good, sensitive,
loyal friend.

This may be a limited view of him but a presentation of
Newman as friend to a great many women is certainly due.
He has been presented and indeed is being presented as a
misogynist. A review of a recent book, (*The Convert
Cardinals: J.H. Newman and H.E. Manning* by David
Newsome, published by Murray, 1993) says of him that he
'recoiled from marriage' and goes on to speak of his 'rejection of half the human race'. The reviewer, (Paul Johnson
in the *Sunday Telegraph*, 26 September 1993) is, of course
summarising arguments in the book. Newman tells us in
the *Apologia* of an early conviction that he was destined for

a life of celibacy. He ratified his decision, never married and never fell in love with a woman. To speak positively – he led a dedicated life and sought God with great single-mindedness. He once set out the negative possibilities of the choice of a single life, saying that it could be unamiable and melancholy if chosen for the wrong reasons, if it were selected to be a state of independence or isolation or barren indolence or crushed affections. These are not the words of a man who was single because he recoiled from marriage. It is a good sign of having found and followed the right vocation when a man or woman mellows with the years. The young Newman was often priggish and some-times chilly but as an older man he was more relaxed and sympathetic in his pastoral care.

That he did not reject half the human race is obvious from the contents of the many letters he wrote to women. These friendships were well within the bounds of Victorian propriety and indeed his correspondents would not have had it otherwise, but he made real relationships. When he heard from strangers he was prompt and welcoming in reply and he had good friendships with those he knew well. In his abbreviations in letters (and there are some curious ones, such as 'Oy' for 'Oratory') he usually wrote, 'Ever yrs affly' – Affectionately. He meant the word and there is plenty of affection in his letters. Of course, much of the correspondence is concerned with religious teaching, advice, the promise of prayers and exhortations to prayer and confidence in God's love and the ladies hoped for just this kind of counsel. None of this religious guidance however, was given in the abstract but was tailored to the needs and situation of each individual and this meant sometimes that Newman's advice and help was practical rather than high-minded, kindly and not at all austere. When he wrote to Lavinia Wilson, an Anglican nun who had left her convent to become a Catholic and who was finding the transition a great strain, he was chiefly concerned that she should take things gently and look after herself. One of his most endearing letters was written to his great friend, Emily Bowles, who was living on a small income and who spent much of her time visiting and helping the poor in London. He sent her some money and said:

> I wish it to go in a special kind of charity, viz in the instrumenta, as I may call them, and operative methods, of your own good works – that is, not in meat and drink, and physic, or clothing of the needy, but (if you will not be angry with me) in *your* charitable cabs, charitable umbrellas, charitable boots, and all the wear and tear of a charitable person who without such wear and tear cannot do her charity.[1]

His women friends thought the world of him, were delighted when he was made a cardinal and at his death they would instantly have acclaimed him a saint if their opinion had been asked. They were generally only too anxious to set him on a pedestal and more than once he directly refused to be so revered, writing to one lady, Miss Munro, in 1850, 'I have nothing of a Saint about me.'[2] Reciprocity is part of friendship and it would be difficult to be on really friendly terms if one person were stereotyped as the saintly counsellor and the other as the humble recipient. Newman shared his thoughts and troubles with those he knew best and trusted, and he was a true friend to many, not a distant guide. Of course not all who wrote were part of this inner circle. It has often been acknowledged that he had great influence in his Anglican days, influence over those in Oxford and many others who knew him from books. One fact that emerges from the mass of correspondence written in his Catholic years is the way that people took it for granted that Newman could always be applied to. Only necessity took him from his 'nest' at the Oratory, and indeed had he accepted all the invitations to preach, to visit and to dine he would have done very little work. Yet his reputation and his ready pen kept him very much in contact. He created many concentric circles and on the outer ring were a host of women who wanted advice, to send a book they had written, to tell him that they had always profited from his sermons.

Even distant and passing acquaintances were rarely

forgotten and to the nearer friends he was very loyal. It would sometimes have been more comfortable to shed them, to retire into some priestly fastness where he did not have to concern himself with them. Of no one was this more true than of his friend, Maria Rosina Giberne (who probably used her second name, as 'Rosina Giberne' is on the flyleaf of her books, though her friends do refer to her as Maria). She herself was loyal, devoted and devout, but she was a singularly tiresome woman, exuberant, tactless and insensitive. She was emotionally immature and given to extremes and, though I have said that these women revered Newman so that they were not in danger of offending against propriety, it must be said that she was an exception. She could be embarrassingly silly and Newman needed to show much forbearance over the years. However, a friend she was and a friend she remained and he did not forget that she did him one great service, at cost to herself. She was a vivid character and in her way a joy.

I have generally called her 'Miss Giberne' and so with the others, using that formal address which was customary. Newman addressed these women formally, unless he wrote 'My Dear Child' and only to the children or to his sisters would he use a christian name. At home they often had pet names, Chattie, Isy, Mamo, Pysie, Gintle, so that there was a switch from a stately reverence to an affectionate diminishment. It is one tiny detail, significant however in the way such things are, demonstrating how matters have changed over the last hundred years or so. Life is very different for Christian women now, with new responsibilities, possibilities, difficulties. The Victorian Catholic ladies cannot be models, but they do often stir one's admiration.

Chapter One

The Family

*Mrs Newman, Harriett, Jemima and Mary Newman,
Maria Rosina Giberne; Mrs Newman, Harriett,
Jemima and Mary Newman at the time of the Oxford
Movement, Maria Rosina Giberne, Emily Bowles,
Mary Holmes*

In 1801 a young mother received an affectionate letter
from her sister-in-law, Mary Fourdrinier, asking after her
health and that of her first baby:

> I quite long to hear from you my love, as I left you so
> indifferent. I trust your sweet little boy is as well as I
> sincerely wish him, and that you mend in the nursing
> way. Pray do not injure your constitution by giving nour-
> ishment too long to that love of a tiger ...[1]

The mother was Jemima Newman, the wife of a banker
living in Old Broad Street, a stone's throw from the Bank
of England. The love of a tiger was John Henry, born on
21st February.

He was a lucky child, born to a loving couple, who had
ample means and a desire to do their best for the children.
His father was bluff, hearty, ready to be proud of his
offsprings' achievements but not over-demanding; his
mother was gentle, affectionate and loyal. They had six
children in all, nicely balanced as to the sexes: John Henry
was followed by Charles (born at Southampton Street,
Bloomsbury, in a fine town house since banker John
Newman was still rising in the world), then Harriett,

Francis, Jemima, and lastly Mary, born in 1809.

If we concentrated on the opening chapters of Newman's *Apologia* we should have a one-sided picture of the child John Henry Newman, the sensitive, imaginative boy who wished the Arabian Nights were true, who 'thought life might be a dream, or I an Angel, and all this world a deception, my fellow-angels by a playful device concealing themselves from me, and deceiving me with the semblance of a material world'[2]. This strong sense of the unseen world that is beyond our workaday existence was always with him but he was also, from his childhood, a person strongly rooted in his immediate surroundings, bound to relations and friends, to home and even to inanimate and trivial things that signified home and those dear to him. In later years he drew together the two strands, the sense that the world is a veil between us and the real world of the spirit and the strong apprehension that all the circumstances of our everyday lives have importance.

> I think nothing more interesting, and it is strange to think how evanescent, how apparently barren and resultless, are the ten thousand little details and complications of daily life and family history. Is there any record of these preserved anywhere, any more than of the fall of the leaves in autumn? Or are they themselves some reflection as in an earthly mirror, of some great truths above? So I think of musical sounds and their combinations – they are momentary – but is it not some momentary opening and closing of the Veil which hangs between the worlds of spirit and sense?[3]

His memories of childhood were always clear, investing tiny details with beauty and significance. In particular he recalled the country house at Ham, near Richmond, that he knew as a young child. He remembered the trees, acacias, a Spanish chestnut, a large magnolia flowering up the side of the house. Coming down stairs, one step at a time and reflecting that this was June. Lying in bed in the early morning listening to the swish of a scythe. Playing at being Ulysses, by the river. Bowers and shrubberies.

Picking wild flowers and sending violets to his mother by a servant. He sent a broom-flower to her when his sister Jemima was born.

His brothers and sisters were constant companions, intelligent, articulate, not allowing the eldest child to win every argument or have things entirely his own way. When it came to school there would be a separation of girls and boys, but for the earliest days and holidays, and particularly when the young Newmans roamed and played round Vine Cottage at Norwood, a later country house bought by Mr Newman, they were very much one group. One summer they could not go to Vine Cottage, a little house set on a remote heath (described by John as a '*terra incognita*, the wild beautiful haunt of gypsies') and Harriett wrote that they 'sighed at being separated from the freshness and freedom'[5] of that beloved place.

Besides their parents there were two relatives who played a great part in their lives, their paternal grandmother and their father's sister, Elizabeth, known as Aunt Betsy. They had a house at Fulham and later moved to Vine Cottage. The children often stayed with them. John's recollections of the Fulham house – and he could not have been more than four or five when he was there – illustrate the tenacity of his memory and his deep affections. He wrote to his aunt in 1844, having revisited the house which had become a chemist's shop at the front.

> I wanted to have a peep at the house, but the good chemist, civil as he was, did not take my hints – so I saw nothing, except the hall through the door. I saw too the staircase which I had forgotten. But I described to him the lie of the house, which he confirmed. I told him where the kitchen was, where I recollect you going to superintend the making of apple puffs. And the room opening on the garden where were the two cardracks with a lion (I think) on them; and the pictures of the prodigal son, and giving alms to the poor and the unjust steward, or some one or other paying a number of people. There you used to breakfast – at least I recollect coming down in the morning and seeing the breakfast

things looking bright and still – and I have some vague reminiscence of dry toast. And I have a sort of dream of my father and mother coming one day to call, and the room being crowded.

I told the worthy man also where the drawing room was – and I spoke of a sort of loft above, in which I have a dim vision of apples on the floor and a mangle. And of the garden – the summerhouse, he said was gone, but the drying ground behind it remained ...

How strange it is, I wish I could describe it, to stand in a house which was so much to me, as that house was, and it so different, and I so different! Whatever good there is in me, I owe, under grace, to the time I spent in that house, and to you and my dear Grandmother, its inhabitants. I do not forget her Bible and the prints in it ...[6]

Newman says in the Apologia, 'I was brought up from a child to take great delight in reading the Bible'.[7] The earliest teaching aids, we note, were the pictures on the walls of his grandmother's house and those in her Bible. In another letter, written when he was in his fifties, he says that he has just been looking at that Bible, sent to him after his aunt's death. He looked again at the pictures 'and when I came to the Angel inflicting the pestilence on David and his people, I recollect I used to say "that's like Mr Owen". This must have been *dormant* forty six years in my mind'.[8]

Impressions cut so deeply into his mind because he was so affectionate and places and objects spoke of his relations. Influences were of course from the male side of the family as well as from the female: John Newman senior, though he was ultimately a failure in business, was no cipher in his household, and John Henry sparred intellectually with Frank and Charles as much as with Harriett, the most argumentative of the girls. But there is no doubting the importance in his development of the women in his family, grandmother, mother, aunt, sisters. Life in a boys' school and then at Oxford (exclusively male) never eradicated those first impressions.

He went to Dr Nicholas' school in Ealing when he was seven and boarded there. The building was crowded and at first bigger boys teased him but he was happy there and the regime was less harsh than at the big public schools. He learned much Latin and Greek, took up the violin, encouraged by his father who delighted in music, wrote, read and debated in his spare time and greatly enjoyed appearing in school plays. Francis and Charles followed him there.

What of the girls' education? At one time Aunt Betsy ran a very small girls' school and they boarded there but cannot have gained much from the experience for Aunt Betsy was ineffectual as a schoolmistress and her establishment soon folded. There is no mention of a governess in the family letters so their education must have been much as Elizabeth Bennet described her own and her sisters' in *Pride and Prejudice*: they were always encouraged to read and those who wanted to learn (as the Newman sisters did) never wanted the means. They read assiduously. All knew French. Harriett read Italian, working at Tasso and Manzoni's *I Promessi Sposi*, while Jemima knew some Latin and had a taste for mathematics.

No doubt they learned their letters in the first place from their mother and, if their own practice when they were young mothers is anything to go by, they learned when they were very young. Jemima's eldest, Herbert, began his lessons when he was not yet three and Grace, Harriett's only child, helped her mother at the village school when she was six, teaching addition, the map of England and the journeys of St Paul. Did they, like the Bennet girls, have masters to instruct them as they grew older? Jemima must have had a music teacher: she was an accomplished piano player, doing much more than offering a little entertainment at evening parties as most young ladies did. One master they certainly had, from their own family – their eldest brother. As, in poorer households, frocks and jackets were handed down, so also education was handed down from boys to girls, particularly if a boy was studious and well-disposed towards his sisters. It is a pattern found in the novels of Charlotte M. Yonge, where it was accepted without question. John Newman instructed by letter, through his own school days and university course, and presumably school holidays and university vacations meant more intensive coaching. He sent from school, in 1816, a list 'of the quantities of the terminations of as many Greek words as I could collect without trouble'[9] with the inscription 'To my Sisters Harriett and Jemima – Improvement is everything!' Nor did they find such enclosures officious because study lists arrived, over the years, when they had been requested by one of the girls.

There are no portraits of the Newman children but we have a good idea of what Harriett, Jemima and Mary Newman looked like as young women. Harriett was small and slight, with a febrile prettiness. She had a small elfin face, as her mother did, with blue eyes, pink cheeks when in health, and quantities of fair hair. When the fashion was for curls, Harriett had them in abundance. She had a child-like appearance, but also looked sharp. Jemima too was small but much plainer, with the big nose that distinguished her eldest brother. Mary seems to have been taller, dark, more of a Newman that a Fourdrinier, but with handsomer features than Jemima.

Harriett was probably the most intelligent of the sisters with a quick tongue, a critical eye. She was not at all strong, nervous, prone to insomnia and to severe colds and headaches. She was active and determined, however she felt, and may be forgiven for being more than a little waspish at times. She was fond of 'putting down' those she thought required it and boasted once of shutting up Hurrell Froude, her brother's brilliant Oriel friend: as one chronicler observed, would not most people be better pleased to get him to speak?[10] Jemima was much more quiet, sober in manner, expressive and passionate only in her music. Amongst themselves they had nicknames. Harriett was 'Harry' or 'Bird' and Jemima was 'Cat' (her second name was Catherine) and sometimes 'Mum'. Was this last name an indication that she often kept mum when others chattered? Mary was eager, full of joy and affection. She was not renowned for any great talent but had a directness and sweetness of character that made her greatly loved.

Letters went to and fro between home and Dr Nicholas' school and later Trinity College, Oxford where the eldest brother was an undergraduate. Besides instruction for their own studies, he treated them to accounts of his own reading and activities. Sometimes he joked, sometimes he used a pompous style that shows him to be at that stage of development when the clever boy or girl must elaborate, practise new and grandiloquent phrases and show off a little to the juniors. Even the jokes were ponderous, as when he told Jemima from school that her message that they all sent their love with his affectionate sister J.C. Newman led him to believe that the lumbering heavy lump at the bottom of the parcel was Jemima herself. Lo! it was a cake. He was obliged, though he found the cake rather too much done. There is no doubting the affection and the interest that each member of the family had for the others. In particular Mrs Newman, like a benevolent spider at the centre of the home web, sent out the lines of communication and concern. She was very much a woman who lived for her family.

Financial disaster befell them in 1816 when Mr Newman's bank failed. Mrs Newman, who had been used to security and a comfortable style of living, did not complain but was as supportive to her husband as she could be. The house in Southampton Street was let. The girls went to Norwood but Vine Cottage too had to be given up after a short time and they then joined their parents at Alton in Hampshire where Mr Newman set up as a brewer. 1816 was a most notable year for John Henry, not so much because of the change in the family fortunes, but because of a deep change within himself. He says, 'I fell under the influences of a definite Creed, and received into my intellect impressions of dogma which, through God's mercy, have never been effaced or obscured'.[11] This conversion could be variously described. His own description is in the *Apologia*, the history of his religious opinions, and emphasises the intellectual side. It was also a change of heart, a personal commitment to Christ. Besides being of profound importance to himself, it was the beginning of a life of dedication that was to affect the hearts, minds, lives of thousands of other people. It was also Newman's first adult act of choice, his first step away from the family. He stayed on at school in the autumn of 1816 as the others shifted about. He was worried and sick and it was trouble that in the first place opened his mind to the teaching of a clergyman, Walter Mayers, who was teaching at the Ealing School. He lent young Newman books of a strongly Protestant cast and influenced him profoundly. It was to Mayers that he confided his innermost thoughts at this time, not to his relations.

The family fortunes continued to decline when Newman was an undergraduate at Trinity College: Mr Newman's confidence was sapped by the first failure and he took up a business in which he had little in the way of skill or luck. After three years in Alton the family moved back to London and he had a brew-house at Clerkenwell. He was declared bankrupt in November 1821 and the family drew closer in their trouble. John reminded his mother that troubles without were easier to bear than those that rent a family within, such a serious disagreement and separation. He was high-minded about the matter, 'convinced that nothing can be a greater snare and evil to a person than unalloyed prosperity'.[12] His parents tried to be high-minded too – but they undoubtedly suffered more than he could realise in his youth and evangelical priggishness. His father had to bear the burden of failure and shame and both parents felt that their children would suffer more than the loss of house, furnishings and ready money. Mrs Newman said, 'I anticipate in my anxiety for you all many evils that it may please God to avert, but yet I hope pardonable in the nature of a Mother's feelings – the decay of friendships from which youthful expectations may have augured comfort and delight through life'.[13] Her convoluted style makes this hard to interpret but she seems to fear that now the family is sinking so low the boys will lack influential friends and the girls will not have suitors. We think of the Bennet sisters again.

John wrote from Oxford that Harriett (described as a kind comforter) must take her own place at home and supply his too. In other words she was to be the eldest child there. Where, meanwhile, was Charles, the next in age to John? It would be another couple of years before Mr Newman delivered it as his considered opinion that Charles would never make his way in the world but already, at the time of the crash, they must have known that he would be a liability rather than a help. It is hard at this distance and looking back at an age that did not diagnose mental disorders with any exactness to say what was wrong with Charles Newman. He was above average in intelligence, well-educated at the school in Ealing and his elder brother described him as being 'upright, sensitively honest, generous, openhanded and affectionate.'[14] But he was incapable of supporting himself and it was gradually borne in upon his family that they would have to support him just as if he were a cripple or bedridden. The nearest to a definition of his trouble is John's comparing him to a character, Baldassarre, in George Eliot's novel, *Romola*, 'whose memory and mind gave away suddenly whenever he had come to the point of reaching some decisive act'.[15] So, in any employment, he reached a point where no task could be satisfactorily accomplished and then he abused anyone who tried to help him, turning on employers and particularly on his relations 'as a relief to himself of the irritation, the fierce indignation ... at his own distressing impotence of mind'.[16]

Poor Mr Newman in his failure and in his heavy responsibilities! Even his able sons caused him to break out in anger at times. The kind of Anglicanism that John Henry had learned from Walter Mayers was evangelical, that is low-church and puritanical, unlike the more easy-going, tolerant kind that John Newman senior espoused. Frank too had imbibed evangelical ideas. One Sunday John was called downstairs at home to give his opinion as to whether it was a sin to write a letter on a Sunday and found that Frank had already refused to copy one. A painful scene ensued, but they were reconciled the next day. John Henry admitted his own deficiency in meekness and patience (so angry words were probably returned when his father exploded) and said in his journal that his parent's forgiveness of his righteous sons was an example of 'very striking

candour, forbearance and generosity'.[17] In the same
month he also noted in his journal that when he informed
his mother that he and Frank intended to take the
Sacrament once a fortnight she 'seemed to think I began
to be righteous overmuch and was verging on enthusiasm'.[18]Mrs Newman never made a scene but she was as
much against what she considered excess in religion as her
husband. Also she thought John was leading Francis – not
astray, but down a very narrow path.

That journal would have made her fear the more if she
had trespassed there. It was an intimate and detailed
account of John's inner life, castigating himself for his sins.
He was particularly conscious of his pride. It was this that
made the time of his conversion in 1816 a real break with
the past – not that pride was conquered from then on but
that the boy he was before that time was content to rest on
his own abilities and on his own moral insights without
acknowledging his dependence on God. There is more to
the journal, though, than accounts of failures and
bewailing his faults. There are heartfelt prayers and positive moves forward. The account of the brush with his
father over the Sunday letter is chiefly remarkable for the
speedy and hearty reconciliation. In the matter of the
financial crash and the time that followed, one may feel
that the eldest son, sheltered by his Oxford life and his
academic pre-occupations, was sometimes priggish in his
expressions of sympathy and in his counsels, but he acted
decisively and with great unselfishness to help. The year
after Mr Newman's bankruptcy, 1822, was the year of John
Henry Newman's triumph when he gained his fellowship at
Oriel, against the odds since he had taken a poor degree.
Again, one may view the matter from different perspec-
tives. It was an academic triumph. It opened up his career,
placing him (to use his own measured phrases) 'upon the
high and broad platform of University society and intelligence, bringing him across those various influences,
personal and intellectual, and the teaching of those
various schools of ecclesiastical thought, whereby the religious sentiment in his mind, which had been his blessing
from the time he left school, was gradually developed and

formed and brought on to its legitimate issues'.[19] It was also, in more mundane terms, the securing of a post that would give him a place in the world and would pay him good money. He determined that he would work hard enough, taking on private pupils, to see Frank through Oxford, and he assured his family that they could rely on him. His mother was delighted and preached to her husband on the text that John must be left alone to manage. "For many months I always begin and end by saying 'I have no fear, John will manage'".[20] Every Oxford don was an ordained priest in the Church of England and to the new Oriel Fellow that was his real vocation, not a formality. He was ordained Deacon in 1824 and Priest in 1825, dedicating himself with the greatest seriousness. He summarised, in an autobiographical note, the further stages of his Oxford career, writing in the third person:

> In the latter year (ie 1825) he was appointed Vice-Principal of Alban Hall ... This office he held with his fellowship, and resigned it in the following year, on his becoming one of the tutors of his College. In 1827 and 1828 he held the office of Public Examiner. In 1828, on Dr Hawkins being elected Provost of Oriel, in the place fo Dr Copleston, promoted to the see of Llandaff, he succeeded him in the Vicarage of St Mary's, which he held till 1843. In 1829 his name occurs in the list of the majority, who place Sir Robert Inglis in the representation of the University instead of Mr Peel, in the famous contest occasioned by the latter statesman to the cause of Catholic Emancipation. At this time he was a member of the Bible and Church Missionary Societies. From 1830 to 1832 he was one of the Select University Preachers. In 1831 he resigned his Tutorship at Oriel. In July 1833 the Tract Movement began with a Sermon preached by Mr Keble before the judges of Assize, and afterwards published under the title of National Apostasy.[21]

There we have, in summary, the record of an arduous life (it does not take in all his pastoral duties as a clergyman, nor his writing), and indicates the outward events that show his growing influence. It would take much more to show the swelling tide of thought that led up to 1833 and to set out all that is included in the laconic phrase 'the Tract Movement began'. Frank Newman, meanwhile, was also establishing himself in the world, beginning with a brilliant career at Worcester College, and Charles was fulfilling his father's prophecy that he would never make his way.

What was happening to the girls? They were leading nomadic lives. Oxford, where the snapdragon grew every year in Trinity College as a sign of continuity, was not for them. After Alton the family was in various London houses, and on the death of their father, in 1824, the three girls and their mother crammed into the little house at Strand-on-the-Green where Aunt Betsy and Grandmama lived. Aunt Betsy was perpetually in financial trouble and Mrs Newman's income was small. John provided. After a year she took a house at Eastern Terrace, Marine Square, Brighton, and she never really liked the location. She had said she would live anywhere so long as the air was good but the winds of Brighton were too much for her.

Harriett, Jemima and Mary must have suffered from their father's failure, illness and death, from their mother's anxiety and from insecurity but they seem to have weathered storms with youthful cheerfulness. They had a great capacity for enjoying themselves, with walks, with visits and with small social gatherings. Sometimes they were girlish and silly and sent letters full of news about pelisses, muslins, ribbons, and the bonnets which were new and of the style called cottage slouch and quite the prettiest that season. Harriett wrote with arch instructions – the others must have been about to go to a party. 'Mary! take care Jemima's hair is neat and her ringlets disposed hubschly! Jemima! curl pins! Francis! take care of your sisters and do not be late! ... Mary! do not walk in your new gloves! Mind you both behave pretty and play if you are asked, there are *good* children'.[22] They must have chattered when they retired for the night and doubtless they giggled. As an old man John Henry said of another household of girls that he knew what it was like when sisters got upstairs together.

As for the social gatherings, they occasionally had some sober warnings from their eldest brother.

As I am on this subject let me remind you, though you hardly need reminding, that some danger always attends that promiscuous intercourse with society which such visits necessarily involve. We are so apt to be led away, to become fond of worldly things and to imbibe feelings hostile to spiritual religion that it is well to be doubly careful in examining ourselves and watching our thoughts and actions when we are in new and pleasing company.[23]

He did, however, modify these views when appealed to for a rule about mixing in society or abstaining, refusing to lay down a strict rule. 'I think,' he said, 'it highly desirable that all of you should see as many persons as you can – though *not all at once.* People get contracted notions and narrow ideas by being always at the bottom of a sugar canister or sewed up in a pincushion'.[24] The image of the pincushion would come readily to his mind: it was an ever-present commodity, together with needle and thread, for a woman in the nineteenth century and must have been there in any Newman sittingroom. Moreover, a prodigious worker himself, he was impressed by the way women rarely sat idle, but would talk or listen to a book being read with a piece of sewing in their hands. He advised his sisters to take their work with them on visits and eschew those large gatherings where one could not sew. And, strict keeper of Sunday though he was, he really wondered on his pastoral visitations whether it was altogether wrong for women to lay aside their work on the sabbath. 'Having been used to it all through the week, they cannot attend so well to (hearing) reading without it. Having nothing to do, they become drowsy. Sunday becomes a weariness'.[25]

The Newman sisters were certainly not always mewed up. Harriett was in London for the coronation of George IV and reported that the whole procession, apart from the Marquis of Londonderry, were a plain set of men, the King looked old, ill and ugly and Prince Leopold looked sulky.

She also went to the theatre, visited the British Museum and thought little of the Elgin Marbles, and saw a Mr Graham ascend in his balloon. Mary reported in May 1824 that the weather was bad and though she could not go out she had been much taken by Papa's account of the Oxford rowing match, rowed against time from Oxford to London. Cheers and brandy revived the crew at Vauxhall Bridge but they were so exhausted that they had to be lifted out at the finishing post and all put to bed. A few days later she went out and shopped for a pocket book, ascended the Monument (310 steps with ten corkscrews), and was taken by Charles to see the Custom House. Mary's style is usually slightly breathless, as though events and impressions rush upon her and she grasps them with pleasure as they pass.

Occasionally, very occasionally, her eldest brother too was in high spirits and effervescent in his letters. When he wrote home to give the splendid news that Frank had achieved a double first, in classics and mathematics, he made the central announcement clear but set it in a passage of witty nonsense. The resultant letter could have been written by Edward Lear. A young person was to be sent to Mrs Newman from Oxford and he should be kept quiet and lodged in a back building. 'He can mend shoes, string pianos, cut out screens, and go on errands – the last is his forte – employ him in errands while he is with you and the time will pass pleasantly enough – I forgot to say he can sharpen knives. – He is very docile, while kindly treated, and quite harmless. – Do not frighten him.'[26]

John's friends provided society and fresh experiences. One friend was Samuel Rickards, a married parson at Ullcombe, near Maidstone in Kent. The girls visited there several times, one and another, the whole group, with John or without him – a chart of visits to Ullcombe would help to show the number of times they packed their bandboxes for they never seemed to be in one place for long. Mr Rickards was mildly eccentric while his wife was kind and charming. In 1824 John 'did duty' for his friend there and took Harriett to keep house. They had many callers and Harriett drove about with a Mr Brownless to see the Kent countryside. She also helped in the parish, castigating the singing in church which, she said, left her mangled.

John had his own clerical duties besides these forays into other parishes. He. was first a curate in St Clement's Oxford, when he was a deacon, and worked amongst poor· people, tradesmen, artisans and the like. He gathered the children for catechising and was helped in this work by the Misses Gutch, the daughter's of the old Rector who was too infirm to do much in the parish. The parishioners eyed the new curate, a new broom ready to sweep very clean, and planned a match between him and Miss Gutch. To no avail. Since Newman was young and inexperienced, he had his troubles, partly of his own making. He was high-handed with the choir who walked out on him and threatened action; nothing came of it but there were mutterings against young curates who thought they knew best. He was very assiduous in visiting – indeed, his father thought he overdid it and advised against anything that was 'ultra'. Occasionally, again through inexperience, he made mistakes. He was bamboozled by a Mrs Bradby who spoke very piously. He was surprised when a sick girl that he visited said she did not like this outwardly estimable woman. Years later, when he had his parish at Littlemore, outside Oxford, he saw Mrs Bradby again and revised his opinion: 'She has a nasty smooth unnatural manner, and I cannot conceive how I could have been taken in by her. But I took things in faith – i.e. I had faith that God's presence ever was, where people talked in a certain way'.[27] He had his successes too, though success was an inappropriate word for what he sometimes saw – poor ignorant people, often with painful illness, strengthened by his visits, by the prayers he used and the Bible passages that he read to them. He made copious notes on his visits. 'Mrs Stuchbery – woman of about thirty – inflammation of chest – very ill – churchgoer etc but conscious that she had not served God in the spirit – Visited her constantly till she recovered – she very grateful – and I trust will walk in the ways of peace and holiness'.[28]

In August 1825, a few months after his ordination as priest, Mrs Newman and her daughters came to stay in Oxford for two months. He administered the Sacrament for the first time on their first Sunday there, Jemima and Mary receiving Holy Communion for the first time and from his hands. He wrote in his journal about the occasion adding, 'We all partook of it also the last Sunday they were in Oxford. O how I love them. So much I love them, that I cannot help thinking, Thou wilt either take them hence, or take me from them, because I am too set on them'.[29] On his birthday, the previous February, his sisters wrote to send their good wishes and he said, 'What am I that I should be loved and looked up to?'[30] These words are in his private journal and he was not so ready to speak them aloud. Reserve lay on him, as on Harriett, who had more feeling than her sharp manner denoted. But the love was there, a great web of sensibility that lay over them all.

Probably he loved and admired Mary most, having more than once a presentiment that this most attractive girl would not be with them long. This feeling was not based on evidence of decline or physical weakness but it was strong, reinforced perhaps by a sense of the fragility of life as he attended his parishioners' deathbeds. He had a special feeling for Harriett too, the nearest in age. In one of his most open utterances he wrote to her 'I cannot say how I love you. No calamity I think, could occur to me here so great, as to lose your love and confidence. For of all my brothers and sisters (from one cause or another) you alone know my feelings and respond to them'.[31] Her reply is very revealing, showing the lack of self-confidence that lay behind her competent, critical exterior:

> I cannot tell you how dear to me is the assurance of your affection. I hope you loved me, dear John, whenever I thought of it – but I could never persuade myself that there was anything in me that could inspire the same feeling towards me that I feel for others. I cannot persuade myself now.[32]

There was a great deal in John Newman's life that he could and did share with his sisters. For all their chatter about bonnets and jokes about Mr Rickards, they were serious-minded young women. They were devout members of the

Church of England (though without a deep conversion experience and probably sharing their father's view that ultraism was a mistake), genuinely interested in theological talk and speculation. Also they were intelligent and continued to read deeply and widely, the advantage of the sort of informal education that they had had being its openendedness: since schooldays did not end, study continued.

Their brother took it for granted that they would like to hear about his life in all its aspects. For all his intellectual subtlety he had a certain simplicity in his loves and friendships, confiding his thoughts and describing his activities freely. Of course he was selective, as all letter writers are: when he wrote to his women folk about his first days at Oriel he did not enlarge on his difficulty at relating to the other Fellows, being at that time shy and socially inept, and when he wrote about the parish of St Clements he enlarged on the need for a new church building rather than talk about the private and spiritual concerns of the people. But he shared much of his experiences. The response was interested and vivid. Mary was keen to know what his rooms at Oriel were like, but she gave his arrangements a qualified approval:

> I wish I *could* see your rooms. Are they generally called by the titles you give them? I hope the 'brown room' is not quite so grave as the name would lead one to suppose. At least Harriett would not be in the number of its admirers. You know *brown* is not a great favourite of hers. I had no idea you lectured in your rooms.[33]

It is clear what his rooms were like, the unexciting, dingy apartments of a scholarly celibate, where he could house many books and have solitude for study and prayer. The only concession to appearances was in fact a towel, kept handy for dusting the precious books.

As for Mrs Newman, her responses were always affectionate and interested but never lively since they were always couched in a prosy style. She was a very devout woman, glad to have her eldest boy a clergyman. Not long before her husband's death she confessed her own pain of mind and felt that some comfort was beginning to reach her sad heart.

> The effort and the resolution to persevere have been so much above human power, that I do not fear saying there is nothing too hard to be effected through His assistance.
>
> I thank you for your Sermons. They arrived at the happy moment to be valuable to me; they all accord with my opinions, but those I most particularly admire are 'Wait on the Lord', 'Man goeth forth to his labour', and the one on Prayer. I am very loth to part from them.
>
> ... I am sanguine to hope you are blessed in various ways so peculiarly, and placed *unexpectedly* in a Profession where you may be the happy monitor and guide to many; if this hope should be realised, which I do not fear, what a recompense to your labours!! Pray take care of your health.[34]

John's opinions, here according with her own, were different from those of his evangelical period. He thought more of the Church, of the Christian faith as an objective body of teaching handed down from one age to another. He no longer believed, as evangelicals did, that the saved and the sinners were clearly divided, the former assured of their reconciliation with God in this world and salvation in the next by faith working in their hearts. This change in his opinions came with the influence of his Oriel friends, Hawkins and Whately, and from a new and increasingly close friend, Pusey. It also came from his close observation of the parishioners of St Clement's. There at the sick beds or praying with them in their close little rooms, he found he could not divide them neatly into the saints and the sinners. 'Calvinism', he wrote, 'is not a key to the phenomena of human nature as they occur in the world'.[35] This is not a theory derived from books but a lesson learned from those like Mrs Stuchbery, recovering her health and struggling to serve God though she had lapsed in the past, and from young Mrs Flynn who died in peace, and from the women who came to be churched, the couples who brought babies to be baptised. 'I found many', he said, 'who in most important points were inconsistent, but whom yet I could not say were altogether without grace. Most indeed were in that condition as if they had some spiritual feelings, but weak and uncertain'.[36] He could not now be counted an evangelical but he never ceased to be grateful to Walter Mayers, the evangelical who had led him to conversion as a schoolboy.

This Mr Mayers was now a parson at Over Worton in Oxfordshire and had married Sarah Giberne, a young woman from an evangelical family of French and Huguenot extraction. There was an obvious link between the families and Frank, who had also known Mayers as his schoolmaster, visited Over Worton where he met a sister, Maria Rosina Giberne, and was greatly attracted to her. There now enters on the scene one of the most colourful characters in the whole Newman saga. She was a handsome, striking brunette, with a tall figure, a fine bust. She was a young Juno, calculated to turn the heads of the men; she knew her powers and expected flattery. At Frank's insistence, the Newman girls were asked to stay at the Gibernes' home in Wanstead. She thought Mary sweet, rather like her Frank in appearance, but objected to the other two who, she thought, were worldly in their style of dress and mode of talking. Mary's visit was brief but Harriett and Jemima stayed for a fortnight. They did not please in their attitude to religion for they were reserved, backing away from pious and fervent talk, but increasingly Maria Rosina found matter to admire in the two sisters: they were devoted to each other and did not talk disparagingly of other people. She felt conscious of Frank's superior intelligence and felt that his sisters were more clever than she was, and in this modest estimate she was right.

It seems that, during this visit, Maria Rosina and perhaps the whole Giberne family judged behaviour by set evangelical rules and, curiously enough, young Mary's mind had fixed on this idea. She wrote to her sisters:

> I must tell you my dream of the other night. I thought I
> was with you at Wanstead and that the Miss Gibernes
> were drawing up very neatly on *ruled paper* the *tests of
> friendship* by which we were determining to regulate our
> ideas. I approved entirely of their judgement in the
> execution, my only objection was that I feared a strict
> adherence to the rules might make us somewhat
> mechanical and formal.[37]

Maria Rosina was not an intellectual but she had talents
and great vivacity. She played the harp, drew and painted
and with some skill, able to catch a likeness when she did a
portrait. Her outstanding characteristic was her tendency
to strong, romantic feeling (which might be for a man or
for a woman), gushing out, a river that was forever over-
flowing its banks. Her feelings seem to have been very like
those of any adolescent, real enough but immature, difficult to canalise, expressed with artless fervour. Frank
proposed to her but she turned him down, choosing
instead a young officer called Robert Murcott who went to
India, hoping to make his fortune and return to marry her.
She led Frank something of a dance and an interesting
hypothetical question still lingers in the air – if Robert had
returned would she have married him, and satisfactorily?

She met the eldest Newman brother the next year, at
Brighton where she was staying at her aunt's house, and
was ready to dislike him, having heard that he was a 'stiff
churchman'. She was curious about him when she went to
drink tea at the Newmans' and not a little put out to find
that he paid more attention to his mother and sisters than
to her. He offered to escort her home and she feared that
the walk would be in silence. And so it was. When they
neared her aunt's house she thanked him for his escort
and said she would not give him the trouble of coming any
further, having already anticipated his response which
would be something like, 'Oh, Miss Giberne, it is no
trouble. Indeed it is a pleasure to be with you'. However,
he said that since he had come so far he might as well
continue.

She maintained, when she wrote down the incident, that

his reply so lacking in gallantry and so foreign to her experience, showed him to be true and sincere and that is why she noted it particularly. Did it stick in her head because she was so rebuffed? Or did it in fact make John Newman of particular interest because she could not snare him? She wrote of her first dislike of him and then added, 'Has he not heaped coals of fire on my head by laying me under an eternal obligation to him! Bless the Monk!!!! In spite of my ill-will to him! Oh! Oh!'[38] The style is the woman.

All the same, Maria Rosina Giberne was not all silliness. She seemed to play with love and to play at being religious, but there was more loyalty and devotion beneath her handsome but foolish outer self than any reasonable observer might suppose. She was to be Newman's friend for the rest of her life, which was nearly as long as his.

In January 1828 she was in Brighton again, this time staying at the Newmans' house with a friend, Fanny King. John was there; he was recovering from a breakdown that had come upon him at the end of '27 when he was acting as University Examiner. The family sat down to dinner with Maria Rosina and other guests. The scene was vivid in her mind when she wrote to him some fifty years later. She said that Mary sat between them and turned to her, looking pale and with a dark ring round her eyes, saying that she felt ill. She went away and the guest wanted to go with her but was afraid to make a stir. The family too were constrained by politeness though Mrs Newman followed her daughter and then returned quietly to say she thought the doctor should be called. John joked that she must not forget his fee. The next day Harriett walked with Maria Rosina and said that Mary had had a bad night. The visitor then went off for a painful session at the dentist's, and to a dinner engagement.

In the late evening she returned to Eastern Terrace with her friend and was met by John, very pale, forced into composure. He stood against a table and told them the doctor said Mary could not live. Still playing the game of watching for correct evangelical behaviour, Maria Rosina asked him to pray for Mary with them ('Now I shall see by his prayers whether he is like other religious people who, at such a time, would pour out their feelings at the throne of grace').[39] He answered that she had gone already. Maria Rosina, writing it all down years later castigated herself for concentrating in this petty way on John Newman's style of prayer. 'Stupid fool that I was!!! Unfeeling hard-hearted wretch!!!!!!'[40]

She was lost in admiration at the family's restraint in grief and at their kindness to herself and Fanny King. She did them one service before she left, making a drawing of the dead girl. Mary Newman was just nineteen, full of vitality, removed from life with shocking suddenness. It is likely that she had appendicitis. When she knew she was dying she said she wished she could have more time to be with her family, more time to prepare for Heaven, but that she had total faith in Christ and was convinced that to be with Him was far better. When she was in pain, during her last night, she repeated Keble's hymns and had much comfort from them. 'And so she departed', said her brother, adding that 'she was gifted with that singular sweetness and affectionateness of temper that she lived in an ideal world of happiness, the very sight of which made others happy'.[41] He had been so struck by the beauty and guilelessness of her character that he had been convinced that she would not live long.

The Victorian era was not far away when Mary Newman died, that era which has in its novels and biographies countless descriptions of pious deathbeds. These accounts usually fill the twentieth century reader with embarrassment. The story of Mary's death, however, is genuinely touching for something of her own guilelessness and truth comes across, just as the reality of the event and the goodness of the Newmans in their grief and acceptance of mortality blew away Maria Rosina Giberne's religious sentimentality.

Jemima Newman, nearest in age to the girl they lost, was very hard hit. She wrote to John with the faintest hint of reproach that he did not customarily speak out what he felt and hinting too that his growing separation from them, with his Oxford life and his theological schemes, meant that he lost touch:

I cannot bear to think that I should ever cease to feel as much towards dear Mary, as I have all my life; but I think I am sure I shall not. I dare say strangers think us much at our ease, and in good spirits; but I always wish to say, when I speak to anyone who did not know her. Ah you little think what she was to herself and to us all. Dear John, how you delighted me once when you said 'she was so singularly good'. I never heard you speak so much about her, but I was sure you thought so; and indeed we, John, know more of her than you could know; I especially, who have been always with her.[42]

He could have replied with truth, though he did not, that he did not have to be with Mary every day to know her worth and to love her. The death of this dearest sister was a major event in Newman's life. Her loss, together with his breakdown in the Examination Schools, were blows that brought him to his knees: it was a second conversion. His sense that the world was a veil, a beautiful veil between us and the real world of the spirit was strengthened, but at the same time he was revitalised. He felt that he had some great purpose in life; cloudy shapes of more work to come were on the horizon.

He was more than ever busy with the mundane tasks of house-hunting, making arrangements to move goods and chattels, finding the money. Mrs Newman got her way – she had wanted to be nearer John. He found them cottages to stay in at Horspath and Nuneham Courtney, villages four or five miles from Oxford, and rode over to see them: Jemima remembered him at Nuneham – 'coming romping over hedge and ditch now and then'. Then they returned to Brighton. Mrs Newman made it plain that she disliked being there: the coastal winds blew and made them ill, and she felt the separation. She said she often wished John to be present, then argued herself out of her mood and was glad he was absent. Eventually he capitulated, the Brighton house was let and he found them a house at Rose Hill, between Iffley and Littlemore, not in Oxford but near enough to see its spires and towers. After two years they moved a little nearer to the city and settled in a house

called Rose Bank at Iffley. The nearness to Oxford suited
the girls because it meant Commemoration Week, parties,
picnics and walks, sun on the river and the company of
young men.

Miss Giberne once sketched a quiet scene, showing them
gathered, Mamma, Francis, Harriett, John and Jemima,
with sewing and books: it is a picture of domestic harmony.
However, the moving near to Oxford and John's work was
not an unqualified success. He put down the reasons years
later.

> It was a great mistake in all of us, though a very natural
> one, to fancy that, if my Mother and sisters came nearer
> to me, they would see more of me ...
>
> When they were at a distance, I went to see them
> from time to time for weeks together ... but when they
> came near to me they came to the seat and scene of my
> occupations, and when they still found me at a distance
> from them practically, as it was not a distance of the
> body it seemed to be one of mind. And when they, in
> their kindness, tried, however delicately and consider-
> ately, to overcome what was to them an invisible
> obstacle, then I got worried ...[43]

At Christmas 1832 there was no John, no Francis to visit.
John had set off on a voyage to the Mediterranean with his
friend Hurrell Froude and Archdeacon Froude, his father.
Francis too was far away, His religious opinions had
changed and he, as well as his brother, had departed from
the tenets of the Evangelicals. His opinions were to be
increasingly heterodox. At this time he was a disciple of
J.N. Darby, a clergyman who left the Church of Ireland to
lead a return to what he considered to be primitive christianity. His sect would later be known as the Plymouth
Brethren. Darby was leading a team of missionaries to
Persia and Frank had joined the expedition. John's travels
were more in the nature of a holiday but Mrs Newman
would have been in fear for both her sons if she had known
that her eldest was to end his visit to Italy with a solitary
journey to the wildest parts of Sicily where he fell ill and

just escaped with his life. History and literature have many examples of men setting out for battle and adventures while the women wait anxiously for their return: this is another telling of the ancient pattern, with Newman's ship, the *Hermes* launched on the seas in early December, Frank heaven knows where, and the trio at Rose Bank waiting for letters.

The letters came in profusion from John, with vivid extended descriptions of new sights and experiences, and verses that laid open his mind. The journey to the Mediterranean was an intense and important episode and his thoughts encompassed so much that apparent contradictions rise up in his narrative. He was fascinated by the strangeness of what he observed – he had never been abroad before – and yet, so concerned was he with Oxford and the Church in England that sometimes he seemed to be ever sending his thoughts homeward. He saw Roman Catholicism in action and hated and feared it and yet he saw aspects of Catholic devotion in Italy that attracted him in spite of himself. The painful, lonely months in Sicily meant a new phase of dedication, a new conversion, so that he was to return to Oxford a different man. He would belong to his family less.

Yet, in these foreign places, memories of childhood rose up again and again. When he sighted Ithaca he remembered playing Ullysses as a child and when he was ill in Sicily his small room reminded him of the cheerless sickroom at school. The famous verses that he wrote on his way back to England, when the sailing ship was becalmed, have home and his youngest sister as themes, with much else. Everyone has heard or sung the hymn *Lead, Kindly Light* (with its lugubrious tunes) and interpreted, correctly, the line, 'I am far from home' as a metaphor by which the Christian pilgrim contemplates his distance from heaven and goes on to affirm his trust in God's guiding light through darkness and a difficult terrain. It also means something concrete and could be expanded to mean: 'I am far from England where I have a work to do, and, after travel, illness and fatigue, I dearly wish the ship could move on the return journey'. The last lines are weaker than the rest of the poem, being obscure and a shade sentimental to modern taste (the Victorians loved this verse) but it has great biographical interest. The 'angel faces' are perhaps his earliest companions, seen as angels by the imaginative child whose spiritual perceptions were so precocious, or the verse simply refers to Mary who was 'loved long since and lost awhile'.

At last he arrived, to great rejoicing at home. Frank arrived at the same time, from his missionary expedition. He thought of Maria Rosina Giberne often on his travels, tried to propose to her again by letter (and was circumvented by her parents) and tried again on his return. She saw how moved he was and noted that his handshake was icy. But she turned him down, although she had lost Robert Murcott. The year before, when she was making her trousseau, her mother received the message that he had died of a fever and had to break the news to her daughter. Maria Rosina prayed that night that she might see him again and did dream of him. He did not come as a gruesome phantom, as in some of the old ballads when a girl sees her dead lover, but as she had known him. Years later, writing in French, she said, 'Voila que J'ai vu mon Robert'.[44] In the morning she drew his portrait, and kept it. Robert Murcott left her his money. This would be a splendid gift for anyone, as well as a pledge of great affection, but for a young woman in the early nineteenth century it was an inestimable boon: it meant that she could live independently.

John unpacked presents. Undoubtedly there were some for the women in the family but what they were is not recorded. He brought Miss Giberne a cameo from Rome and took a parcel of oranges from the orange boat that had, slowly, brought him from Italy to France, in order to give them to some little girls in Oxford. But he was not inactive at home for very long. The Sunday after his arrival Keble preached the sermon on National Apostasy, in St Mary's, Oxford, and Newman put down the marker exactly there for the beginning of the Oxford Movement.

‹⊙⊙›

Of course, women had no direct part in the formation or the conduct of the Movement, that call for reform in the Church of England and for a return to the ideals of the early years of Christianity. Many devout women were involved, however, learning the tenets of Tractarianism from the famous Tracts themselves from books, from the clergy. Some became deeply involved because of the involvement of their husbands or brothers. Trollope, a novelist with a keen eye for what was topical on the social and ecclesiastical scene, poked gentle fun at Eleanor Arabin in *Barchester Towers*: she had married a man who had been an ardent Tractarian and at one time had nearly succumbed to the charms of Rome. Now 'she likes his adherence to the rubric, she specially likes the eloquent philosophy of his sermons, and she likes the red letters in her own prayerbook'.[1]

The women who doted on the outward forms, mistaking the shell for the substance, were good matter for the satirist (Newman laughed at them in his novel *Loss and Gain*), but there were plenty of women outside the pages of novels who found in the Oxford Movement a spur to real personal devotion and knowledge of doctrine and scripture. Such was Maria Pusey, the gentle wife of Edward Bouverie Pusey, one of the leaders of the Movement. She, with her husband, gave up entertaining in order to give money to church building and to charity and she sold her jewels to the same end. She did not, however, shed gloom around her: Newman described her as a very pleasing person. Her early death in 1839 caused her husband such grief that he determined to live in penitence thereafter, though both Keble and Newman urged him not to see such an affliction as a punishment from God.

Whole families became adherents, such as the Bowden family. Newman's great friend, John William Bowden, the companion of his undergraduate days at Trinity, was a Tractarian. He married Elizabeth Swinburne (of the same family as the poet), a cultured, elegant woman who also became Newman's friend and shared his and her husband's views. The family all met at the parents' home in 1834 for the sad reason that Bowden's sister was dying of consumption and even the patient herself was concerned to be praying for the cause, that is the Movement.

Another Tractarian, Tom Mozley, an Oriel man and a clergyman, who had been a pupil of Newman's, later wrote reminiscences of his day and of the Oxford Movement. He included a section on Maria Rosina Giberne who had become a Tractarian and a keen one. Tom Mozley's narrative is not wholly to be trusted but what he says of her squares with what we know of her character. He admired her statuesque looks and called her the *prima donna* of the Oxford Movement, a grand and ornamental figure. According to him 'her interest in the whole circle was insatiable'.[2] On one occasion she, with some other ladies, was invited to breakfast in the Oriel common room. When Keble crossed the quad she was unashamedly keen to have a good look at him and rushed to the window, the others following suit.

She was, as usual, prone to excess, going in for penances such as sleeping on the floor and whipping herself with the cords off her trunk. She carried little parcels of the Tracts with her when she went visiting and unloaded them on the maid to be handed on to the mistress. Fervour was needed and a spirit of independence since she lived with her stricly evangelical family. They teased her about her correspondence with Newman, suggesting that she had turned down one Newman to entrap another. This she stoutly denied and went on writing. She asked Newman whether she should attend the evangelical Bible Society and he replied that she should go among its supporters, making clear her disapproval. He added: 'the more havock you can make among them, the better'.[3]

Newman's mother and sister were by no means so devoted to the cause. As early as 1832 Harriett was saying she had a difficulty in speaking to her brother because of the great difference she saw in their opinions on many points. In 1835 he gave his mother the latest volume of his sermons with the remark that he knew she did not have any particular interest or sympathy with his opinions. This called forth the reproach which is at once just and pathetic. 'My dear John, I would ask you, who of your friends anywhere, who have equal means of judging with yourself, agree with you in everything? Is it then wonderful that I, unschooled in your learning, should not always be able to follow you close? ... I know I am a very weak arguer, and on most occasions, feel much more than I venture to express'.[4]

He was to say, looking back on those years, that 'from the first they did not like the distinctive principles of the Oxford Movement; and the more it developed, the wider did their difference from me in respect of it grow'.[5] He also said that they did not like some of his friends, though he did not specify which friends they were. These statements have to be taken as true (for who should know better than Newman himself?) but they are summaries of a situation spread over years, global and delivered with hindsight. His mother and sisters certainly did not dislike *all* his friends and, if they disliked the principles of the Oxford Movement, they were not totally out of sympathy with his ecclesiastical concerns. Jemima, for instance, found his University sermons, which she was reading in 1843, attractive and satisfying and commented that he made deep things so very simple. Harriett was to marry a tractarian clergyman and busy herself in parish concerns without demur.

It was with the practicalities of parish life that they were most at home and there they gave Newman help and encouragement. He had continued his pastoral work, after St Clement's, with the parish of St Mary's in the High Street and at Littlemore, the village outside Oxford which was also in his charge. The Oxford Movement was not simply a matter of theory but a blue-print for the care of souls in the Anglican Church and Littlemore was an embodiment of its principles. Newman took it for granted that it could not prosper without the help of some women and when Frank objected to the expense of keeping up a whole house for the females of the family, his elder brother (whose expense it was) replied, 'if they had lived in lodgings where would be the kitchen for Littlemore, with broth and messes? Where the rice and tapioca from the housekeeper's closet?'[6] This conjures up a splendid picture of the ladies transporting stews and nourishing puddings to the sick and needy of the parish. Harriett and Jemima also helped with the teaching of the children and did it with devotion.

Littlemore had no church when Newman was first there but he saw to it that a church was built. The list of subscribers to its building is kept there, and Mrs Newman laid the foundation stone. In 1835 she wrote in a pocket-book diary: 'July, Tuesday, 21st. A gratifying day. I laid the first stone of the church at Littlemore. The whole village there. The Hackers, Thompsons, Keble, Eden, Copeland J.H. a nice address. Prayers, Creed, and Old Hundredth Psalm'.[7] There is a sketch of the scene extant, variously ascribed to Jemima and to Miss Giberne – probably done by the latter, since the drawing is quite skilful. The villagers, with a great many children and babies in arms, are clustered round a crater while Mrs Newman, in a splendid bonnet and pelisse, waits below, with two gentlemen in tall hats, for the stone to be lowered. One of the attendant gentlemen must be 'J.H.'.

This was one of her last gratifying days and there was a rift between her and her eldest son even as they celebrated the new church together. He said, 'she thought I was surrounded by admirers and had everything my own way'.[8] He also said, with a curious obliquity of phrase that indicates that she was not totally opposed to what he believed and taught, 'my Mother has much misunderstood my religious views, and considered she differed from me'.[9]

Another bone of contention was his attitude to his brothers. It would not be quite true to say that the women in the family were on the side of Frank and Charles whereas John was intolerant towards them: even gentle Mrs Newman acknowledged the hard edges to Frank's character and knew that Charles was impossible to deal with, and their elder brother tried to be forbearing and was at all times very generous to them, nobly so since he did not reproach them nor demand thanks when he was spending money on the family. But he did condemn their heterodox religious views and the ladies thought him hard on them.

Frank did not in any way follow Charles' path to insolvency and dependency; he taught Classics at Bristol, became Professor of Classical Literature at Manchester and was later appointed to the Chair of Latin at University College, London. When he knew that Miss Giberne certainly would not have him, he married a Maria Kennaway. She was a devout Christian all her life and it grieved her that her husband gradually abandoned his Christian beliefs, becoming eventually a Unitarian. In old age Frank Newman espoused a variety of causes, including that of women's emancipation, but he was not always sensitive to individual women. When Maria died her husband composed an epitaph which set out her virtues but began with the phrase, 'with no superiority of intellect'. This seems a curiously insensitive way of celebrating a loved wife.

Charles had shown his heels immediately his father died, saying he could not bear to live any longer with such a pious family. He espoused the cause of socialism but it was not the noble side of socialism that attracted him, the desire to help the unfortunate by distributing wealth more evenly: Charles Newman's theory translated into the assertion that he was as good as the next man and this emboldened him to be impossibly rude to his employers in the bank where he first worked. He declared himself an atheist and was proof against his elder brother's arguments for Christianity.

Mrs Newman did one very foolish thing in an effort to keep Charles housed and fed and out of trouble. She had a dowry of five thousand pounds which she had kept intact through all the financial disasters and she gave Charles a thousand pounds, his inheritance in advance, intending that he should live on the interest. She might as well have thrown a bag of sovereigns into the depths of the ocean; he spent the capital, rapidly, and soon presented himself penniless again. John probably took issue with her over this.

The poor woman had one great cause for rejoicing in 1836, though she was then in failing health. Jemima was to be married and married well. Her fiancé was John Mozley, the brother of Tom and of James, another Oriel man; they were three of a family of ten, the children of a wealthy printer in Derby. The Mozleys were more like a tribe than a family, numerous and closeknit. John was to inherit his father's business and was managing it. He had visited Oxford the previous year and reported home that Miss Jemima Newman looked like her famous brother, was plain and was certainly a very pleasing person. By the autumn they were engaged. Jemima made her preparations and went round the Littlemore parish to wish them farewell; her sister said poor Cattie had her worst time parting with the children she taught in the school, who sobbed inconsolably. Free bread and ale were to be given in the village in honour of the wedding day.

This was in April and all went happily, except that Mrs Newman was not well enough to be at the church. Mozleys were there in force and some of Newman's friends, including Henry Wilberforce. He and his brother Robert, sons of the great reformer, had once flirted with the Newman girls but nothing had come of it. Now he and the waggish Tom Mozley caused a minor upset for Tom, who was assisting at the marriage ceremony, was nearly late because he was retrieving his best trousers that he had lent Henry the evening before the party. Mr Newman, according to a female Mozley, cut the bride cake in style, and the happy pair went off in a post-chaise.

A month later Mrs Newman was dead. Her last illness was brief and John and Harriett were with her at the last. They were shocked at the suddenness of her death for, though she had been ailing, she had not seemed mortally ill. He, in particular, was grieved to think of recent misunderstandings and seized on a phrase that one of the Wilberforces had used, 'in heaven there will be no misunderstandings'.[10] At the funeral he stayed on in the church, lost in prayer and memory. This was noted by Anne Mozley, Jemima's sister-in-law, an intelligent and kind young woman who had stayed on after the wedding to keep Harriett company.

Harriett, however, was not to be long on her own. Tom Mozley proposed by letter, and she accepted him in July. John felt that a six month's interval of mourning for their mother would be proper but Harriett would have none of it; she and Tom were married in Derby late in September, their old friend Samuel Rickards officiating. She was ready to be happy with Tom, glad to get away, but had bouts of depression, apathy and jumpiness since she was still suffering from her mother's illness and death. Materially she was not as lucky as Jemima, now settled in her large house in Derby. John did what he could for the couple, persuading Oriel to give Tom a living in Cholderton, and giving Harriett the family plate.

Cholderton is a village in a fold in Salisbury Plain, then a very remote spot so that life in the Rectory was by turns peaceful or boring. The living was not a rich one and Tom had his difficulties with some Wiltshire opponents of the Oxford Movement. A local Mr Humphries who met clergy at dinners (either third rate or dissipated hunting dinners, said Harriett scornfully) observed that they were soon tipsy and 'how can you call these men descendants of the apostles?'[11] However, Tom became popular in the village in time and they needed some tractarian zeal in Cholderton because before he came people sat on the altar in the tiny church and put their umbrellas in the font. Harriett helped in the parish and made life as sociable as she could with many visitors.

She had warned Tom before the marriage that Shakespeare's line had been applied to her, 'And though she be but little she is fierce'. He had his fierce fits too. Anne Mozley, on a visit, reported that he had been whipping Harriett round the garden with the new whip from the pony carriage and often threw her very nearly out of the window. Harriett herself said that he lifted her into a sheepfold, high on a Wiltshire hill, and would have left her there if they had not been expecting someone for dinner who would have wanted to know her whereabouts. This was not reported as a complaint about persecution by a cruel husband – it was admired as masterful horseplay. The Thomas Mozleys do not fit the stereotype of a clerical pair: quiet Jemima and staid John Mozley looked the part of Rector and his wife far more satisfactorily.

So their brother John was relieved of anxiety about his

sisters' future and also relieved of a financial burden. Dear, kind, impecunious Aunt Betsy too was no longer a drain on his income; she went to live with Jemima in Derby. He was now quite alone and he told Jemima that God meant him to be lonely. This was a statement that he intended to live single, one of the things that had distressed his mother who would have liked to see him passing from an honoured position at Oriel to a country parsonage with a suitable wife, as Keble had done.

He had felt a personal religious call to the single life from the time of his first conversion. He says in the *Apologia* that the anticipation that it would be the will of God that he should lead a single life 'was more or less connected in my mind with the motion, that my calling in life would require such a sacrifice as celibacy involved; as, for instance, missionary work among the heathen, to which I had a great drawing for some years'.[12] Thoughts of the celibate vocation had strengthened over time and had been reinforced by his long, formative study of the early Fathers of the Church and by the influence of his friend Hurrell Froude who 'had a high severe idea of the excellence of Virginity' and 'considered the Blessed Virgin its great pattern'.[13]

He had certain pragmatic considerations too, with reference to the Oxford Movement and the good of the Church. He believed that a band of picked men would be the ones to convert the great cities by putting before the people the ideal of self-sacrifice and being free from the responsibilities of a family. The image was not of a patriarch settled with his family around him but of a prophet, free, on the move and able to be zealous and poor.

He had a liking for military comparisons when thinking of the Oxford Movement and this and his zeal led him into one distasteful metaphor where women are described as camp followers – 'The Church wants *expeditos milites*, not a whole camp of women at its heels, forbye brats'.[14] This phrasing has, of course, to be set into the context of the time with its limitation of the scope of women's activities: an earnest Tractarian woman could in no sense fight in the front line but had to confine herself to moral support, the stitching of altar cloths and carrying the Tracts in a reticule or muff.

Newman was aware, or became aware, that it was possible to choose the single life for selfish reasons, to choose isolation or independence, to shut up the human springs of sympathy and affection, and he rejected all but the highest motives, to choose celibacy in order to love God and to serve others. In his novel *Loss and Gain* he was to make his young hero, Charles Reding (who is not Newman but who has much of Newman in him) discourse on the ideal of the celibate life and its 'high ethos' and listen to a great many objections. At one point he says to his Anglican friends that they are telling him 'that any one is a black sheep who does not marry'.[15] It is a fair point. Newman's beloved early Fathers and the medieval church which Hurrell Froude admired certainly overemphasized the desirability of the celibate vocation but in Newman's own time and since there have been those who call all celibates black sheep: they must be psychologically disordered or people who hate the opposite sex. At best they must be homosexual. It is not fair to affix any of these labels on Newman, not so much because of what he said about his own motives as because his life, taken as a whole, gives evidence of singleminded longing for God and loving service to his fellows.

He was not desirous of making the Anglican clergy a celibate body – in fact he thought 'country parsons ought, as a general rule, to be married'.[16] But he did expect his own friends in the Oxford Movement to stay with the picked militia and he was disappointed when they decamped to get married. He was decidedly cool when Keble married. One of the young Tractarians, a pupil of Froude's who was destined for holy orders called George Ryder spoke publicly on the ideal of priestly celibacy and then fell in love. Newman wrote to him in highly reasonable terms, assuring him that he was of course free to marry and to go into the church but disapprobation was in the air. Perhaps he was remembering Ryder's change of mind when he later wrote a comic passage in *Loss and Gain*. A character called White, who had earlier thought he might be a

Cistercian and who had talked with a young lady intending to be a nun, appears again at the end of the novel with the same girl. Charles Reding sees them entering the book-shop where he is busy himself:

> He heard the shop door open, and, on looking round, saw a familiar face. It was that of a young clergyman, with a very pretty girl on his arm, whom her dress pronounced to be a bride. Love was in their eyes, joy in their voice, and affluence in their gait and bearing. Charles had a faintish feeling come over him; somewhat such as might beset a man on hearing a call for pork-chops when he was sea-sick.[17]

Of course Charles does not feel sick because he sees a happy newly-married couple – he feels disappointment because he thought these two had pledged themselves to the 'noble demands' of the religious life. His reaction does rest on the assumption of a hierarchy of values: marriage is good but celibacy, undertaken for the right reasons, is better. A literary critic might make some objection because the situation is not really credible. Newman has set two characters who are burlesqued beside a serious, central character, Charles Reding. Their commitment to celibacy, described in very exaggerated and comic style, could never be believed by anyone with any sense, and Charles is no fool.

Ryder (to return to reality) was marrying Sophia Sargent, the daughter of the Rector of Lavington in Suffolk, where a young Tractarian was curate, one Henry Manning. Sophia, herself a beautiful girl, had three equally beautiful sisters. Manning (who was to become Cardinal Manning) married one of them, Caroline. Henry Wilberforce, much closer to Newman than George Ryder, fell in love with Mary Sargent and, fearing disapproval, kept the engagement to himself. As is the way with such secrets, gossip found it out and Henry, with consummate foolishness and some unkindness, did tell his friend's sister Harriett. Newman denied rumours of the engagement in Oxford on the grounds that Henry would have told him if the tale were true. Harriett triumphed, and spitefully, and a blow was dealt to a friendship. The main point at issue was the tactless secrecy, though Newman regretted Henry's choice of a state in life. They did mend their fences and Newman was godfather to the first child of the marriage, a baby who, it was hoped, would live up to the names John Henry William, after his famous grandfather and his father's friend. Like many children of that era, however, he did not live long.

The year 1836 that saw Mrs Newman's death and the marriage of her daughters was indeed a year to presage loneliness. Hurrell Froude, friend, mighty influence, one of the chief men of the Oxford Movement though his work was curtailed by his failing health, died late in February. Despite the trip to the Mediterranean and a later stay in Barbados, tuberculosis, that scourge of the time, killed him at the age of thirty three. Newman confided to Miss Giberne:

> As to dear Froude I cannot speak of him consistently with my own deep feelings about him, though they are all bright and pleasant. It is a loss such as I can never have again. I love to think and muse upon one who had the most angelic mind of any person I ever fell in with – the most unearthly, the most gifted. I have no painful thoughts in speaking of him (though I cannot trust myself to speak of him to many) but I feel the longer I live, the more I shall miss him.[18]

The Movement continued and Newman was busier than ever, writing, preaching, organising and increasingly facing attacks, from liberals, Bishops, the Heads of the Oxford Colleges and indeed from the country at large. Pusey was now a staunch ally. Attacks did not daunt them too much: Newman maintained that the ability to rouse wrath in different sets of men meant that they were succeeding in stirring their minds.

Increasingly Littlemore became home. He took lodgings there until he had his own establishment, the set of converted stables that became 'the College'. As part of his pastoral work he took on the education of the Littlemore children, and felt the lack of his sisters' expertise. He got out his violin and taught his small pupils 'Gregorians'. Also he catechised them in church, getting them to take. an interest in the subject matter. But there were few girls and the ones who came were dirty, so that he had to turn from chants and catechism to lecture on the necessity of washing hands and faces and keeping their knitting and sewing clean. There were no ladies at hand and the schoolmistress was hopeless so he laboured manfully on his own, giving material for neat white pinafores to be worn in church, which the girls were to make themselves. He sent off to a friend's wife for a pattern, drew up some prayers on a model of prayers written on cardboard, to hang up, done by some ladies in Sussex, and sent a hopeful call to Jemima. 'I live in hopes of your or H's coming through this place in the summer and giving my girls a polishing up'.[19]

There were some happy times at Littlemore: he wrote to Jemima at Easter 1840, with his curious and constant presaging of ill when times were good, 'We are all so happy we are afraid of being too happy'.[20] He could look with pride on the children who sang as he had instructed them, the girls in white pinafores and pink bonnets. The church was decked with sweet-smelling flowers 'as if to remind one of the holy Sepulchre',[21] and there was a new and splendid altar cloth sewn by Jemima and the other Mozley ladies. Mrs Barnes, Newman's landlady, was so struck with the beauty of that altar cloth that it haunted her dreams.

One young woman who came on a feast day to the little church at Littlemore was called Emily Bowles. She had heard of Newman through her brothers, Henry who was at Oriel and Frederick who was at Exeter College. No portrait survives of her in later life but there is a tinted drawing of her as a young girl: she looks plain, with straight hair looped back and a very direct gaze. It is the picture of a young bluestocking and she was undoubtedly very clever and desperately serious. When she was forming her own opinions (perhaps at fifteen or so, like Newman) she doubted Christianity and was given to reading Carlyle's *Sartor Resartus* but her brother Henry later introduced her to the Tracts and they talked earnestly of religion on their walks and rides; she said, 'the Oxford Movement began to fill our little world to its centre'.[22] He brought her a copy of the *Lyra Apostolica*, the verses of Keble, Newman and other Tractarians, meant to be an exposition of tractarian themes and a kind of devotional book too. She was much moved by it: 'it was as if a thunderbolt had fallen at my feet'.[23] It was not Keble's gentle poems that impressed her but Newman's more rugged verses and she was curious to see the writer and to hear him preach at Littlemore.

The experience was overwhelming. His appearance was impressive, powerful and a little forbidding, and when he preached, taking out his sermon from a little black-covered case and then standing still, with no histrionic gestures, she wept with emotion. The famous voice affected her, the voice that Maria Rosina Giberne described as '*douce et belle*' and that Emily called 'exquisite'. Lunch was served after these devotions and the exalted experience in church was followed by anti-climax. When Newman bent down to her with the mystic words, 'Will you have some cold chicken?' she could not answer him and her Mamma had to reply for her.

Emily was already an ardent Tractarian: she said, 'Catholic doctrines took root in me' and 'the language of the Tracts became a familiar tongue'.[24] She was converted to Roman Catholicism about two years later than her encounter with Newman, partly through the reading of a novel called *Geraldine* by a Catholic lady called Miss Agnew, and partly through her friendship with the Eystons, an old Catholic family. The Bowles family lived in Abingdon in Berkshire, not far from the Eystons at East Hendred. She was received into the Church of Rome by Cardinal Acton in 1843, when she was twenty five. She did not expect to see Newman again.

The note of adulation is clear in her account of the Littlemore meeting and this was to sound more clearly in the voice of another devotee, Mary Holmes who was a governess. She had accepted the doctrine of the Tracts in 1839 and began to correspond with Newman a year later. She had a great opinion of him as a spiritual director and must have been pleased to be invited to meet him in Oxford in 1842. He asked her to lunch, prudently inviting another male friend. Unlike Emily Bowles she was not impressed. He was younger than she expected and much more unassuming, not the venerable guru she had pictured.

Somewhat tactlessly she let him know what she thought – she had put him on a high pedestal and now felt disappointed. Newman would not have undue devotion and, not for the last time, he discouraged it.

> As for myself, be quite sure that if you saw me again, you would just feel as you did when you saw me before – I am *not* venerable, and nothing can make me so. I am what I am. I am very much like other people, and I do *not* think it necessary to abstain from the feelings and thoughts, not intrinsically sinful, which other people have. I cannot speak words of wisdom; to some it comes naturally. Do not suffer any illusive notion about me to spring up in your mind …[25]

Mary Holmes was sincere and very intelligent, but somewhat lacking in common sense and with a certain nuisance value. She was always moving from one job to another and consequently had her employers constantly in mind – either thinking of the current ones and wondering if she would go, or of the ones she might apply to for her next post. She involved Newman in these affairs, which was hardly discreet. Like many a conscientious clergyman he was caught, because he would not cast off a good person who needed him. When she became a Roman Catholic in 1844 she endeavoured to have her cake and eat it too by acquiring a priest adviser but continuing to apply to Newman. Then he did turn on her quite sharply, saying he had borne the burden long enough. She had Catholic priests to help and advise: their duty lay in being patient with her. He felt he had been patient beyond his duty.

In general, however, he was acquiring correspondents and disciples rather than losing them and one of the reasons for his long hesitation in breaking away from the

Church of England was his fear of letting them down, because he felt strongly that those who had committed themselves to a particular form of Christian life might lose all faith if their trust and certainty were disturbed.

Littlemore meant loneliness, solitude and austerity – it also meant a gathering of friends for others came to join him once he had set up 'the College', or as some called it, with reason, 'the Monastery'. It was a repetition of the pattern of his childhood when he had been at one and the same time the boy who was so conscious of the reality of God and of himself and yet was a member of a vigorous, close-knit family and the kind of child who would be a leader when he got to school. He seemed made for both solitude and friendship.

Harriett, rather surprisingly, was full of praise for the Littlemore College, which she visited in May 1842.

> John's new rooms are in a place neither you nor I knew. It looked like a wall. Now it has a dozen windows – one storey. Inside it is very pretty and neat – just my fancy. I do not wonder at John's present enthusiasm. There are four or five sets of rooms – sitting and bedroom – all on the ground floor – the door opening into the verandah which runs all along, a length of the diagonal of Oriel quad. The kitchen is in the middle – a pretty little garden before the verandah. At right angles is the library, a large pretty room with a nice roof, the sides covered with books. Inside, another small bookroom and above a spare bedroom ... The new windows were putting up – very old and handsome looking ...[26]

But Harriett was to lose all patience with her eldest brother, even before the conversion to Rome in 1845. The trouble really came to a head because of Tom and it all started with a holiday to France in the summer of 1843. Harriett, Tom, little Grace and her nursemaid set off in July, crossing to Le Havre and lodging at Ingouville above the town and the sea. Harriett's first visit to a French Roman Catholic church evoked mixed feelings, but her principal reaction was admiration at the sincere devotion of the worshippers. She wrote to Jemima:

We went into the large church (or small Cathedral) last evening in the dusk. No service going on – no priests – but many in pews and at the side altars – in the last people seem most engrossed – almost always on their knees on the floor. A good deal of noise with people's creaking boots in walking, else it was a solemn scene and one to make one feel more and more the sinfulness which somewhen or other brought on the present state of things as regards ourselves – for it seems to me no church man can doubt but that here they have us at a great advantage, and one must have a feeling of being in the *wrong* as it were – just as one feels in a quarrel, though ourselves may be every so conscious of having the right on our side, and that on no account, under no temptation whatever, must one yield up one's cause. There is nothing striking or exciting in the churches here to rouse any such extraordinary feelings – only the view of simple devotion in individuals as one *never* can see it exhibited at home cannot fail to affect ...[27]

They met several priests, quite agreeable men, who knew all about the 'Puseistes' and were excited to meet the sister of M. New-man. They charged the Anglicans with the enormity of having a young woman at the head of the church, but Harriett retorted that in France the clergy were paid by the State. They went on to Caen and to Langrune, seven miles away on the coast and became friendly with a Mlle Tyrell, who introduced them to two priests, Achille and Hyacinth de Valroger, who were holidaying with their mother and sister. 'They make no show of their hopes of converting us, but their hearts are full of it',[28] said Harriett. They also met some aristocratic people, Mme Polignac and her daughter and son-in-law, who also believed 'that England is going to turn Romanist all in a "coup"'.[29] Harriett was drawn to Mlle de Valroger, her health improved and she was enjoying herself.

Again, on visiting the churches, she was struck by the numbers who attended church, the 'incessant scattered worshippers' during the week and the general air of devotion. But she was sure that the French hopes of the English coming over to Rome in a body were delusions and she disliked the services she saw:

> The infinity of these ceremonies and forms and the complication of these traditional services, is something I had no conception of – and the notion of our doing anything of the kind in any one of our churches, too monstrous to dream of. There is nothing for those who would have such things but to go over at once to Rome. To think for instance of any English bowing towards the altar and equalling the salaam they contrive to make here. I hardly know how it is done.[30]

She also noted, with disapproval, that the people were not expected to join in the prayers at all. 'The whole is as opposite of our notion of common prayer as anything can be ...'[31] Newman's hero, Charles Reding, hears of just such a celebration of Mass from the lips of an enthusiastic convert – it is a famous passage – where each is in his place 'not painfully and hopelessly following a hard form of prayers from beginning to end' but each with his own prayers 'separate but concordant'.[32] It is an irony of history that Harriett's perception of the necessity for common prayer should have been shared by the reformers of the Second Vatican Council so that she would not be so alienated today.

Harriett and Grace stayed on in Langrune when Tom went home to attend to business. In September came a letter that shocked her to the core. Tom announced that he wished to become a Catholic. She replied, and with some justice, 'it seems to me the most treacherous thing in the world to have persuaded me to stay here against my will and then to go home, and in my absence without a word of preparation to take so grave a step'.[33] After this she did not wish to continue her friendship with the de Valroger family and spoke of their wretched religion. 'Every hour is showing me what a showy, fallacious, false and hollow system it is'.[34] She went off to stay with the Polignacs at the Chateau d'Outrelaise for a fortnight and was pleasantly entertained but secretly very worried.

John, at home, believed that Tom was acting precipitately and persuaded him to wait for two years before he joined the Church of Rome. One would have thought that Harriett, back in England, would be mollified by such persuasions but she somehow thought that her brother was to be blamed for the whole affair. Tom never did become a Catholic and Harriett's letters to John petered out. After his conversion to Rome she did not see him again.

Jemima was not so hard-hearted. She suffered blow after blow as her brother was denounced over the famous Tract 90, as he confided his doubts about the Church of England, as he severed one link after another with his Anglican and Oxford life. One of her troubles was that the Mozleys were concerned and she had ever to be looking over her shoulder to see how they reacted to events: women were then surrounded by family, often supportive but also demanding, forcing opinions, modifying reactions to fit some family pattern. Jemima had to take thought too for Aunt Betsy, distressed over her favourite nephew.

Letters went to and fro in the crucial years 1844 and 1845: on Newman's side they were frank and loving and Jemima's letters were sorrowing, eloquent and sensitive to his troubles and to his conscience. All the same, she had some harsh things to say about the Roman Church which he was increasingly drawn to. 'I cannot help feeling a repulsion from that church which has so many stains upon her',[35] she wrote, and later, 'I feel a strong and what seems an insurmountable disapprobation of her, as of a guide with whom one dared not trust oneself'.[36]

In March 1845 John wrote:

As to my convictions, I can but say what I have told you already, that I cannot at all make out *why* I should determine on moving, except as thinking I should offend God by not doing so. I cannot make out what I am *at* except on this supposition ... I am distressing all I love, unsettling all I have instructed or aided. I am going to those I do not know, and of whom I expect very little. I am making myself an outcast and that at my age. Oh, what can it be a stern necessity which causes this?

Pity me, my dear Jemima ...[37]

She did pity him and, though she could not see the stern necessity herself, she was willing to believe that he truly felt it. On 8 October, 1845, Newman wrote a sheaf of letters and of course there was one for Jemima.

Littlemore Oct 8, 1845

My Dear Jemima,

I must tell you, what will pain you greatly, but I will make it as short as you would wish me to do.

This night Father Dominic the Passionist, sleeps here. He does not know of my intention, but I shall ask him to receive me into what I believe to be the One Fold of the Redeemer.

This will not go, till all is over.

Ever yours affectly John H. Newman[38]

Harriett was in no mood to show pity. She wrote to Jemima, 'I do not always understand, dear Cattie, how it is you always say of J.H.N. "I am afraid," "I fear he will be disappointed," etc. Surely you do not desire he should be satisfied?'[39] She maintained he was acting against his reason and was like a man who must abide the consequences of making a disgraceful marriage. He returned some papers to Tom in 1846, ending his note, 'Do not suppose I do not think of you and Harriett continually, because I do not write'. He signed himself, 'Ever your constant friend and brother',[40] a phrase that was meant to take in Harriett as well as Tom, but evoked no response. We should have some pity for her in all this because she was lashing out at someone she loved because she felt threatened and no one need suppose that she lost all feeling for her brother, though she locked herself into the estrangement.

In after years, Jemima kept up a correspondence with John though they both had topics on which they kept quiet. She lived on in Derby and had six children, Herbert, John, Henry, Jane, Francis and Alfred. While they were growing up she did not invite her brother to visit the family. There was plenty of intelligence amongst the young Mozleys: Herbert for instance, became a lawyer and a very good mathematician.

Harriett and Tom left Cholderton for London where he gave up his work as a clergyman for a time to turn to journalism, writing for the *Times*. Harriett's health was never good and indeed, in her letters from Normandy, on that notable holiday, there are so many references to her dreadful insomnia that it is surprising that she kept going at all. While on a visit to Oxford in 1852 she became seriously ill and was taken home to London. A maid sat up with her one night but, seeing her mistress sleeping in the early morning, slept herself. Later, when they tried to rouse Harriett they found she had died of a heart attack. She was forty eight. Newman wrote to Henry Wilberforce, that friend who had shared the scenes of their youth: 'I daresay I have spoken severely of her to my sister Jemima before now – but I am not aware that I have ever felt unkindly. Poor Harriett, what a change from what it was when you first knew us! What a world this is'.[41] Old Aunt Betsy died too, a few weeks afterwards.

Grace, Harriett's one child, was made much of by her parents, treated like an infant prodigy by her mother who was always reporting her exploits and her cunning ways. She suffered from her mother's death – she was only twelve – but she and her father were very close (she wrote to him, when a very little girl, 'I love you most stremely').[42] She grew up to be a very sociable young woman, emigrated to Australia and married a doctor.

Chapter Two

The Converts

Elizabeth Bowden; Emily Bowles, Cornelia Connelly,
Mary Holmes; Maria Rosina Giberne; Catherine
Froude and her family; Other converts – Eliza Ward,
Lady Lothian, The Marquise de Salvo, Jane Todd,
Catherine Ward, Lavinia Wilson

At the end of a piece of autobiographical writing done in 1834 and called *My Illness in Sicily* Newman added in 1840 a passage about his own loneliness.

> The thought keeps pressing on me, while I write this, what am I writing it for? For myself, I may look at it once or twice in my whole life, and what sympathy is there in *my* looking at it? Whom have I, whom can I have, who would take interest in it? I was going to say, I only have found one who even took that sort of affectionate interest in me as to be pleased with such details – and that is H. Wilberforce and what shall I ever see of him? This is the sort of interest which a wife takes and none but she – it is a woman's interest – and that interest, so be it, shall never be taken in me. Never, so be it, will I be other than God has found me. All my habits for years, my tendencies, are towards celibacy. I could not take that interest in this world which marriage requires. I am too disgusted with this world – And, above all, call it what one will, I have a repugnance to a clergyman's marrying. I do not say it is not lawful – I cannot deny the right – but, whether a prejudice or not, it shocks me. And therefore I willingly give up the possession of that

sympathy, which I feel is not, cannot be, granted to me. Yet, not the less do I feel the need of it. Who will care to be told such details as I have put down above? Shall I ever have in my old age spiritual children who will take an interest such as a wife does? ...[1]

This is interesting for all sorts of reasons: it is a very clear statement of his views on celibacy, for himself and for at least many of the clergy and it shows that he felt that, when Henry Wilberforce married, if he had not lost a friend he had certainly lost an intimacy that he valued. He asked the question about the spiritual children he might have. As an Anglican leader he had many such; followers, devotees, men and women who asked his advice and relied on his guidance. As a Catholic he was to have even more: especially he was consulted by the flock of converts who left the Oxford Movement at much the same time as he did or some years later. Who more obvious as a guide? Much of his direction was given by letter and since he was an excellent letter writer as well as a wise counsellor and since so many letters are extant, the fears, difficulties, joys, lives and fortunes of the converts are there for all to see. There is much that is sad in the tale of Newman's conversion: the years of doubt, the pain of separation, his cry that it was like going on the open sea. With hindsight the modern reader of his letters sees Newman setting forth on his Catholic life with difficulties ahead and the partial rejection of his great gifts by the Church of his adoption. Yet there is always that second part of the title of his novel about conversion to be considered – the gain that accompanies the loss. In the months that followed Newman's reception into the Church of Rome, he visibly relaxed. He delighted in the services, was unspeakably consoled by being able to pray in chapels and churches before the Blessed Sacrament. He no longer had to argue for his celibate vocation or debate whether it was right to invoke the Virgin Mary and the saints. He said it was easier to direct people when they were accustomed to reveal their inner lives in the confessional.

So it is easy to see how the great convert would collect

other converts about him – he would not need to gather a flock because they would come quite naturally. In that revealing passage, however, he is not considering what he can do for his spiritual children but is thinking of what they may do for him. Human relationships need to be reciprocal. He notes that sympathy, attentiveness to the details of another's life experience are talents that women have in particular. At the end of the *Apologia* he pays tribute to the Oxford friends from times past and, more emphatically, to the priests of the Birmingham Oratory, his spiritual children in a special sense. He singles out one great friend, Ambrose St John, who was at Littlemore with him and became his constant companion for ever after, Ambrose 'whom God gave me when he took everyone else away; who are the link between my old life and my new ...'[2] The gracious rhetoric obscures the fact that there were others who served as links between his Anglican life and his Catholic one.

One of these was Elizabeth Bowden. Her husband, John, had been so much Newman's companion when they were both undergraduates that the story goes that he sometimes addressed his wife as 'Newman'. She did not seem to mind, had no jealousy, and accepted Newman as her own friend. She and her John had a nickname for him – the Great Man. This was at once a teasing tribute and an ironic phrase because he did not behave as a great man when visiting them: he related well to the family situation, to Elizabeth and to the children. There were two boys, John and Charles, and two girls, Marianne (or Maryanne) and Emily.

Their mother, though rich enough to employ the best governesses, taught the children herself, the boys eventually leaving her care for public school. Harriett visited them when they lived at Roehampton and reported on the schoolroom, where the three younger ones were employed.

Mrs Bowden is teaching the three children in the same room. Her management seems very good in all ways. Charlie has been saying his French and other lessons in

a merry chanting tone. Mary Anne aged ten is reading
French verse very nicely. They are very plain in dress etc.
Too much so for my taste – i.e. their hair is cropped
close like old Charity School children. I have no doubt
their Mamma is a most thorough governess. The Papa
looks – oh so much older! but is well and strong – and all
is pleasant and zealous as possible.[3]

The reference to the health of 'the Papa' is significant,
because John Bowden came from a family prone to
consumption. He, like Hurrell Froude, was to die young of
that disease, a scourge of that time. Newman went to see
him in 1844, knowing that he did not have long to live, and
was impressed by his calm and cheerfulness. He described
for Keble the little scene at night when Bowden was carried
upstairs by two servants, his wife going ahead with a candle,
the invalid joking about his 'procession' and making sure
that his friend, at the foot of the stairs, saw that he looked
at him as he went. He died in September and Newman's
grief was compounded with his own doubts and distresses.
He could not have disturbed his friend's rare tranquillity
by telling him of his doubts about the Church of England
and he felt that Bowden went to God leaving him 'still dark
as to what the way of truth was'.[4]

Bowden had told his wife to take Newman as her guide,
and it troubled him to think that he must break it to her
that he was on the brink of joining the Roman Church. She
was distressed and both of them were in a painful and
emotional situation where he wished to help and she
wished to follow her husband's leading – and yet this division of thought, in the most important area in their lives,
opened like a chasm before them. Newman wrote: 'Unless
my heart is very self-deceived I most profoundly wish to be
a servant to you. O do suffer me to be such, and take me
for what I am, though I cannot be all you might have
thought or could wish'.[5] Affection and a desire to be open,
on each side, preserved the relationship.

Newman was very concerned for the children too. He
was fond of them and worried about them, particularly
about Marianne, because they were not strong. Early in

1845 he visited the family, then living at St Leonard's, but all the children were 'in the measles'. Then Elizabeth herself caught it, so the visit was hardly a success. As her mother took to her bed, Marianne emerged from seclusion and took on the role of hostess. She was a gentle girl of fourteen, learning gracious ways. Newman wrote to her mother, 'Dear child – I took her by surprise and wished her goodbye on the staircase – and her manner was so kind, and I wished so much our custom was to give a blessing on leave taking.'[6]

After his conversion Newman left Littlemore for Birmingham and was housed, with his companions, at Maryvale, a house which had been the Catholic seminary before a new and more extensive college had been set up at Oscott. He wrote to Mrs Bowden from there when he had newly arrived and all was in disorder. He told her that he did not mind the confusion because of the blessedness of having a chapel containing the Blessed Sacrament. 'I could not have fancied the extreme, ineffable comfort of being in the same house with Him who cured the sick and taught His disciples, as we read of Him in the Gospels, in the days of His flesh'.[7] He added that he did not mean it to be a proselytizing letter 'but really, while there are few pesons to whom I could say what I have said, I cannot keep from saying it where I can say it'. In other words, she sympathised with his religious position enough to be a fit recipient for such confidences.

By March 1846 she was writing to him that she was thinking of becoming a Catholic and he urged her to take her time coming to a decision. However, she was not left in peace to make up her mind because her brother-in-law, Henry Bowden, was vehemently against her taking such a step, particularly since her conversion might turn his nephews in the same direction. Henry was a Captain in the Scots Fusilier Guards and he laid about him with military firmness. She could not come to a right conclusion, said Henry, since she could not read all that could be said on both sides. Newman's advice was delivered fully in June.

Use the means which God has given you, as you have

hitherto done. As far as I know your course, you have almost grown of yourself into what you are – in the course of many months, first by the example of myself and others, next by your own judgement on the present state of things, further by the general impression made on you by history, and not the least, by your knowledge of the gradual tendencies of dear John. Here is the legitimate way in which you are called upon to use your reason. God will bless you in such calm spontaneous use of it – But as to your being driven about hither and thither, by opposite disputants, I cannot bear to think of it. It is meant kindly, but for me, I am not capable of stunning you with arguments, or stifling you with folios, or subduing you by an urgent tone or a confident manner. The first Volume of Collyer! it is wonderful! when would you have done it?[8]

Collyer or Collier wrote The *Ecclesiastical History of Great Britain to the end of the Reign of Charles II* and the nine volumes were being republished. He was, presumably, recommended as useful reading by Henry Bowden. Newman was making a practical point here: how could women, even intelligent women like Elizabeth Bowden, without technical training at university level in evaluating evidence, be expected to wade through great volumes and in any case, was not her time properly spent in supervising her household and looking after her delicate children? He was also considering a deeper psychological and religious question which was to occupy him for years and issue in a book, *The Grammar of Assent*, published in 1870. What is the nature of belief and what is the connection between faith and reason? It is not a book to be summarised in a sentence or two: suffice it to say here that the lines of the developed argument agree with what he said to Elizabeth Bowden – we cannot prove religious truth as we would prove mathematical theory, but probabilities accumulate to make revealed religion worthy of our credence.

She was received into the Church in July, 1846. The three younger children followed her, the girls being willing converts and Charlie, Newman's godson and not very old, going with the family tide. John, the eldest, who was seventeen and at Eton, was a very different case. Newman counselled that he should not be urged or preached at, though there was the difficulty that he would be lectured and urged in the opposite direction by his uncle. In the event he did become a Catholic two years later and eventually, after all the fuss, so did Henry Bowden and his family. One of Newman's company, John Dalgairns, said of the first Bowden conversion, that of Elizabeth, that she and all her children were born and cut out by nature to be Catholics, as anybody might judge by their very looks. He did not extend this astonishing statement to define the looks that proclaim a Catholic.

At the other end of the scale measuring enthusiasm for conversions to Rome, Harriett had commented tartly in a letter to Jemima; 'By the bye I suppose you see in the papers that it is said "Mrs Bowden and family" have gone over to Rome. I have not had it confirmed and if I went by *words*, I ought to be amazed etc. etc. – but though her words in our late meeting were against Rome, her heart I saw went the other way, so I cannot be surprised. Also, J.H.N. was staying with her, which I thought very suspicious, on more accounts than one ...'[9]

The house where he was staying was the Bowden family house in London, in Grosvenor Place, described by Harriett, again in sour mood, as an area that had been grand but had become 'sadly second rate now, and I had rather live in any fourth rate square than in such rattle of vehicles ...'[10] When in London on business or in transit, Newman often stayed in the Bowden house, as he had done years before when John Bowden's father was alive.

In the first years after Newman's conversion he was very much on the move, packing up to go from Littlemore, travelling about England to meet Catholics and see houses, institutions, churches and chapels, making a temporary home in Maryvale with his little community and visiting Oscott and then, after some deliberation, going to Rome to study for the Catholic priesthood, taking Ambrose St John with him. It is movement and travel that calls forth a certain vivid kind of letter writing, with descriptions and accounts of the traveller's reactions to new experiences. Newman had other matters to discuss too, since this was a time of decisions about the life ahead of him: he decided to be a priest but he was debating whether he would join one of the Religious Orders.

He wrote to Mrs Bowden from Milan, greatly impressed by the Duomo and by High Mass in another church where 'the floor was covered with people, as thick as they could stow'[11] and, in the midst of a great eulogy on St Charles, told her that he had thought of 'dear little Charlie' and she was to tell him so. Once arrived, with Ambrose, at the *Collegio di Propaganda* where they were to stay and study in Rome, he told her in detail about the arrangements made for their welfare. There would be no chance of their following a strict Lenten regime, as at Littlemore, for 'they seem to treat us like wax dolls or mantlepiece ornaments'.[12]

He informed her of his ordination and told her in some detail of their plans to bring the Oratory of St Philip Neri to England, the Oratorians being secular priests living in community. He added:

> You will be disappointed, I fear, to be told what our duty will be – it will be to plant ourselves in a large town, say Birmingham, and attempt to get hold of those classes which at present are anything or nothing, members of clubs, mechanics – institutes etc. etc. Not that this is not a great object, but perhaps you would not wish it for me. But it has great recommendations for me personally – It gives me what I want, active work, yet as much or as little as I wish – time for reading and writing – and a rule without being a very severe one. It will associate also together persons of very different tastes – as we want to argue, to preach, to sing and play, and to train young people.[13]

In the same letter he asked particularly for her prayers because he was feeling old, played out and lacking in confidence. 'I cannot realise to myself that my time is not past'. It was the sort of thing he could not now say to Jemima.

When he returned to England he arrived in London on Christmas Day and Charlie Bowden proudly served his Mass.

~~∞∞~~

Elizabeth Bowden had her difficulties as a widow with the responsibility of children but she had ample means, status and the protection (albeit an ambiguous one) of Henry Bowden. Single women had more difficulties to face and there were many of them in the middle of the last century. A census taken in 1857 revealed that in the over twenty age group women outnumbered men and many articles and pamphlets appeared on the subject of single women and their problems. Such publicity must have made them feel they were like unwanted mechandise, surplus to require- ments. Two of Newman's friends from the tractarian days are examples of very intelligent unmarried women whose talents were not fully used and who suffered in conse- quence: they are Emily Bowles and Mary Holmes. They are alike in being intelligent, in the fact that they had a great admiration for Newman and were in touch with him for most of their adult lives. They both entered the Church of Rome before he did. They were, however, quite different as to background. Mary Holmes, the governess, did not have much influence and she had no money of her own beyond what she could earn in her lowly capacity as a teacher in the houses of the wealthy. Emily Bowles came from a large, well-to-do family and the range of her friends and acquaintances, some of them very influential people, was considerable.

One new possibility was opening up for devout unmar- ried women, to join a Religious Sisterhood. Pusey was one strong advocate for the restoration of Religious life in England and by the eighteen forties Anglican Sisterhoods were being founded. Catholic non-monastic Congrega- tions, engaged in such good works as nursing and teaching, were also appearing on the English scene. Some of them were from Europe and some grew up on English soil. Newman was greatly in favour of these developments

though, English to the core and with a certain John Bullish
distrust of foreign ways, he tended to look with more
favour on the native communities. He wished Miss Holmes
would consider Religious life and he did make the suggestion to Miss Giberne that she might be interested in the
new Congregation being planned by Cornelia Connelly, an
American lady. He wrote, in a tone of approbation that the
first object of this Religious Institute would be 'instructing
girls, principally of the middle and upper classes' and that
'the person who begins it, is in the truest and best sense an
enthusiastic person – of education and great influence in
her circle.'[1]

The story of Cornelia Connelly is an extraordinary one.
She came from Philadelphia and grew up to be both
cultured and beautiful. She married an Episcopalian clergyman, Pierce Connelly, and in the mid-thirties they both
became Catholics, being received into the Church in
Rome. Lord Shrewsbury was Pierce Connelly's friend and
sponsor and he stayed with him at his great house, Alton
Towers. In 1840 Connelly expressed a desire to be a priest
and, incredibly, despite the fact that he was married with
three children, permission was granted, provided that his
wife agreed to total separation. At first she demurred but
came to the belief that God was asking this sacrifice of her.
In 1844 a deed of separation was drawn up in Rome and in
the next year Pierce Connelly was ordained. His wife had
entered the Society of the Sacred Heart in Rome but she
was not settled there although she was firm in her determination to remain in Religious life. England needed a
Congregation whose main object would be education and
she was encouraged to found her own community there:
from the start she meant it to be based on Jesuit spirituality
and she was to lay down broad and firm principles of
Christian education. Her Congregation became the
Society of the Holy Child Jesus.

On 18 August 1846, Mrs Connelly arrived in
Birmingham, lodged at the usual staging post, the Convent
of Mercy at Handsworth or the house next door, and met
Newman at Maryvale. He was to say later that he did not
like her and rather rudely described her as a Yankee. She

probably meant to continue the acquaintance but he was due to depart for Rome and she, now staying at Spetchley Park in Worcestershire with a Catholic lady, Mrs Berkeley, was deep in plans for taking a building in Derby for the first convent.

Meanwhile Miss Bowles, now twenty-eight, was often in Birmingham, visiting Oscott and Dr Wiseman. At that time England did not have its own hierarchy and dioceses but was divided into districts. The Central or Midland district was presided over by Bishop Walsh, with Nicholas Wiseman, who was also president of the seminary at Oscott as his coadjutor. It is easy to gather from descriptions given by Newman himself and by other converts how exciting it must have been to see Catholic houses, communities and churches beginning to flourish all over the Midlands. Pugin was putting up his gothic churches, such as St Chad's in Birmingham. Aristocrats like the Earl of Shrewsbury were making their houses Catholic centres and Pierce Connelly was there as chaplain at Alton Towers. Spetchley Park, a gracious Georgian house, was another lovely setting for Catholic worship and Mrs Connelly must have been glad to rest for a little while there, with her children, the youngest only five years old. Dr Wiseman, an enthusiast, was full of plans and the new congregation was part of his schemes and his hopes.

While Miss Bowles was visiting Oscott she happened to be with her friends in the gallery of the chapel and saw Newman being catechised by an Italian priest. This must have been one of the occasions when, to use his own words he was 'a spectacle for Dr Wiseman to exhibit to strangers,' 'a wild incomprehensible beast'[2] that had been captured by the triumphant hunter, Wiseman. She said, 'It was almost more than I could bear to see the great teacher come out to be questioned and taught as a little child.'[3]

It was not Newman but Wiseman who advised Miss Bowles to join Mrs Connelly's venture. She was likely to be a great asset since she was devout, talented, had already written for publication and, in addition to all her good qualities and gifts, had a knowledge of English society and English ways. She could advise Mrs Connelly in many

matters. Here lay the source for future trouble though no
one saw it at the time. Mrs Connelly was to be the superior-
general of the new Society and with her lay the power and
responsibility. But her first recruit was intelligent, articulate, versed in many customs and attitudes that Mrs
Connelly was new to, and, moreover, was to prove,
according to one of the next recruits, Maria Buckle, very
argumentative and quite prepared to disagree with her
superior about the way things should be.

When they went to Derby Mrs Connelly's five year old,
Frank, went with them. The older children, a boy and a
girl, were packed off to boarding schools. Frank too would
soon be parted from his mother and Miss Bowles advised
that this should be as soon as possible because English eyes
would be upon them and English sensibilities were ultra-
sensitive where Catholics were concerned. There was
ignorance and suspicion abroad and the sight of a nun
with a small son would provoke malicious gossip. As a
judgement about English reactions, this counsel of Emily
Bowles seems eminently reasonable and accurate, but she
does not seem to have had much regard for the mother's
feelings. 'Emily is much too anxious *not* to have him'[4] is the
phrase used by Mrs Connelly, discussing plans for Frank
with her husband.

Derby must have been a revelation both to the privileged
young English woman and to the dignified American who
had so far seen only Spetchley and Alton Towers in her
adopted country. It was industrialised, with lace, silk and
cotton mills, with dreadful slum areas that lacked sanitation
or even a proper water supply. The building that they had
been offered as a convent lay among narrow, dirty streets and
the sewers of the town emptied themselves at the end of the
garden. Newman and his new community had much the
same experience when he returned from Rome and set up
his first Oratory house in Alcester Street, in the centre of
Birmingham, in a disused gin distillery. It says much for the
converts, men and women, that they did not turn their backs
on the cities, though little in their background and former
experiences had prepared them for the sights and smells of
the Victorian Midland urban scene.

The new nuns (there were soon seven of them) started on the Poor School and also ran a Sunday School for the factory girls which in time was turned into a night school to teach catechism, the three Rs and sewing. Early in 1848 a small boarding school was opened for middle class girls. There is no question but that Emily Bowles had the skills and the energy to be a most valuable associate in setting up and maintaining such work. Whether, despite her religious earnestness, she was cut out for the life of a nun is quite another matter. Paradoxically enough, since religious rules were strict and obedience was exacted in such a way that independence and originality were severely restricted, she probably chose the Religious life in order to gain some independence.

Mother Connelly's community grew, often recruiting from converts, a fact noted and approved by Wiseman who saw that there was a new reserve of energy and enthusiasm among English Catholics. They moved from Derby to St Leonard's, a small but high class Sussex watering place. One new project was in mind, to begin a teacher-training college, a grave need for the Catholic community, and Emily Bowles and a little core group of sisters were preparing for this. Although St Leonard's was a cleaner and more prosperous place by far than Derby, they did not neglect the poor there and set their sights only on middle class pupils. A Poor School was established and Mother Connelly was pleased to be asked to send her sisters further afield to Liverpool where Irish children, their families fleeing from the potato famine, were in grave want and had no one to offer them education.

She sent four nuns to make a start, one of them being Emily Bowles as the superior. Three more followed and they set about their hard teaching work, directed by Emily herself. A government inspector praised what they had done at the end of their first year. All augured well. In 1853 the secretary of the Catholic Poor Schools Committee consulted both the superior of the Liverpool convent and Mother Connelly about setting up a teacher-training college for women in Liverpool. The idea was welcome but the doubt was where the money would come from and

Mother Connelly made the condition that the Catholic Poor Schools Committee should arrange grants for building costs. A year before, Emily, who had not brought a dowry on entering the Society of the Holy Child, made over £1300 to Mother Connelly, and she was now authorised to borrow £1300 from one of her brothers, Samuel Bowles, securing the loan with the gift already in the Society's possession.

She hunted for a suitable property and, borrowing from Samuel, she paid the first instalment on Rupert House, an expensive purchase at £6000. A provisional grant was allowed. On this slender hope, she then met the rest of the debt by going to another brother, John, and with him signed a Note of Hand for £5000 from a bank. She also contracted for alterations to the house and hoped that this original gift for her of £1300 would pay for this, thus leaving the loan from Samuel with no security. Mother Connelly expressed great apprehension and displeasure at the course that had been taken and removed Emily Bowles from her office as superior in December 1854. The apprehension was well-founded: in the spring of the next year the Catholic Poor Schools Committee withdrew the agreement for the grant because the Sisters of Notre Dame de Namur, an established community with some funds, were willing to set up a teacher-training college for women at their own expense. Mother Connelly now had a large house that she did not want and a massive debt. The first debt to Samuel Bowles she had known about and now acknowledged as money that must be paid by the Society. The second debt, to John Bowles, she maintained was entirely Emily's responsibility. She had acted on her own. The debt was to grow even larger: Mother Connelly gave John Bowles a simple mortgage on Rupert House, or rather a simple mortgage as she thought, whereas the document, drawn up by the Bowles' solicitor under Emily's direction and signed by sisters who did not understand its terms, was a compound one. The house was put on the market but did not sell.

In answer to her cry for help, Newman visited Miss Bowles in Liverpool. Her account of this visit is reticent

about her own situation and this is proper in the circumstances because she was writing a short account of her
acquaintance with Newman, not of her own life.

> For many reasons chiefly arising from my own troubled
> circumstances I did not see him again till 1859 when at
> great inconvenience and loss of time he went all across
> Liverpool to judge of my state for himself and to give
> what comfort and support he could in a crisis of intense
> mental suffering. At that very time he himself was
> suffering from the double strain of being the Superior
> of the Birmingham Oratory and Rector of the Dublin
> Catholic University, which instead of appreciating or
> rewarding his continual labour and anxiety was slowly
> perishing before his eyes. No one then, or I believe ever
> since, knew that my almost unconscious cry of distress
> had brought him at once, at whatever cost to give
> strength and comfort ...[5]

This account demonstrates Newman's kindness. It also tells
us that he heard of the whole affair from Emily Bowles and
at a time when she was in a distressed state of mind. He did
not hear the other side. She then, presumably under
Newman's guidance, applied to her bishop for a dispensation from her vows and left the Society of the Holy Child
Jesus. Indeed it is difficult to see how she could have
stayed. From then on she and her brothers harried Mother
Connelly for a full repayment, threatened lawsuits and
finally had the matter settled out of court, Mother
Connelly doing so at the wish of her bishop, who wanted
the matter settled quietly. The last sum paid to the Bowles
was made over in 1871 – and trouble had rumbled on
throughout the intervening years.

The affair was not entirely clear in its details since it has
many financial and legal twists and turns but there is
enough evidence to make some kind of judgment and in
the main there is not much excuse for poor Miss Bowles.
There is this to be said – that in an established community
with more nuns she would probably not have been
appointed as superior in the Liverpool convent when she

was young in Religious life but would have held a responsible post in the educational work that the Society was engaged in. It was almost inevitable, given the history of the new Society and her temperament, that there would be a power struggle between her and the foundress. William Buckle, the father of one of the first sisters, had the impression at first that she was co-foundress, but she certainly was not. On her own in Liverpool, keen to begin the training college and knowing that the Catholic community badly needed such an institution, she would be tempted to act with great independence.

However, no nun, for whatever good reason, should have engaged in the financial transactions that Miss Bowles took on. Perhaps Mother Connelly did not keep a close enough eye on such matters. For instance, when she had already seen that Emily Bowles had been massively indiscreet in borrowing money, one would think she should have signed the mortgage deed herself. Mother Connelly was a downright woman and not always easy to deal with. But she was honest and entirely consistent in her statements that the second and larger debt was incurred without her consent or indeed her knowledge, and in this she was backed up by George Eyston, the Society's solicitor. The name is significant: the Eystons, as we have noted, were an old recusant family, neighbours to the Bowles family and an influence on Emily's conversion to Rome. He would have been predisposed to take the side of the Bowles brothers and Emily herself because of this connection but he backed Mother Connelly with a lawyer's attention to facts.

Almost the worst part of the business is the long tale of complaint and slander that came from Miss Bowles' pen after she had left the Society. She traduced Cornelia Connelly to Wiseman and to Newman and in bitter terms. Since she had many connections and friends in high places she could wreak damage and she did. Mr Buckle summed up matters neatly when he wrote of her, 'in point of talents and accomplishments she has not her equal but of common sense, judgment and now principles she is wanting.'[6] He was referring to her lack of principles in the matter of the money but her bitter and relentless pursuit of Cornelia Connelly and her Society seems to argue an even more serious fault.

She certainly added to the griefs of a woman who suffered a great deal. Cornelia Connelly's main sorrow was the separation from her three children. This became total when Pierce Connelly reverted to Protestantism, part of his disillusionment with the Roman church being that he was not allowed to have a part in the running of his wife's convent. He sued her for the restitution of conjugal rights. Matrimonial suits were heard in ecclesiastical courts and the case of Connelly v. Connelly was heard in the Court of Arches of the see of Canterbury in 1849, and judgment was given for the husband. Cornelia Connelly was pilloried in the press as one who had deserted husband and children and the fact that the initial separation had been brought about by Pierce Connelly was hardly averted to in any publicity. She made an Appeal to the Privy Council and had to wait for fifteen months before the case came up. When it did the judges took into account the religious aspects of the case and stated that Mrs Connelly's cause should be reconsidered; they further asked that Pierce Connelly should pay the costs of both parties, thus signalling that the law was in her favour. He could not pay and she eventually paid all costs and on 24 June 1858 the case was finally dismissed. Pierce Connelly left England, taking the children with him. It is an extraordinary and harrowing story and it is not hard to imagine the distress that it caused Cornelia. She persevered courageously with the foundation of the Society of the Holy Child but even there she suffered because ecclesiastics harried her. She had left her husband because he wished to be a priest and she began the Religious congregation because she was required to do so by Wiseman. In the first instance her obedience and pliability is hard to accept in modern times, when a different judgment would be made about a husband's ascendency over his wife. Having complied in meekness, she was persecuted both by husband and by bishops for carrying out the work put into her hands. Her Religious vocation was truly her own although Pierce

Connelly had brought about the initial circumstances where a Religious vocation could be considered, and to this calling she adhered at whatever cost.

Emily Bowles' affair was a small matter compared with her large griefs, but it was a long-standing trouble all the same. At one point on the negotiations about the money which were running on it was suggested that Miss Bowles and Mother Connelly should meet. The latter wrote this reply:

> I must decline any interview with Miss Bowles. In all charity and forgiveness, we still feel that she has acted the part of a demon towards us, and the only way to secure charity is to keep apart. The calumnious effects of her many grievous falsehoods can *never* be effaced, nor will it be easy in time to *forget* them, tho I trust Our Lord may remove the Viper of animosity, and help us through the burden of wrongs which must be felt for some years.[7]

This first draft was not sent, and a less bitter answer was written and posted. The original outpouring calls Miss Bowles a 'demon' and though the 'Viper' is animosity it is not fanciful to think that Mother Connelly thought that the erstwhile Sister Emily was the real viper. It is hard to reconcile this picture of her with the Miss Bowles that Newman knew, admired and liked. He accepted her story of events in the convent though he did say once that he had heard only her account.

There was something in Miss Bowles, competent and strong-minded as she was, that required a mentor, a prop, a person to be loved and admired. When she was first in the convent Mother Connelly was such a person, but the relationship changed dramatically. A modern biographer of Cornelia Connelly explains it in these terms:

> If this extremely intelligent, energetic but emotionally insecure woman began the life with even some sense that she was of notable importance to the foundation, and then gradually found herself unable to move it in directions she wanted; if eventually she lost in the

process both the venture in which she believed and the family money she had sunk into it, albeit illicitly; if in consequence she was then deprived of office and status – all this could have generated an emotional conviction and vindictive anger that she had been unjustly dealt with.[8]

Newman, who had always been admirable in her eyes, became her guide and stay but she still yearned for convent life. Twice she asked to be taken back into the Society of the Holy Child Jesus. She thought she might join the Third Order Dominicans at Stone in Staffordshire. She had thoughts of trying to bring some Belgian Béguines to England and herself set up a Béguinage, a community of ladies living in their own little houses but with communal prayers and a rule of life. At her second application to be taken back into her Society, Mother Connelly sent her a kind and sensible letter saying that with her energy and talents she could serve the Church well as a lay woman.

This is what she did. She had a small house in London with one servant girl who was friendless and for whom Miss Bowles felt responsible and there she divided her time between writing and works of charity, visiting at a prison and at a large hospital. The lessons of Derby where the new nuns had learnt what the poor suffer were never forgotten by her. She did not see Newman very often but they corresponded regularly and she liked to think of herself as his 'child'. It was at the Birmingham Oratory in 1856, when she was shown over the comparatively new house and the unfinished church that she learnt of what she called the 'pretty custom' of calling Newman 'the Father' and she took the phrase to herself. Once, though Newman customarily began letters to her 'My Dear Child,' he inadvertently began one with the formal 'My Dear Miss Bowles'. She begged him to use the other form of address, as though it meant a great deal to her.

Once he visited her in London, in 1865. He came to her little drawing room 'which he seemed to fill with his sweet dignity, the singular charm of his majestic simplicity and the magic of his voice'.[9] He did not stay long but they packed plenty of conversation into the visit. Perhaps the little maid, when she next went into the room, was given to understand that henceforth it was a kind of hallowed place.

Mary Holmes, that other admirer of Newman, was also an intelligent woman with a great deal to give to the Church she joined. Newman had a long correspondence with her when she was debating, slowly, prayerfully and intelligently, whether she should leave the Anglican Church for Rome. He copied out the letters in 1863 calling the collection 'A History of a Conversion to the Catholic Faith, in the years 1840–1844 exhibited in a Series of Letters' and he meditated offering it for publication. It never was published but it is significant that it was this correspondence which he thought worthy to record for others.

She had a talent for writing letters and managed to secure some of the major literary men of the day as her correspondents. As well as Newman himself, she had Thackeray to write to, though for a limited period of time. She started writing to him on January 1852, asking him to promote a little book she had written about music and reminding him that she had known him in Devon when she was a girl. She also hoped he would find her employment. He was lonely at the time and replied with candour, writing about his youth and how he had recreated it in *Pendennis*, and the correspondence flourished for some weeks. He sent her some money and in the spring of that year she came to London, stayed for a few days at his house and began to teach music to his daughters. But just as she had had a picture in her mind of Newman before she met him, and laid up a disappointment for herself since he did not look as venerable as she had hoped, so Thackeray thought that this sympathetic writer must be physically attractive. In fact she was plain with red hair and a red nose and he was ungallant enough to note down the fact. Moreover, she would try to convert him to Rome, and the letter writing became one-sided, except for one letter from Thackeray refusing to wear a medal she sent him. When he set off for America in the autumn he took the opportunity to break off the correspondence.

She fared better with Anthony Trollope, writing to him regularly, at a later period of her life. Her letters and his replies span a period of nine years and he said of her, 'I found her letters to be full of piety, good sense, and of most excellent literary criticism ... She was an honest, religious and a high-minded lady.'[10] She did not include only favourable criticism of his novels in her letters. For instance she took him to task over his presentation of a Catholic priest in *The Way We Live Now*. In this novel there is a description of a dinner party at Carbury Manor, given for the Anglican bishop, where a Catholic priest, Father John Barham, makes himself unpleasant. Trollope replied stoutly that he took trouble *not* to draw a Roman priest as 'bad, hypocritical or unfaithful'[11] partly because he had generally found them sincere men and partly because they were not of his church. He reserved his satire for the Anglicans of Barchester and Barsetshire. However, as he told Miss Holmes, he had once met a good priest and befriended him but the priest had taken it upon himself to run down Trollope's religion.

She also took him to task over his novel *Lady Anna*, published in 1874. In this novel the heroine, young, attractive and titled, falls in love with a tailor called Daniel Thwaite and eventually marries him. Many, besides Miss Holmes, protested at such an overthrow of the social mores of the day. Ladies should marry someone of their own rank. Trollope would have none of it.

> ... you've trodden on ever so many of my most favourite corns. Lady Anna is the best novel I every wrote! Very much! Quite far away above all others!!! – A lady ought to marry a tailor – if she chanced to fall in love with such a creature, and to promise him and take his goodness, when she was not a bad lady. That is all! Will you deny it![12]

She also wrote to Sir Edward Bulwer Lytton and had hopes that he might become a Catholic. Newman disabused her of this idea.

Poor Sir E. Bulwer Lytton is, I fear, not likely to be a
Catholic. He is one of the prevailing school, who look
down on all religions, and think they can measure them,
and then go on to assign to Catholicism the first place as
being the greatest idea, faith being the highest exercise
of reason, and (I suppose) *imagination* the second, but,
as imagination does not deal with truths, neither does
faith. When then he recommends you to be *careful* and
jealous of your faith, lest it escape you, it is a quiet hint to
you not to lecture to *him* but be content with your own
great happiness, which he *therefore* only does not envy
you himself, because he has something better, because
truer, though less magnificent, viz philosophy. Again,
not knowing the power and reality of Catholicism, he
may easily fancy that, as you argued yourself *into*
Catholicism, so you may argue yourself out of it.[13]

Miss Holmes shared Bulwer Lytton's comments with
Thackeray too who was not going to weigh arguments but
who thought little of the other novelist's high line. 'So
poor Bulwer wrote to you to hold fast to your Faith – it's
like one of his grandiloquences ...' He went on: 'I'm not
going into Controversy be sure of that. I'm sure Newman's
is a great honest heart. So is Frank Newman's. I'm very
glad you haven't a vocation for my part. You haven't – I
must stop this chattering and go to work – Dr Newman's
letters read very honest – better than that poor Bulwer with
his bosh. It is very difficult for literary men to keep their
honesty'.[14]

The reference to the vocation is there because it was at
this time that Newman was urging her to think of considering the life of a nun. He was not pushing her into a
convent because he saw no signs that she had such a vocation but he would have been pleased if she had – it would
mean that she was anchored and fully useful. 'It is to me
quite miserable,' he said, 'that you should go on
wandering from place to place. I do not like to see real
good mental stuff, which might be made useful, wasted.'[15]

It was ironic that she thought as she did about Trollope's
Lady Anna, defending the social system with such vigour

when it was that very system, which considered rank and money more than scope for talent, which constrained her to be a governess. She was perpetually discontented, forever moving on, writing to her influential friends to find her new employment. There is no tale of cruelty or the kind of harrassment that the Brontë sisters suffered, but Miss Holmes was dissatisfied with every post she had. Perhaps she was constitutionally restless, perhaps teaching was not really her forte. It is doubtless a mistake to move a person in imagination from one century to the next, but it is hard to banish the thought that if Mary Holmes could have lived in later times she might have found a place as a professional woman, as a musician or perhaps as a teacher in a different setting.

Newman's thought of 'real good mental stuff wasted' is typical of him. One of his favourite words was 'object': everyone should have an object in life, tasks that are commensurate with one's abilities if possible. He had great sympathy with those who were, through no fault of their own, afflicted with what he called 'helpless idleness', such as the convent clergymen who had lost their employment and had the responsibility of the support of their families and also the distress of their own lack of usefulness. He did not like people to roam about because it meant that they would not settle to their work and, with something less than his usual exactness and originality of phrasing, he once told a young man who had emigrated to New Zealand and thought of coming back again that he should remember that a rolling stone gathers no moss. So he wrote to Miss Holmes in 1865, 'If I were you, I should make it a resolution, as a matter of conscience, that, when I got a situation, for at least two years I on my part would do nothing indirectly or directly to close the engagement'.[16]

It was to no avail. She was here, she was there. Just before she started her brief friendship with Thackeray she was thinking of going to Spain. She was in Ireland. She was in Boulogne. She was off to Italy. Newman, who did not envy English expatriates, did not encourage such ventures. He wrote, when she went to France, that he thought the longer we live in our own country, the less we like to be in another where the ways are different from our own. When she was about to go to Rome he wrote:

> You cannot expect too much in a supernatural line – but, according to my impression of it you gain that privilege by a great many human and earthly discomforts, which make it, as it should be, a place of pilgrimage. The climate shifting from heat to cold, the heavy and insidious atmosphere, the alternative of whisking dust in clouds and ankle deep mud, and the ever lively ever hungry insects, make it pre-eminently, to me at least, a place of penance – and the want of pavements, the water pipes emptying the clouds upon your head, if you walk in rain, the forlorn, untidy, ruined palaces, and the faded churches, would be insupportable, were not the ground you tread on the dust of martyrs, and the wonderful dome, which you see from all parts of the city, the roof over the body of St Peter.[17]

However, Miss Holmes was not deterred from moving about. Once he lost track of her completely so that he wrote, when a letter came from her, 'I am glad you have at last come to light, for I did not know whether you were in Italy, France or Ireland.'[18] He went on in the same letter, 'I was pleased to find that you seemed more satisfied with the family you are now with, than with those before them for some time past.' The phrasing suggests a long line of Miss Holmes' employers, stretching out like Macbeth's vision of Banquo's descendants. He suggested once that she might set up as a music teacher independently, so that she did not have to live in all these households, but acknowledged that this would require capital which she did not have.

Not all these exchanges were about her affairs and her complaints about her situation. She was alert to what was happening in the Catholic world and intelligently interested in Newman's work and his problems. He sometimes shared with her his thoughts about such matters as the conflict between the two Oratories – for instance in a detailed letter sent in April 1859. It is a cool letter, saying in a dispassionate way that he could not trust Father Faber any more than he could trust the Cardinal (ie Wiseman). They both had many good qualities but did not have the kind of character that made those who knew them trust them. As for the London Oratory – if they would cease their constant talking about the difference between the two houses the difference, the appearance of a quarrel, would cease. It is the kind of letter that is very informative to historians now and it is informative, indirectly, about Miss Holmes for it required intelligence and sympathy to draw out such confidences. Thackeray had been touched to the same kind of response, but he was not proof against her plainness and her proselytising fervour.

So she went on from place to place, with her devout spirit, her sweet singing voice, her plain face and her carrotty hair. In 1860 she wrote to say that she was leaving the service of Mr Gainsford in Sheffield and wondered what Newman could do to help – presumably in the way of recommending her to other Catholic families. He replied that he would do what he could and commented sadly:

> I look to the future for you and, while I see how easily you make friends and how you interest persons in you, it distresses me to think that you do not seem to advance towards anything settled and permanent.[19]

She was to have a temporary job in Scotland with the family of Lord Henry Kerr that same year but it came to nothing. Newman's letter, with his regrets about this, has a sentence about Miss Bowles: 'In one of your letters you spoke of Miss Bowles – she is a very great friend of mine – very good, very clever and very active.'[20] So the two women are there linked, and the same phrase of being 'very good and very clever' was used at another time when Newman was recommending Miss Holmes to a friend. Neither of these women found a satisfactory niche for herself and neither of them made full use of what was 'real good mental stuff.'

❧

Another person who was a link between the old life and

the new was Maria Rosina Giberne. She had continued as a
fervent Tractarian and went on with her correspondence
with Newman, adopting sometimes a robust and bantering
tone. This sometimes called forth a sharp and amusing bit
of satire from him, as when he described the Evangelicals
to her as putting him in mind of 'a naughty child, put atop
of a bookcase, very frightened but very furious.'[1] She still
moved in evangelical circles and was a temptation to young
ministers because of her good looks and lively air and also
because of the attraction of the forbidden, since her
tractarian convictions would render her dangerous. One of
her suitors informed her dramatically that his infatuation
had come to an end by quoting the verse from a psalm that
proclaims that the snare is broken. She was thankful that
he was delivered and that she was delivered too, for she
cared for none of her admirers.

She left the family home to share a house in Cheltenham
with a friend, Selina Bacchus, and was happy there, though
as time went on she was increasingly disturbed by
Newman's doubts about the Church of England. As long as
he was confident about his position she could laugh at
attacks on the Tractarians, maintaining, for instance, that
she enjoyed the row made over the famous Tract 90, but
when Newman to whom she looked for what she considered near-infallible guidance, was in mental turmoil, she
felt as though her world was breaking apart. When he
became a Catholic she (and Selina) wondered if they
would follow, and Newman was convinced that what held
her back was not genuine doubt but a nameless fear of the
foreign and unknown. Pusey warned her against following
Newman's example but she disregarded his advice.

There was in London, in Bolton Street, a Mr Brownbill, a
Jesuit priest much in demand for receiving converts into
the Church. He received Henry Bacchus, Selina's brother,
though Selina herself was hanging back and did not
become a Catholic until 1848. Newman met Miss Giberne
in London and whisked her off in a cab to Mr Brownbill,
who she thought of as 'the terrible Jesuit.' He turned out
to be mild and not at all alarming and shook hands, which
seemed a reassuringly English gesture, so although she had

hung on Newman's arm at the beginning of the interview, she agreed to call again, without her prop. The Jesuit did receive her into the Church of Rome, in December 1845, just two months after Newman's reception. She was alarmed at having to make a general confession into Mr Brownbill's large red ear but felt a great peace and contentment when all was over.

As a spiritual advisor, however, the Jesuit was not wholly satisfactory. She asked Newman in a letter in January: 'Do you think Mr Brownbill a clever or deeply learned man? I do not.'[2] To this he replied that he was known as a 'clever, sensible, good director'[3] and nothing was reported as to his being learned. Newman added, obviously smiling as he wrote, 'Has he been speaking against my book, that you write as you do?' She answered this letter at some length.

> I have nothing to say against Mr Brownbill – far from it – He is all kindness and consideration – but he seems to imagine that Protestant converts know nothing at all of the Doctrines of the Catholic Church – He prosed on for an hour of things that anyone who is at all up to the religious topics of the last ten years must be supposed to know if he has ever thought at all before entering the Catholic Church. This makes me think that he knows nothing of what has been going on among us and that he can have read but very sparingly of your writings. He talked to me, you know, as if I was a child. I mean as to *topics* and did not solve any one difficulty for I could not make him take my meaning. If he were *stern* instead of *stiff* I could manage better ...[4]

Newman poured oil on these troubled waters by pointing out that many converts were partially informed and that Mr Brownbill had to assure himself that all doctrinal ground was covered. However, the kernel of her complaint tells us as much about Newman as about the unlucky Jesuit. Newman did not treat enquirers as if they were children and he answered difficulties systematically without 'prosing on.' Selina Bacchus was married in 1846 to George Copeland, a doctor in Cheltenham who was the brother of

William Copeland, Newman's curate at Littlemore and a lifelong friend. Miss Giberne found it hard to rejoice at her friend's happiness because the marriage left her bereft and homeless. She wrote to Newman with artless frankness.

> It was only my Selina that made this a home to me ... She is the only person in the world that has ever felt for and with me entirely. Such sympathy existed between us as is seldom found here. Her love and affection has soothed all my sorrows, mental or bodily. For five years I have scarcely shed a tear and now I never cease crying except when she is by, lest I should grieve her. I cannot tell you how I love her and how it sometimes agonises me to see her living for another as she used to live for me. I know you will think me very weak and very wicked. It breaks my heart to keep it in any more so I have inflicted all this on you as the only friend I have now to whom I can write from my heart.[5]

Newman did not stigmatise her as weak and wicked but tried to comfort her by reminding her that he was in like case (though he admitted in another letter that it does not always help to be told of the troubles of others). He too had lost home and friends. 'And so in your own case, depend on it, God's mercy will make up to you all you lose, and you will be blessed, not indeed in the same way, but in a higher.'[6] She replied gratefully, thanking him for his 'dear kind letter.'[7] Sincere but always effusive, she went on. 'May nothing ever separate us, for though we meet face to face but seldom, I always feel as if you were my strong hold. You have never failed me, and you never will, for I have always loved you in Christ and for him.'

Cheltenham was no longer home and living with her family proved impossibly difficult. She came to Birmingham, where Newman was now installed at Maryvale and, in June with the rain that was pouring outside she wept in the parlour. Newman restored her with tea and a visit to the new seminary at Oscott and an introduction to Dr Wiseman.

She lodged, in Birmingham, at the house of Mrs

Wilkinson next door to the Convent of the Sisters of Mercy in Handsworth. Helen Gladstone, the sister of the great politician, had been there just before her and her troubles were more acute: she too was a convert, lived in fear of her brother and suffered ill health, treating nervous attacks with opium. Two years later she was cured and went off to live in Germany, spending her time in works of charity.

This was the question that had to be answered by these single ladies who were converted to Rome: how were they to spend their lives and how were they to be useful in the Church? Newman did wonder whether Miss Giberne might wish to be a nun but at that time she felt no call to enter Religious life. Instead she went off to Rome, lodging with the Colonna family. Since Newman was also in Rome it sounds as though she moved in order to be near him but in fact she was entering on a period of great independence. She supplemented her income by painting, leaving aside her pastels or 'chalks' and turning to oils which she used to copy the religious pictures that abounded in Rome and then offer her copies for sale. English Catholics were pleased to have them for their new churches and chapels.

She had been thrilled to attend High Mass and Benediction at Oscott in Pugin's neo-Gothic chapel and the churches and the services in Rome must have been like a perpetual feast laid before her. Also she was carried away with enthusiasm for the Pope, Pio Nono, described by Newman as a vigorous man with a very pleasant countenance, friendly to the English converts.

She did not look after herself well, cutting regular meals and sometimes eating an apple or a piece of bread in the street. Newman rebuked her, not for impropriety but for being too careless about keeping warm in winter and reasonably fed. Tom Mozley, in his gossipy way, told of her appearance and habits when in Rome, though some of his descriptions may apply to a second period she had in Rome, in the fifties, staying with the Borghese family. She walked every day between her lodging place between the Quirinal and the Forum of Trajan to her studio which was a room in the gallery of the Palazzo Borghese. 'She moved along like a divinity,' said Tom Mozley; 'no one thought to interrupt her stately passage and no rough Roman dared to molest her.'[8]

It was the custom in Rome for small boys to attend a festival in the church of Ara Caeli, between Christmas and Epiphany, and each to preach a sermon. Miss Giberne took in a poor child, aged about eleven, trained him as a page and further trained him as a preacher for this event. His skills were displayed to visitors and his utterance and use of gestures were impeccable.

She had always had some talent for portraiture and not all her paintings were copies. Again according to Tom Mozley, she drew Cardinal Antonelli and sketched Pio Nono on a mule. She also did a portrait of Newman with Ambrose St John, in oils, both seated at a table and clad in voluminous black cassocks. The picture is lightened in colour by an apparition of Our Lady floating above them, which is not meant, presumably, to indicate that they had visions but that they were under the protection of Mary. It is slightly reminiscent of later Hollywood versions of the story of St Bernadette. This picture has some importance among Newman iconography. There are earlier portraits of Newman the Anglican leader and many of him in late middle age and old age, photographs in the sixties and formal paintings made when he became a Cardinal. Miss Giberne's Roman picture is between times and though sentimental in conception is probably accurate, showing a dark and beaky Newman and a fair, cherubic Ambrose St John.

Many of her pictures found their way back to Newman's Oratory in Birmingham. He wrote in 1850, for instance:

They tell me you have not received news about your pictures – but I thought I had been very careful in writing about them, as far as I knew. Your St Philip (Guido) is in our Chapel – your Sta Croce Madonna is opposite me as I write, in my room – and a beautiful little picture without history came to me *with* the Madonna – viz our Lady and Bambino and the Baptist. We made great use of it at Christmas, not having a Cave.

It was beflowered and belighted, and the people all but worshipped it – or sang hymns before it out of hours up to the Octave of the Epiphany.[9]

She was deeply interested in all that was going on. When Newman and his community were first set up at Maryvale she had to be warned that ladies could not go all over the house – in her enthusiasm she would have wandered freely. When she was in Rome and Newman back in England and had moved into the first Oratory house in Alcester Street in the middle of the city, he sent her detailed descriptions of the timetable, the names of the new Oratorians, the plan to set up a second Oratory in London, the finances, the rooms and disposition of the house and the numbers of those attending services and the evening school for poor children. He ended, 'Now you see how much I have gossiped about ourselves and myself, but I thought you would like to hear everything.'[10] He was entirely right in supposing that that was just what she wanted.

He added in a postscript that 'I thought F Ambrose or F Frederic would have finished this – but they are so busy with the approaching functions they cannot – and I don't like to delay this having kept it back yesterday for the purpose.' It is not the only letter that reveals that the other Oratorians added news for Miss Giberne or sometimes sent whole letters of their own. She was treated as if she were part of the family: like a cousin or an aunt she might be tiresome at times but she was always kept in mind and treated to all the news of the household.

In 1850 she returned to England from Italy and Newman was very welcoming. Her return was in one respect a sad one because her dear friend Selina, Mrs Copeland, died that autumn, leaving two little daughters. That same autumn witnessed the beginning of a troubled time for all English Catholics with a great campaign against 'Papal Aggression.' A new Roman Catholic hierarchy in England was established in September, Wiseman was made a cardinal and wrote the triumphant pastoral letter 'from out the Flaminian Gate' which was published in October and roused great fears throughout Protestant England. Anti-Catholic feeling, still very strong, came to the surface and there were violent scenes in the streets, as well as violent and satirical attacks in the papers. Newman reported, in a jesting mood, that the brother of one of the London Oratorians, was surrounded by an angry rabble because he wore a long cloak and was taken to be an Oratorian in Religious dress. 'He faced round, pulled aside the cloke, and showed his trousers – When they saw him all sound below, they gave him a cheer and left him.'[11] His wit was also evident in the letter he wrote to the *Morning Chronicle* when questions had been asked in the House of Commons about his new Oratory building in Edgbaston. There had been dark suggestions that cells had been built under the house, doubtless for some sinister purpose. Newman explained that they were to serve as a larder, a coal-hole, a brew house and so on. He was not gravely troubled by the verbal attacks – indeed, he thought the persecution of Catholics that had been stirred up might be exploited by using it as an excuse for lectures, for increased Catholic lay activity and for a determined attack on the problem of Catholic lack of education. He set about lecturing himself with addresses delivered in the Corn Exchange, later published as *Lectures on the Present Position of Catholics in England*. During these lectures he attacked an ex-Dominican friar, an Italian by the name of Giacinto Achilli who had been condemned in Rome for sexual misdemeanours. He then became a Protestant and was brought to England by the Evangelical Alliance to tour England, denouncing Rome and claiming that he had been condemned for heresy. Wiseman had already denounced Achilli and Newman took legal opinion on the advisability of his own public attack on the man; he was assured that it was a safe move since Wiseman could produce proof of his statements.

In the event, Wiseman let him down, losing his papers and being dilatory about obtaining other documents from Rome. Achilli brought a charge of criminal libel against Newman and, in the frenzied anti-Catholic atmosphere of the time, things looked very black indeed.

It was at this point that Miss Giberne's great adventure began. She tells the beginning of the tale in a lucid and fascinating document which describes the whole episode in detail and with great care. Her style crystallises and gone are the bursts of exclamation marks which she used to describe her first encounters with the Newman family at Brighton. She wrote her journal at the end of 1852, not long after the events.

> I had several times expressed my wishes, that the Father would make use of me or my money, to help him in the threatened trial, for the *so called* libel against Dr. Achilli ... At length one evening, after my confession (I think it was), the Father said: 'I think you might be of great service to us in this affair.' I rose up from my chair ready for anything though not guessing what it was I could do. He then told me it was to go to Italy, and bring away the female witnesses who would not be so likely to come without a woman to conduct them. He added that the committee would decide and he would let me know as soon as possible.[12]

Friends had rallied to Newman's side – hence the committee – and money was being collected for the great expense of the trial. A good sum would have to be paid out for Miss Giberne's expenses. It was Newman's idea to ask her to go to collect up some of the women who had been seduced by Achilli and it was a good choice: she was used to travel, spoke fluent French and Italian and was singularly intrepid. She did not hesitate although she did not know at that first broaching of the subject that she did not have to search out these women. Others would take on that task and it would be her job to bring them to England. She went straight back into the church to thank God for giving her the chance to help Father Newman, 'my spiritual father.'

The committee approved Newman's idea and Miss Giberne packed a carpet bag. On Monday the 8th December, 1851, she came to the Oratory and the Father gave her Communion. After breakfast she set off, accompa-

nied by another devoted friend of Newman's, Mrs
Wootten, who saw her as far as the railway station. The next
day Newman wrote to George Talbot, an important cleric
in Rome, with information that he was to hand on to a
lawyer, Mr Harting, who was acting for Newman in Italy. It
was news of a young woman called Elena Giustini, née
Valente, who had been seduced by Achilli in Viterbo, in
the sacristy of a church. She could be tracked down, given
the directions they had received. Newman added:

> Miss Giberne started yesterday and was to cross to
> France today – on the mission of persuading the women,
> either at Viterbo or Naples, or elsewhere – a most diffi-
> cult job, but necessary, if we are to ensure success.
> Nothing will resist such a witness, but nothing short will
> be sufficient – though many things will *mitigate* the
> sentence, when pronounced against me. If I am to be
> acquitted, we must have the women or some of them in
> court. Miss G. is very eager the Borghese should know
> the fact of her coming.[13]

A visit to the Princess Borghese had already been in view
so, if questioned, Miss Giberne could explain why she was
off to Italy without disclosing her main purpose since
secrecy (adding some spice to the affair) was essential. She
arrived in Folkstone and had to linger there until two in
the morning at a hotel before she would start the crossing.
Since she had no maid and was travelling light, the people
at the hotel took her for a lady's maid and invited her to
dine in the servant's hall. She said piously in her journal
that she was glad of this little humiliation but she took
good care to explain that she was not a maid. Moreover,
when she landed at Boulogne and the men set her aside
with her carpet-bag and attended to other luggage and
other passengers, she marched up to those in authority
and 'began a discourse on the politeness of the French
nation formerly – now they, instead of attending to one
lady who most required their protection, left me standing,
while others arriving after me were let pass before me.
They stared and immediately settled the matter.'

She arrived in Paris and visited people she knew. Pausing for breath there, she made up her mind to recite certain prayers every day for the Father and the trial's success. She kept a New Testament in her basket, near at hand, and kept up a regular pattern of prayers and meditation during the whole journey. When on the road again, to Chalons, she spoke to fellow travellers who seemed well disposed, telling them that they must pray for a great event in England, 'a fight between the devil and God's angels.' If they continued, she would see to it that the Pope would give them a blessing. Their prayers must have been shot through with speculations about the nature of this English struggle, but dark hints were all that Miss Giberne gave them.

At Chalons a diligence was starting at once for Marseilles and, with no time for refreshment, off she went again and had two days of uncomfortable travel, being tired, cold and hungry. Her reactions were typical of her – an artless admission of being extremely uncomfortable and full of a spirit of complaining, a fulsome piece of piety in which she identified herself with Mary suffering with Jesus, and a wholly admirable determination to go on and endure. Her good spirit within her bade her be content, 'and so I was content, and loved to suffer for the moment till a new sort of trouble began and then began again my struggle and consolation.'

At Marseilles she stayed in a hotel where she met two Irishmen, described as two Paddies, who were bound for Leghorn to fetch the body of their father who had died there. They were amiable but inefficient, at one point offering to take Miss Giberne's passport with their own to obtain a visa for the next part of the journey and then having it wrongly made out, which caused her some trouble. She compared them very favourably, however, with a Protestant gentleman, travelling with his bride and her maid, and also staying at the hotel in Marseilles. He was rude and a grumbler, and these faults were connected in Miss Giberne's mind with the fact that he was a Protestant.

They all took the boat at eight in the morning and Miss

Giberne went to her cabin before it had left the harbour and wondered whether it would be wrong to mend a hole in her glove since the day was Sunday. A loud report made her think that something had fallen on deck. Then she heard screams and saw water streaming down the cabin portholes, so she went up to the deck through hot water which was coming down the cabin stairs, could see nothing through a cloud of hot vapour but heard repeated screams and began to feel suffocated. The ship's boiler had burst. She regretted that she did not have her crucifix with her since it was blessed for the hour of death and uttered some simple and heartfelt prayers to Mary: 'Maria, take care of me and don't leave me. I am alone with you. Don't let my dear father be too much vexed and grieved at my death.' The vapour cleared a little and she saw the dreadful sight of people scalded in the accident – twelve died from their injuries. The cross Protestant was a little scalded about the head and face and his hat was rolling on the deck. Miss Giberne comforted the poor wife and saw the maid 'standing fixed upright and skinned.'

The two Paddies were unharmed and received a lecture from Miss Giberne on their merciful escape which should make them reflect on their missing Mass that Sunday morning. They replied that they relied on the prayers of their good mother and sister but she said that she saw 'they only talked in that way.' The Captain of the second boat was much impressed by Miss Giberne's likeness to the first Napoleon and asked her whether she was related to the Buonaparte family! She had made the transition from the first wrecked boat to the second in apparent calm and presence of mind but, not surprisingly, she was very nervous all her time on board and 'kept as much as possible at a respectable distance from the boiler.'

She travelled from Leghorn to Rome, via Florence, having some difficulty in getting transport, partly because of her incorrect visa, and she 'inwardly growled at the stupidity of Paddies in general, and these in particular,' thus lumping together all Irishmen as she had made the tribal generalisation that Protestants are likely to be unpleasant and Catholics are likely to be good. She met the pair again in Leghorn and her heart softened towards them since they were about to meet their widowed mother. It was a cold Christmas eve when she got to Rome and she was treated like a poor woman at the Minerva where she stayed, as she had been before. It was at church that she met her aristocratic friends, the dowager Princess Borghese and the Prince. He sent her in a carriage to fetch her bag from her lodgings, her stock went up and so did her bill; 'I grumbled, but paid and went off.'

It was a day or two afterwards that she went to see Elena (whose familiar name was Gippina or Giuseppina) who was waiting for the English woman. This young person had been speculating on the reasons that had impelled Miss Giberne to come so far and concluded that she must be one of Achilli's victims. She was surprised to hear that her new acquaintance had never seen him (one can imagine the vehemence with which this was stated) and, according to Miss Giberne's opinion, thought her a fool for taking on such a business.

It crossed Miss Giberne's mind at this point that she had indeed taken on a load of trouble and that the difficulties and discomforts of the journey, made as quickly as possible, were all nothing compared with what was to follow. 'I began to feel,' she wrote, 'as if the realities of life were grappling with me and as if a weight of responsibility had fallen upon me – a thing I had been trying to avoid all my life.'

She ingratiated herself with Elena by getting her a special pair of shoes with a high heel because she walked lame, having one leg longer than the other, and found her lodgings near the Palazzo Borghese where she was living herself. Elena was out for what she could get, so Miss Giberne surmised, though she talked of coming as she was asked to do 'solely for the glory of God.'

Then a second party arrived from Viterbo, Elena's husband, and another family belonging to Alessandra who was to be a second witness against Achilli. Miss Giberne was in a perpetual pother lest they should decide not to come to England and only kept herself reasonably calm because she was shored up by an English lawyer and various priests.

The two families got together and stirred up doubts amongst themselves. Alessandra, who was pregnant, decided she could not travel and that family determined to return to Viterbo, despite urgings from Miss Giberne and her supporters. She gave Alessandra a dress and twenty five scudi. Elena and her husband then turned restive and swore they would not come unless they received a certain sum of money. Miss Giberne, with some cunning, maintained that bribery would spoil all but that they could trust the English to see that they would not lose out if they made the required journey. Monsignor Talbot counselled a speedy departure, Miss Giberne prayed mightily, and her charges seemed more settled. However, they had no passport and she had to pull every possible string, religious and secular, to get one speedily. Get it she did and was much admired for her pertinacity. Monsignor Talbot had organised a private audience for her with the Pope but such was her state of mind that she did not really want to go and when she got there 'said nothing that I recollect.' She did remember, however, when she wrote her journal, that the Pope gave his blessing, for her, for 'the Father and all who prayed for the trial.'

There were troubles and delays getting a visa, the post carriage they travelled in was a poor one and the postillions were impudent and demanded more money. Nor was that all:

> I did not sleep all night, being far too anxious. The harness broke once, and when the carriage stopped my companions woke out of their sleep; and the man, thinking there were robbers, exclaimed in agony 'Misericordia'.

At Civita Vecchia they took a steamer and had a very bad crossing to Marseilles. It was anxiety that wore Miss Giberne down, rather than hardship, fearing that her charges would be indiscreet, that they would decide to go home or make demands that she could not satisfy. She threatened Elena with Achilli and his friends, saying that to prevent her witness they might kill the whole party. At

Marseilles they took the railway train to Paris and all was harmony because she had provided herself with a bottle of spirits and a little glass from the Borghese palace and small doses made Elena and Vincenzo sleep like tops. Just before they reached Paris an official jumped into their first class carriage, stared at the occupants and busied himself with a portfolio. Miss Giberne, sure that all was discovered, stared into space and uttered a prayer of thanksgiving when he jumped out again.

At Paris, after an uncomfortable short stay in a damp hotel in the Rue du Bac, they all moved to the house of one Mrs Foljambe with Miss Giberne's one bag and the Italians' few possessions tied up in a handkerchief. Mrs Foljambe was just furbishing her house to open it to Catholic converts who had nowhere to go and it was Monsignor Talbot who had put the two ladies in touch. Elena was employed to make curtains and they settled in, though Mrs Foljambe was in some doubt when her first convert lady moved in lest she should find the Italian guests too rough. Elena found that French church services were not identical with Italian ones and was much amused at the differences. Vinci did not seem to go to church but went out on his own, leaving the women to their devotions. He was a great smoker and Elena insisted he should not have more than two cigars given him at a time: 'There are three persons in the Holy Trinity but two cigars will do for Vinci.'

It was in these days that Miss Giberne got to know Elena. She could be very tiresome and she had a way of folding her hands under her apron that indicated that a bad mood was upon her. She had said at first that her husband was an angel to have married her when she was poor and dishonoured but when she was downcast she would tell Miss Giberne it was 'that man' that made her depressed. Vincenzo was not above taunting her with her past life when they had a row, though Miss Giberne thought he was really quite fond of his wife. 'I think she hoped,' she wrote, 'by always complaining of the hardships of the married life, to excite my compassion and make me give her plenty of things and money.' She did provide her a pair of stays that opened in front and a box or two of magnetic fishes and ducks.

Newman wrote in the middle of January:

I have just received your welcome letter from *Paris. All*
your letters have come safely. I could not answer you in
time – I have written to you in Rome since you left.

I have sent up to Town to have £20 sent you.
Meanwhile, I suppose you can get credit. Do not be
sparing in kindness to the two poor people.

You have done exceedingly well, and our Lady and
St Philip have been with you. I congratulate you, and
truly condole and thank you for your sufferings ...

I will let you know at once what you had best do,
and whether you need to be a jailer a whole month! If
the man likes *reviews* and other pageantry, there will be
plenty of them just now at Paris. I *don't think* there is any
chance of their meeting any one they know.[14]

He wrote again two days later to tell her to make sure that
Elena understood the seriousness of taking an oath in
court and added a postscript to say that a second witness
had been found, Sophia Maria Balisano, née Principe,
from Naples.

Meanwhile Miss Giberne was busy writing to him,
describing the way she was entertaining her charges: 'they
like very much to go in "legno" [a carriage] ... for the man
I allow him two sigars a day, and for anything more he has
no taste – he sits wrapped up in his cloak and does nothing
except put coals on the fire when he is asked.'

Newman replied to this information:

We think you don't allow Gippina's husband cigars
enough – let him have an unlimited supply. Let him
have anything else he takes to – perhaps he would get
tired if he rode in legno every day – but is there nothing
else? is there no equestrial exhibition? no harmless play?
no giant or dwarf? no panorama, cosmorama, diorama,
dissolving views, steam incubation of chickens, or
menagerie (the jardin des plants!) which he would like to
see. Surely beasts are just the thing for him. I wonder he
has no taste for a review. I should not *ask* him but I

should *take* him to the jardin des plants, as if I wished to see them myself.[15]

There was talk of more witnesses having been found, perhaps as many as four ('It amuses me,' Newman wrote, 'that you should be thought capable of such a tail'). She did not have such a tail to cope with but Sophia Maria came from Naples with her mother and a very little girl, not much more than a baby, hideously dirty and with a cloak and pointed hood that made her look like a tiny pyramid. Miss Giberne washed the child (called Nannie – or perhaps this is an Anglicised version of her name) the next day and persuaded her mother to wash her every day thereafter. The two Neapolitan women, however, could not be persuaded to take a bath until two months had passed.

The trial was to have been in February but Achilli's lawyers brought about delays by various shifts and Miss Giberne had to break it to her party that their sojourn away from home would be longer and then entertain them as best she could. The Neapolitans were easier to deal with than the pair from Viterbo and Miss Giberne became very fond of Nannie. The two families sometimes fell out, and Vincenzo became more and more surly. Elena frightened Miss Giberne by saying that he was probably about to go out of his mind and she did what she could to keep him on the rails: 'I kept an anxious eye upon him, and dosed him, and soothed and flattered him by telling him how 'capace' he was in finding his way and making himself understood in French and told him to take care of the women when they went out.' Then, as if the Italians were not enough to strain Miss Giberne's powers of pacification, a French maid arrived who taunted the Neapolitans and provoked a small racial war. Miss Allen, Mrs Foljambe's first convert lady, graciously gave up her front room to the women from Naples who sat in the window for hours, knitting stockings and looking into the street, and some peace resulted though Miss Giberne had to keep Elena at bay (she behaved with grandeur towards the others) and also keep out the French maid by doing the sweeping herself. Just once the poor woman, worn by such irritations, thought to herself 'why should I endure all this – why do not I go clean away and leave them to their own devices?' The answer to the thought was obvious, and she banished it.

This plain statement of her feelings and the generosity with which she quickly resolved to get on and make the best of things shows Miss Giberne at her best. Unfortunately she followed this with an extraordinary piece of piety, likening her experience to that of Mary who suffered for her Son. Newman, in this use of religious identification, becomes her son. Not only is the comparison dubious in that it matches small things with great but the picture of son and mother is bizarre – Newman and Miss Giberne were the same age, or rather she was a year younger.

The trial was put off and put off – Newman and his friends suffered by the delays and dodges of the law as the characters in Dickens' *Bleak House* did. Father Ambrose came out to give Miss Giberne support. 'While he remained,' she said, 'I felt quite a different being – that *cold paw* of anxiety and responsibility no longer seemed clawing and pinching my heart, and I felt a tinge of spirit and hope diffuse itself through my life.' She wrote to Newman that she had found a new way of entertaining her gang. 'It is to begin to take their portraits one after another and have all in hand and none finished till near the time to go.'

When news came in April that there were further delays she talked much of the pleasant weather they would have in England in May and a calm sea for the crossing. She also urged prayer and offering up their trials in waiting about; all were impressed by this except Vincenzo who found her piety oppressive. He liked to hear of the wonders of England, however, and especially of the excellence of its knives and razors. Mrs Foljambe grew impatient and they all transferred to the poor *Missions Etrangères* and complaints abounded from the Italians. Father Stanislas had arrived from the Birmingham Oratory and treated the complaints with cool male insouciance. 'I thought,' said Miss Giberne, 'I had been giving myself a deal of needless anxiety and worry.'

They set off for Calais about the 12th of May, arrived in Dover and spent a few days in a hotel, until a house was found in Marine Parade, facing the sea. Unfortunately, Miss Giberne's sister-in-law was holidaying in Dover, with three aunts and they met by chance; she was hard put to it to explain what she was doing there with five Italians without telling a lie. Nannie enjoyed herself having donkey rides and Vincenzo lolled about the beach smoking. British wine was unacceptable to the party but Vincenzo took to drinking beer and enjoyed the heavy meals with plenty of meat so much that his waistcoat had to be undone at the end of dinner and his shirt issued in several places. He burst the buttons on his trousers so Miss Giberne wrote to Newman for permission to spend money on a new outfit, and Vincenzo was fitted out, though he had to be persuaded by her and by the tailor not to discard his old clothes in the parlour. He looked so smart that the English aunts quite admired him when he took off his hat to them. The women were busy making dresses for themselves and for Nannie, all material being supplied by Miss Giberne who wrote that she enjoyed giving presents, adding artlessly 'it is a fine thing to be generous with other peoples' money.' The cost of travel, accommodation, presents and clothes must in fact have added up to a considerable sum – all to be added to the legal costs.

The party transferred to Ramsgate where Vincenzo, overcome by beef and beer, spent much time stretched out on the sofa. The Neapolitans, who were very simple people, liked to go out to marvel at the tides of the sea, the pretty English cottages and the vegetables in the fields – they said they would all have been stolen in Naples. The old mother thought England poised between supernatural forces of evil and good: the telegraph service was surely the work of the devil, according to her, and, like St Gregory before her, she thought the fair children were angels. She began to pray for the conversion of the English. Lawyers were now arriving to take affidavits and Miss Giberne was constantly afraid that 'Achilli's people' would find them out and suborn the witnesses. This anxiety had some foundation – it was not simply due to her propensity to fuss. A more

immediate source of distress was that Nannie fell ill of a
swelling behind her ear and had to be operated on, Miss
Giberne being employed to hold the child who, mercifully,
recovered.

At last they moved to London. Vincenzo looked at the
column in Trafalgar Square and wanted to know what saint
was at the top. Miss Giberne said that the English
honoured their heroes but cared little for saints. By this
time she was feeling ill with anxiety. The women were led
off by two lawyers' clerks and she stayed to mind the child.
News got back from time to time that the trial was going
badly. All her hopes and prayers seemed cast away. She
wrote:

> The last evening when all my witnesses were done with
> and I could leave them safely, I went to the Oratory in
> the tribune. Close behind me sat the dear object of all
> our cares, pale and still calm and heavenly. He retired
> soon after and at the beginning of one of the hymns,
> Father Ambrose came and said – All is lost and the
> Father thinks you had better take the people to
> Boulogne lest they should be imprisoned for perjury.

She had some soothing words from Newman himself and
made ready for departure the next day. Vincenzo then
turned very threatening and demanded his money but Miss
Giberne, who had been tying up a parcel when he came in,
answered him roundly and made a little scourge of her
string to drive him from the room, 'not striking him but
flickering it.'

Father Joseph Gordon saw them all as far as the boat at
Folkestone – which was a more complicated matter than it
should have been because the carriage taking the
Neapolitans went to Dover by mistake. This Oratorian was
all for going home again but Miss Giberne, now at the end
of her tether, demanded that he should make the crossing
with them, and so he did, 'and was very kind and pleasant
all the way.' The Italians were to be met in Paris by a Mr
Reynolds and Miss Giberne managed to find an Irish priest
who would escort them there. Before they went she paid

them each £15 in gold. Elena, at parting, went on her knees to beg pardon for any bad conduct and the other women followed suit. Vincenzo however stood aloof! Miss Giberne was sorry to part from Nannie but her main feeling was of exhilaration that they were fairly out of her hands. She returned to Rome, still very anxious about Newman, and learned there 'that he got off well and had won the field morally in the eyes of all, though not legally.'

Doubtless the story was filled out rather more when it was told to her. Her witnesses did quite well, though Elena had to endure a long spell in the witness box, and English women testified that Achilli had made improper advances. A prejudiced jury, however, brought in a verdict of guilty, which was all that poor Miss Giberne knew when she set off in haste with her charges in June. Newman was to be sentenced in November and, though his lawyers pleaded for a new trial, the plea was not granted and he faced judgment in January, '53. In the event, however, though Newman expected to go to prison, he was only fined. Moreover, the *Times*, immediately after the trial, strongly criticised the Judge's conduct of it and made the comment that Roman Catholics could not have faith in British justice. This was a ray of honesty in the gloomy scene compounded of Achilli's villainy and the general air of bigotry. Miss Giberne's own anti-Protestant bias can be understood: violent prejudice always begets prejudice and she knew full well what a miscarriage of justice the whole affair was.

Her own part in the matter was not inconsiderable, and she came out of it well. Her demonstrations of piety like her demonstrations of feeling for Newman were often excessive and doubtless tiresome to the beholders – but she truly prayed with fervour and she carried out her task with courage. She fussed, but she did what she had to do, under God. Moreover, she was careful not to utter plaints to Newman while she was employed in journeying and guarding the witnesses, thinking that he had enough anxieties without that. Heaven knows what memories the Italians had of this extraordinary episode in their lives and of the English woman who had shepherded them like a strict and pious governess but had been generous, efficient and warmly concerned for the small child.

Newman was grateful to her for her help and perhaps this gratitude went to her head. When there was trouble in the Oratory in 1852 over a lay brother who was overcome by an excess of what he called 'spiritual love' for Mrs Wootten (a most devout lady who lived in Birmingham and was in charge of the domestic arrangements in the Oratory School) Newman's thoughts flew to Miss Giberne as he contemplated the case of Brother Bernard:

> I suppose Miss Giberne has encouraged him. Doubtless she has talked to him in the most idiotic way of her spiritual love for me – and doubtless B. has thought that my impatience *at* seeing her rose from my fear that I felt too much spiritual love for her.[16]

One of the days Newman himself or one of the Oratorians would have to bring her down to earth. Meanwhile, Miss Giberne herself was taking up the cudgels for Newman in Rome. He had been asked to begin the foundation of the Catholic University in Dublin but was kept hanging about at the end of 1853, not yet publicly recognised as Rector. In Rome, apparently, the delay was visited on Newman himself. Newman told Ambrose St John that he had heard from Miss Giberne. 'Talbot has been at her, asking her if it would do to put me to Dublin – whether I should not retire into myself and do nothing. She recollected herself for a moment, to say nothing out of propriety – and then fired a broadside into him so effective that she saw nothing of the wreck and does not know what became of him. Not content with this exploit, she followed it up by going to Cardinal Antonelli and complaining of Talbot.'[17]

She was deeply interested in the new Chapel at Edgbaston, sent vestments and pictures and received detailed news of its opening from Father Ambrose. In December '53 Jemima passed through Birmingham and visited her brother at the Oratory and sat for some hours, uncomfortable ones for both of them. Miss Giberne was a link with the old family days and one of the few people

Jemima seemed interested in. As he told her: 'She inquired much after you and took down your direction. She would not ask not a single question about my friends here whom she had known. She would not return a civil answer to a proposal I made about Mrs Wootten – she would not ask a word about Ireland – she would not notice even the house, except to ask how high the room was. We had the greatest difficulty to find talk; for all subjects were forbidden of any interest.'[18]

Miss Giberne was to see Newman in Rome again, at the beginning of 1856 and she found lodgings for him and Father Ambrose at 47 Piazza di Spagna. He was in Rome because of a dispute with the London Oratory and its Superior, Father Faber, and he believed that the London community was out to gain ascendancy over the Birmingham house and to obtain from Rome a modification of the Rule which would apply to both houses. On this particular matter, Newman was eventually satisfied but the causes of the dispute lay deep and members of the London Oratory were prone to oppose Newman, maintaining that their notion of an Oratory was more true to the spirit of the founder, St Philip Neri, and that Newman was *il Babbo*, an old Daddy who lacked the thrust an fervour of his sons, particularly those in London.

One would expect that in any dispute between the two Oratories Miss Giberne would be firmly on the side of her dear Father, as she had been when she blew Monsignor Talbot out of the water. However, most uncharacteristically, she became the champion of the London party and told Father Hutchinson, of the London Oratory that when Newman was young he always had a shocking temper. This Oratorian said something which gives a clue to her attitude. 'She also is in a row with him. He picked a quarrel with her, or Ambrose did for him ... and he has not written to her since.'[19] What the quarrel was we do not know, but one of Newman's biographers surmises that the subject was her 'spiritual love' for him. 'Grateful as he was for her loyal help in the Achilli trial, Newman had certainly been embarrassed by her uninhibited devotion just afterwards. If St John had spoken to her on Newman's behalf on this delicate subject, she may well have felt very cross with him. It would be humiliating to her enthusiastic temperament to find her feelings considered more natural than spiritual, especially if common sense suggested it might be true.'[20]

She took to visiting the lodgings of the London Oratorians, Hutchinson and Stanton, when they were in Rome, and played hymns on the piano, in between times agreeing with them that in many matters Newman was sadly in the wrong. When she had a letter from Birmingham asking her to pray for more novices for that house she told Ambrose St John to ask Father Faber to pray for them, for he obtained whatever he prayed for, whether for cures or for conversions.

Meanwhile Newman thought of her, living in her lodgings in the Palazzo Borghese and not thinking of her own comfort and he took the liberty of a very old friend to tell her that if she did not eat properly her spirits would sink and she should indulge in the pleasures of the table a bit, cover her floors, buy a writing desk and enough candles. Decent meat should be bought, not cat's meat, and she should remember the cartoon of old Lord Eldon who was presented by his admirers with a large cheshire cheese – and was depicted sitting before it saying, 'My cheshire cheese is now my only consolation.'[21]

No one knows if she took any notice of this sensible advice, but her fit of indignation wore off and she continued Newman's enthusiastic friend, as before.

∽∾⊙∾∾

It is not to be thought that Newman, with his choice of celibacy, his high regard for that state and his relief at belonging to a church that demanded celibacy of its clergy, was one to think little of the married state and to turn aside from married friends. He was on friendly terms with a great many married people and was deeply interested in their family concerns. Some of his friends from his Oxford days were married, he knew many married converts and with the setting up of the Oratory School, next door to the Oratory itself and employing lay masters and with the

Catholic University in Dublin employing lay tutors, more families came within his circle of friends. There are countless indications in his letters that when something of note happened to one of these families – when there was a marriage, when an adult son or daughter chose the priesthood or religious life, when there was illness or anxiety, Father Newman was one of the first to hear about it and a courteous and sympathetic note always followed. Heaven knows how he managed to say all the Masses for people that he promised them. Sadly, there was often news of the death of a child. Sometimes there was news of a wife who had died in child-birth. Mortality was high and families, even the relatively well-to-do and wealthy families that he knew, with access to the best medical help, had little expectation of rearing all their children.

Hundreds of messages of good wishes, of prayers promised, have inevitably a certain formality and the reader would dearly like to know more of the family in receipt of the kind phrase. There is no doubt, however, of Newman's sympathy. When a daughter was off to a convent, his thought was for the parents, particularly her mother, who would in a sense be losing a child. The girl herself, though making a sacrifice, had the interest and fulfilment of a new life but those left behind needed consolation. He wrote from the heart when a young life was cut short, as when he wrote to the Marchioness of Lothian whose son John, aged nearly fourteen, died of pneumonia at Ushaw, when his mother was in Rome. He said that he had been thinking of the child ever since he heard that he was ill and went on:

> I saw him last year at Ushaw and was so struck by him that I talked of him to others for some time. He came into my room of his own accord, and made friends with me in an instant. For him, how can I but rejoice that he should be taken out of this dark world in the freshness and bloom of his innocence and piety. But it comes over me most keenly that if once seeing him made me love him so much, what must it have been to you?[1]

There were plenty of cheerful congratulations to be sent too, as on marriages and births. Just as the old Catholic families, knit together by their religion and by the disadvantages of recusancy, formed a network, inter-marrying, knowing one another socially, so the new converts were often linked. George Ryder's daughter, Caroline Alice, was also Mrs Henry Wilberforce's niece. If she looked like her mother and aunt, two of the famous Sargent sisters whose beauty lured earnest tractarians' clerics from celibacy, she must have been a lovely bride. When she married Henry Clutton warm wishes went from the Oratory in Birmingham where her brother was a priest. Newman wrote to Mrs Wilberforce that he and Father Ambrose and probably other Oratorians too had said Mass for her that morning.

Newman wrote to his old Oxford acquaintance, W.G. Ward, with kind thoughts on the birth of his youngest daughter, Margaret, on the 6 August, the feast of the Transfiguration, 1860.

The Oratory Bm August 10, 1860

My Dear Ward,

I waited to answer the announcement contained in your kind letter, till I could tell you that I had said Mass for your and Mrs Ward's intention about the little child. This I have done this morning. I offer you and her my best congratulations, and I earnestly pray that the Festival on which she was born may over shadow her all through her life, and that she may find it 'good to be here,' till that time of blessed Transfiguration when she will find, from experience, that it is better to be in heaven. Give me your good prayers in return, and beg that I may spend the rest of my life to God's glory and believe me to be,

My dear Ward, Affectionately Yours in Xt
John H. Newman of the Oratory[2]

This is such a gracious letter that it would have been sad if it had to be followed by condolences – but the child, Margaret, throve and grew up to be a nun. Many years later she was celebrated in a book by Maisie, W.G. Ward's grand-daughter. The pleasant irony is that Maisie Ward was one of those frail babies that Newman prayed for. But fears for her were groundless – she had a long life and became a well-known writer.

Of all the families known to Newman none is more interesting than that of William and Catherine Froude. He was one of Richard Hurrell Froude's brothers. Oriel was the Froudes' college and their father had been there as an undergraduate, going on to take Orders and to become Archdeacon of Totnes and Rector of Dartington in Devon. With ample means he was a cultured, country gentleman, a parson of the old school and a loving father to a large family. His wife died when their eldest son Hurrell was still a boy. The youngest son, James Anthony, also at Oriel, became a noted historian, writing a history of England and becoming Rector of St Andrew's University and eventually Regius Professor of Modern History at Oxford. The two brothers who left their mark so decisively, Hurrell and James Anthony, were very different in their attitude to religion: the eldest was one of the founders of the Oxford Movement, Newman's friend, each influencing each other profoundly, and the youngest of the family was a sceptic.

William, the fourth son, was different again. He was, inevitably, an undergraduate at Oriel and Hurrell was his tutor for a time. We first meet him in Hurrell Froude's letters as 'Master Willy'. When Hurrell was at home in Devon, during term time, and William was to come into residence at Oriel, Newman suggested he should come up on his own: he, Newman, would keep him in order, making him write his fingers off and 'he shall come regularly to me and receive his periodical rowings as good as you could administer.'[3] When the eldest brother died, nursed tenderly by the Archdeacon at Dartington, it was William who acted as messenger, coming to Oxford to clear up his brother's rooms, telling Newman all that the Archdeacon could not convey in letters.

William was very clever in his own line and became a most distinguished man. He gained a First in mathematics and went off to become a railway engineer under the great

Brunel. Then he went back to Dartington for a time to be with the Archdeacon, then over seventy. Later he took up naval work and became well known as a naval architect and engineer, working for the Admiralty. Quite early on in his career, under Brunel's direction, when his main work was with railways, he was investigating the movement of ships and in time warships and mercantile ships were more stabilised and made greater speed because of William Froude's investigations. At the end of his working life he gathered many honours and gave important evidence to a Royal Commission on scientific research.

He married, in 1839, Catherine Holdsworth, the daughter of Arthur Howe Holdsworth of Dartmouth who was the Member of Parliament for that rotten borough and later Governor of Dartmouth Castle. She met Newman before her marriage – it must have been at a gathering at Dartington where there were young ladies, the Froude sisters and visitors too, and where Newman showed himself skilled at writing verses for their albums. Both William and his wife corresponded with him regularly. Devon was their home and after the Archdeacon's death in 1859 William built a house in Torquay and named it Chelston Cross. Newman, when he visited in his youth, found Devon rich in colour and marvelled at the brightness of rocks, of a beetle, of flowers. He thought it a lovely, sensuous place, overpowering and even stifling. He wrote years later to Jemima, 'When I went down to Devonshire in 1831 with H. Froude, the rich depth of the vegetation stifled me – I could not enjoy a leafy feather bed.'[4] William and Catherine Froude did not give the impression of people who always breathed enervating air: he was unusually active and practical, they were both intelligent, downright and sensible.

Although Newman was very fond of William and their friendship dated back to the time he was a boy and then Hurrell's pupil, the greater friendship was with Catherine because of their shared religious concerns. She was a devout Christian who gave long consideration to the question of the validity of the Anglican Church and the claims of Rome. William Froude loved his wife deeply, loved and admired Newman but he could not share their faith. In the later part of Newman's Anglican life he expressed himself freely to these friends, particularly to her. He wondered at one point whether he was boring her. 'I really do not quite know why I am going on prosing to you at this rate, and all about myself. I hope it will not look very absurd some little time hence, and I fear it really must be very dull to you. I am sure my last letter must have been a regular quietus, and by its sedative effects must have tended to undo all the excitement I have caused you (as Punch says that a pun of the Duke of W's this day week made the Emperor of Russia go home and sleep sound for two hours) but to proceed ...'[5] The letters to her, in the fateful year of 1844, chart the progress of his mind towards conversion to Rome very fully and it is not surprising that, when retracing his earlier years in writing the *Apologia* he used these letters.

There is a photograph of Catherine Froude, in middle age, kept at the Birmingham Oratory. It shows a thin, elegant lady in a plain, well-fitting dress. She is tall with thin features; an artist drawing her would use lines rather than curves but there is no impression of angularity or meanness. She is fine drawn. There was no gush, no exaggeration about her. She loved Newman and said so, writing to him once, 'you are dearer to me than any person in the world after my husband and children and my dear sister.'[6] Of course, buttressed by William, Newman's old friend, and as a married lady, she had the freedom to speak like this but had she been single she would not have prated of spiritual love, like Miss Giberne or lionised him as Miss Holmes did. Miss Bowles, who was not silly like Miss Giberne, customarily used language about Newman that was so full of admiration that it was, like the air of Devon, over-warm and oppressive. Mrs Froude never did.

She was not a Catholic at the time of the Achilli troubles but she and her husband took Newman's part and wanted to help. William sent £20, then a considerable sum. He was one of the multitude of friends who contributed to Newman's heavy expenses and to the fine imposed on him. When all was over and Newman was low in health he

bought port wine, ordered by the doctor, with money sent
by Catherine Froude.

Newman believed at one time that both Froudes would
in time become Catholics, and their children. He wrote to
another friend and convert, Mrs Francis Ward in 1851 in
confident tones.

> It is very kind in you to tell me about the dear Froudes.
> How is it possible to doubt that they will ultimately be
> brought by God's grace to where we are? They house no
> argument against Catholicism, but it is their imagination
> which starts back from it. They have all their lives been
> accustomed to something so different – the worship in
> the Catholic Church is so new to them, the customs, the
> phrases, the ideas, the tone of thought, that it is like
> forcing what is square into what is round ...[7]

He was wrong about William Froude who set out, with
great openness, his doubts about religion. He believed that
no certainty could be attained by the human mind; in
Newman's words, he believed in the 'necessity of an ever-
lasting suspense.' As for his wife, who was 'Kate' to him, he
said (in 1854) that they had talked together and he had
formed an opinion of her state of mind.

> I fully believe that as far as reasonable or reasoning
> conviction goes, her judgment is against Catholicism –
> as far as feeling goes it is in its favour – the feeling being
> partly what might be called fascination occasioned by
> the magnitude and endurance of the system, and what
> appears to her the adaptations of its ceremonial to her
> own peculiar turn of mind – and partly her entire love
> and admiration for the few Catholics she has known – a
> love and admiration which goes entirely beyond that
> which she feels for any other persons whatever.
>
> My conversations with her, have led me to see that I
> had if anything underrated the force of this fascination,
> and it would not surprise me if it were some day or other
> wholly to outweigh all opposing influences of whatever
> kind ...[8]

He did not like to contemplate the change she would almost certainly make. As he said, in his somewhat circumlocutory style, though her becoming a Catholic would not impair affection it would 'in its very nature make an end of that full communion of thought and judgment in which affection has had such scope.'[9] In fact, though her change of religious allegiance would sharpen the differences, they did not have full communion of thought even then: she was of a religious mind and he was essentially agnostic. Newman assured him that feeling drawn to Catholicism by the love of Catholic friends or even by admiration of its system and rituals would not consitute valid reasons for a change – only a conviction born of judgment would do.

Mrs Froude did become a Catholic, but the transition took a long time. In 1849 Newman expressed himself in very sober and worried terms lest she should have lost faith in the Church of England and was preferring scepticism to Rome. Later, however, he spoke with more calm: 'My dear Mrs Froude, *do* you pray for "effectual grace" –? Suppose I come to a high wall – I cannot jump it – such are the moral obstacles which keep us from the Church. We see the Heavenly City before us, we go on and on along the road, till a wall simply crosses it. Human effort cannot clear it – there is no scaling, no vaulting over. Grace enables us to cross it – and that grace is called effectual grace …'[10] He sent love to William (he no longer expected him to act with his wife, though he always hoped and prayed) and said 'Excuse this Sermon.'

She was painstaking and earnest and not easily satisfied about Roman practices, asking detailed questions about indulgences, about exaggerated devotions, about the use of images. Certainly she was put off by what was strange to her habits of thought and prayer, but it was not simply a matter of accepting what was unfamiliar – her intelligence needed to be satisfied. Newman answered at length, pointing out the difference between what was important and what was a matter of taste. There was no necessity for English ladies to adopt Italianate devotions. Some of the exchanges make the modern reader wonder that Christianity should call out such complicated reasonings, and perhaps Kate Froude, herself a very straightforward person, found it hard to be battling through such thickets. She entered the Church in the spring of 1857, very gladly except for her thoughts of William who, she knew, would be distressed. Both Froudes, and Newman, behaved with the greatest delicacy and with respect for the consciences of those involved and affection triumphed in a difficult situation.

The next question was – what about the children? They were three boys and two girls. The eldest boy was Richard Hurrell, and when he was born his mother had asked Newman if he would be godfather to 'another Richard Hurrell Froude.' He was called by his second name as his uncle had been. He wished to follow his mother's path and Newman received him into the Catholic Church at Christmas, 1859, though not before he had assured himself that this boy of seventeen knew what he was about. William Froude wrote a long letter at this point[11] saying that he knew that his son was acting from conviction and that Newman had acted fairly and with discretion. He set out his own position at great length: as a scientist and a student of 'the mechanical arts' he had come to the conclusion that all ideas and theories must be held with a residuum of doubt and the mind must be ever open to discard one idea for a better one. Hence he would not offer his friend any hope that he would ever follow his family into the Roman church. Newman replied that he understood this line of reasoning, had long meditated on it and, though he thought it a fallacy, was hard put to refute it. He would not put it down with 'a few magisterial words.'[12] Their discussions continued, in the most friendly and honest fashion.

As for Hurrell, he was unable to proceed to one of the Oxford colleges as had been intended and instead he lodged with a Professor Donkin in Oxford and studied there. A difficulty arose over family prayers and the incident illustrates the intransigence that obtained then, both on the Anglican and on the Catholic side. Hurrell was made to attend family prayers – it was Mrs Donkin who insisted – and Newman was equally insistent that he must not join in. He could be there and use his own prayer book quietly – a curious and devious way of behaving but in a sense forced by the insistence on conformity to Anglican ways. Hurrell's mother may have been worried by all this but her attention was much taken up by grief at her father's death in 1860.

The other children chose to be Catholics too, one at a time, as they made their own decision – all except Mary Froude. Her story is a very sad one. The Froudes, like the Bowdens, lived under the shadow of the dreaded disease, tuberculosis. Hurrell Froude, a brother and a sister had all died young of T.B. and a predispositon to it might well exist in William's children. Mary Catherine, the younger daughter, developed the disease when she was sixteen. Mrs Froude had the double grief of seeing her daughter's decline and wishing, in vain, that she could live the rest of her life as a Catholic. She wrote:

> I cannot prevent myself from regretting that the dear child is not a Catholic, as I know she loses *that* which would sustain and cheer her through all she may have to suffer, I feel hopeful that she is careful about saying her prayers – and she is very regular in wishing to have the Psalms and Lessons read to her, which I read every morning to her the first thing; – and then if she is tolerably well, she always wishes for a 'Newman', which (as you may suppose) is one of your sermons – which she always enjoys greatly, – and quite appreciates and seems to enter into the arguments.[13]

Newman did not yield one jot of his conviction that it was 'indescribably better' to live and die as a Catholic but he urged Mrs Froude to have a cheerful hope about this child and 'leave her to that God who loves her more than you can love her.'[14] It was William who wrote to say that Mary had died on the 30 May 1864 and Newman replied at once, 'Dear Child, she is gone to heaven and is safe.'[15]

As for her sister, the eldest in the family, she was healthy, intelligent, a devout girl who had plenty of spring and bounce in her. Her full name was Eliza Margaret but she was always known as Isy. She became a Catholic in 1859,

when she was nineteen. She loved Newman and he was very
fond of her. In fact, though he had the education of boys
in hand and knew and liked a good many of them, he had
a distinct following with little girls and growing girls. There
were Marianne and Emily Bowden and the daughters of
Henry Bowden. Then there was Mary Monica Hope-Scott,
always known as Mamo from her first rendering of her
name. James Hope-Scott was a close friend of Newman's
from their tractarian days. He was a convert, influential
and rich but a man who had great sorrows, losing two wives
and two young children. Mamo was his daughter by his first
wife, the grandchild of Sir Walter Scott by whom he inherited Abbotsford, Scott's home. Letters to Hope-Scott always
sent affectionate messages to her.

When Isy Froude was fifteen she sent Newman a
penwiper that she had made for him. He obviously wished
to reply in grateful terms but equally obviously could not
find the right tone to use to a girl of fifteen. He used short,
stiff sentences, as though simplifying a letter for a child of
eight or nine. 'I am very glad to have your present. A pen
wiper is always useful. It lies on the table and one can't
help looking at it.'[16]

However, Isy was not put off and wrote from time to time
with zest and Newman was very helpful to her – pointing
out to her, when she was received into the Church that she
might feel miserably flat when she had attained her goal
and all the excitement was over. Mrs Froude wrote to him a
little later to give 'very good accounts' of Isy, so she had
been helped over a time of reaction, both by Newman and
her mother. She found out the date of Newman's birthday
and wrote in 1861 in that slightly facetious and flamboyant
style that the young adopt when trying out phrases to say
that it would be a great bore and nuisance to him to have a
letter from her bringing birthday greetings. By this time he
was at ease when writing to her and thanked her charm-
ingly for her letter which had been written 'with so much
effusion of heart'.[18] She was indeed very fond of him.

Charlotte or Chattie Bowden aged fifteen showed her
affection for him by baking him some cakes and the letter
thanking her was in verse and more successful than the

one about the penwiper. It led to some moralising but girls
in Victorian times, like Lewis Carroll's Alice, were used to
having the moral pointed out.

> Who is it that moulds and makes
> Round, and crisp, and fragrant cakes?
> Makes them with a kind intent,
> As a welcome compliment,
> And the best that she can send
> To a venerable friend.
> One it is, for whom I pray,
> On St Philip's festal day,
> With a loving heart that she
> Perfect as her cakes may be,
> Full and faithful in the round
> Of her duties ever found
> Where a trial comes, between
> Truth and falsehood cutting keen;
> Yet that keenness and completeness
> Tempering with a winning sweetness.
> Here's a rhyming letter, Chat,
> Gift for a gift and tit for tat.[9]

The Newman who wrote such a letter was not the great
thinker or the fierce controversialist but the Newman of
the 'Spy' cartoon, a thin cleric in black with a smile of
great benignity. He was amazingly thin in age and, as he
said to Isy, his hair was getting whiter and whiter, and his
fingers thinner and thinner, adding that she should tell
her mother that he would not love her and all the family
less or forget to pray for them though he dwindled and
faded away into a spider's web.

Isy grew up to be very much her mother's companion.
Sometimes they came to Birmingham together to stay a day
or two (probably in the Plough and Harrow hotel near the
Oratory) to visit Father Newman. They went out, as the
Newman ladies had done years before at Littlemore, to
give charity to the indigent. However, they found this
easier to do in Mentone, where they all had long holidays,
because the local people accepted them whereas in Devon

the villagers were suspicious because of their religion.

Isy had a social life of her own too, knowing plenty of people. She visited at Abbotsford and found Mamo Hope-Scott 'sweet and remarkable' and they talked together of Father Newman and said how much they admired him. She went to a ball at Keswick, on one of her jaunts, and danced with a Mr Arnold and as they danced they talked of religion and Mr Arnold seemed melancholy about it. Mrs Froude reported in one letter that Isy had just made a retreat and the priest was admirable because he 'was able to see both sides of the question which is not always the case with Catholic priests.'[20] This remark is typical of Isy's mother. She was not less devout than the other convert ladies but she had a very cool head.

Isy, unlike some of the converts' daughters, did not become a nun. In fact not one of the young Froudes entered the priesthood or Religious life, though they all became good and devout men and women. One boy, Robert Edmund, known as Eddy, the next in age to Hurrell, spent the last of his school years at Newman's Oratory School and at the close of it he made a retreat and came home announcing that he had a vocation. Newman was perturbed at this news, feeling that a genuine vocation must be encouraged but doubting whether Eddy Froude was in earnest since he seemed vague about any distinction between the secular priesthood and the Religious Orders. If this was all an adolescent's reaction to a fervent retreat poor William was to be worried for nothing. He intended that Eddy should study at Oxford but why should he spend more money educating him for the Catholics? In the event, Eddy did not become a priest but followed his father and became a naval architect and engineer. Mrs Froude kept hearing from her Catholic contemporaries of sons who were to be Jesuits, of daughters entering convents and she surveyed her brood wondering if she should feel some sense of shame that they were different. She decided that she did not but was proud of them as they were.

The last boy, Arthur Holdsworth, entered the Navy. He became ill, when he was a Lieutenant, and went home to Chelston Cross. His brother Eddy feared to visit him, knowing that he was seriously ill and remembering that his sister Mary's death had been harrowing, but he did go home and found that Arthur, at twenty four, was dying but in a calm and hopeful spirit. Mrs Froude wrote to Newman:

> I thank God every year more and more, that we have had you for a friend. It is curious to me to see that – although my children are all so different, yet there is something in your writings which fits into their minds in a way that no other serious reading does. I read your books over and over again to Arthur, now that he is ill, and he is never tired of hearing them.[21]

Arthur Froude died that Easter in 1868, and three compassionate letters whent out from the Birmingham Oratory, to William, to his wife and to Isy. A little later Mrs Froude reported, 'Dear William has been more kind than I can say – but you know him – and he has suffered much distress. He constantly says, "dear fellow, how good he was."' She said that she was trying to keep up for Isy's sake. The family were closer than ever in grief.

They were a remarkable family and Catherine Froude was a remarkable woman, fulfilling every Victorian tenet of behaviour as a devoted wife and mother but managing to keep her independence when she chose her own religious way, quite against her husband's philosophy of life. Her William too was the salt of the earth, honest and tolerant in an intolerant age. No wonder Newman valued them. No wonder, either, that they valued him. Mrs Froude always said a great deal when she paid her quiet tributes and she said once to him, '*you* always contrived to say exactly what suited my mind.'[23]

⋘◉⋙

One of Mrs Froude's great friends was a certain Mrs Francis Ward. Her maiden name was Eliza Welsford, her husband was a solicitor and her brother-in-law was Richard Ward, a graduate of Oriel, a curate in Leeds and then Vicar of St Saviour's in the same town. The brothers were both supporters of Newman and in 1857 Francis, Richard and Eliza were all received into the Church of Rome. Newman wrote to Mrs Ward, 'I congratulate you with all my heart on your reception into the Catholic Church and pray, and am sure, you will enjoy to the full those blessings which there alone are to be found.'[1] Newman continued to be her friend, though the friendship was not so close and the correspondence with her not so extensive as with Catherine Froude. The connection between the Froudes and the Francis Wards illustrates the network that so many of these converts formed.

However, not all the convert ladies knew Father Newman well and many of the inquirers or new Catholics wrote for a time, or met him briefly and no strong bond was made. It was bound to be so. The remarkable thing is that so many knew him and admired him, and profited from his care, whether they became friends for life or had only a passing acquaintance with him. An aristocratic lady, Lady Lothian, a widow who had been helped by Manning and received into the Church by the ever useful Father Brownbill, called at the Birmingham Oratory just before Christmas in 1851 when she was a new convert. She wrote to her brother-in-law, Lord Henry Kerr (who was a friend of Newman's) to describe the visit.

> He was most kind. I was nervous, but without cause, for he is so full of sympathy and Christian love that he is the last person one need be afraid of. That which struck me most was his childlike sympathy and humility, and next to that, the vivid clearness with which he gives an opinion. He is a very striking looking person. His saying of Mass is most striking. I do not know what makes the difference, but one is conscious of a difference. It appeared to me very unearthly.[2]

If he answered enquirers and helped them on their way or actually received them into the Church, there is a fixed pattern in his letters, though all counsel was tailored to individual need. Although he firmly held by what he said to Eliza Ward, that blessings were to be found in the

Catholic Church beyond what could be found elsewhere, he was always cautious. Hasty conversions could be most harmful, no one should act from inadequate motives and every convert should know exactly what he or she was in for. He made this abundantly clear in a letter to a priest friend in 1862,[3] tabulating the reasons that Protestants might be disappointed in what they would find in the Catholic Church. They often believed that the Catholic Church was a rich and mighty organisation, peopled with 'crafty Jesuits, with deep, subtle, powerful intellects,' whereas in reality Catholics acted by faith and 'often acted in a second best way in a worldly aspect.' As for money, the Church lived hand to mouth, and as to all those Jesuitical clever minds, English Catholics lacked higher education as far as the laity were concerned and their priests were not so intellectual as others imagined, they did not provide 'a glut of the best direction for all possible persons and cases' nor theological schools. Newman ended by saying that educated converts had to look for supernatural excellence, not natural. But, he added, underlining his words, *'many Catholics do not like to allow this.'*

Potential converts needed to consider the effect their conversion would have on their relatives and this was particularly true for women who were heavily dependent on their families. On the one hand, it was morally wrong to go counter to one's conscience because of family considerations or pressures. Newman was disappointed in an enquirer called Miss Kebbel who was on the verge of becoming a Catholic but then wrote to say that she could not do it in the lifetime of her father who was in Anglican Orders. On the other hand, it was important that converts should act with delicacy and discretion where their relatives were concerned and not offend them gratuitously.

Many of the women converts sifted religious doctrines assiduously but they were also concerned, quite properly, about prayers and devotions. Like Mrs Froude, several were put off by devotional books that came their way via France and Italy, full of extravagant outpourings to Our Lady or in a florid style that stifled devotion rather than fostered it. Newman's general line was that much depended on the individual's leaning and tastes. He wrote to the Marquise de Salvo, an English lady who had married a Neapolitan nobleman, who had been widowed and was a convert of some years' standing but who was still bothered by certain devotions; 'I do not see,' he said, 'that a person ought to force himself into the use of particular manuals or exercises which do not come natural to him.'[4] However, he was wary of a minimalist theory that would lead to a convert's virtual rejection of devotions and customs that were dear to Catholics. He recommended solid prayerbooks like the *Garden of the Soul,* much in use amongst 'old' Catholics and he liked his converts to learn to use the rosary. 'To my own feelings,' he said to the Marquise, 'nothing is more delightful than the contemplation of the Mysteries of the Incarnation, under the invocation, so to call it, of her who was the human instrument of it – so that she who ministered to the Gracious Dispensation itself, should minister also to our adoring thought of it.'[5]

Many and various were the ladies who applied to him for counsel. Besides such grand personages as Lady Lothian and the Marquise de Salvo was a poor seamstress called Jane Todd who lived in Scarborough. She was certainly not illiterate but she was not up to a long and intensive correspondence with Newman; however she had followed his teaching from tractarian days and felt a great gratitude and veneration for him. In those times she thought of coming to live in Littlemore but took rooms instead in York. The Catholic church was nearby and she did become a Catholic in 1847. Afterwards she moved to Scarborough and she was perhaps housekeeper to a priest there for a time. She took a pen with a thin steel nib and in a spidery hand wrote from there what she felt for her spiritual guide.

My *understanding* has seen His truth in you, and never in any other human being. I know you are His Work, and His own Servant – as I feel the sun and the stars are His – and my mind rises to Him in praise and confidence – because He so condescends to show me signs and tokens of Eternal Life.[6]

This was signed, as all her short letters were, 'Yours respect-
fully.' Her gratitude was not confined to words: she sewed
for Newman, making him drawers and waistcoats and
nightcaps, hemming pieces of silk for his throat and urging
him to wear horsehair insoles because the friction kept the
feet warm. Since he lived to be nearly ninety it is difficult to
think of Newman as an old man in his sixties, but he felt
himself to be old (and indeed proclaimed himself old and
failing years before that) and was as he admitted very thin,
fading 'to a spider's web' and looking as if his frame could
hardly support his powerful head. He was not cold in
winter, however, despite the poor covering for his bones.
He wrote to Jemima in 1864, 'There is a lady I have never
seen, who is ever throwing flannels and silks at me, in spite
of my protesting and sometimes sending them back.'[7]

One of his early converts was a single lady, Catherine
Ward – who was no relation of Richard and Francis Ward,
nor of Newman's Oxford contemporary W.G. Ward. She
lived at Norland House, Clifton, the property of her
brother-in-law and her religious history was an extraordinary one. She said she had been brought up 'as a sort of
half church woman, half dissenter', and was sent when she
was twelve years old and thereafter to prove for herself the
truth or falsehood of Calvinism by reading the Bible and
other books and comparing their statements. She does not
say who sent her on this exploration – was it her father,
about whom nothing is known? After years as a self-taught
Evangelical she came to the Oxford Movement, read
Newman's sermons and put herself under the guidance of
Dr Pusey. She said in 1848 that she had made it her aim,
for three years, to lay aside her habit of self guidance and
to practise obedience but she had, increasingly, to 'crush
thoughts of distrust towards the Church in which I have
been brought up.' She said that there was much in the
superstructure of the Catholic Church which both startled
and shocked her but still she felt drawn to it, and she was
able to put her finger on exactly what drew her like a great
magnet. It was 'that wonderful Sacramental system, so lost,
confused, almost vilified in the Church of England and
tho' Dr Pusey and others hold it and give me leave to hold

it, yet it is in such an isolated manner that I cannot feel it as a truth of the Church, but only as held by individuals.'

She set all this out in a long letter to Newman,[8] feeling that he, who had known Pusey for years and admired him, would judge her case fairly and with tenderness to the man she revered and to whom she felt she owed obedience. She was pulled all ways, by her long habit of self guidance, of reading and weighing evidence carefully and making up her own mind, and also by her present resolution to trust authority. What was she to do when she did not trust the authority vested in the Church of England? She said, 'It is an awful question to a lay person who "ought to obey those set over her" to a woman who "ought to learn at home" to take such a solemn step upon her own responsibility ...' Also she felt like a traitor towards Pusey himself who was 'a thousand thousand times holier than I am, who lives in prayer, who breathes the love of God as the very atmosphere of his existence, who has for years lived in the study of the fathers and Holy Scriptures.'

Newman anwered her letter at length and took her point about the holiness of Pusey. But, he argued, Pusey could not be called a specimen of the Anglican Church. Pusey strove for sanctity but an Anglican clergyman aimed to be 'a gentleman, a scholar, a good father of a family, a well conducted, kindhearted, religiously minded man – and little more.'[9] There was grace and holiness to be found in the Anglican Church and elsewhere but that was not proof, according to Newman, of the truth and efficacy of its ordinances, only proof that God 'is merciful beyond His promise.'

The correspondence continued and Catherine Ward laid out her difficulties about the doctrines and devotional practices of the Church of Rome. She was an intelligent and thoughtful woman, reading Newman's *Essay on Development* with minute attention, and making some investigations into the devotional practices of Europeans and finding, like Mrs Froude, that the more extravagant kind, particularly devotions to Mary, caused her considerable disquiet. Again, Newman answered at length and point by point and she seemed satisfied with his replies. At the end

of that year she wrote that she was indeed intellectually
convinced that if she was to continue believing in 'the
Church' she must identify it as the Roman Church but she
felt that she could not trust her convictions because of her
past history when she had changed her creed again and
again. This time she gave more details of her early life.[10] At
twelve she chose dissent. At fifteen she had doubts about
the Athanasian Creed and at nineteen she spent a miserable time trying to shake off all belief. Then she made 'a
kind of religion for myself, a kind of Bible asceticism –
from thence rushing into Evangelicalism with all its
committees and talk and bustle – to Calvinism –
Millenarianism'. Then, thanks to Newman's sermons, she
embraced Tractarianism and then read Dr Pusey's sermon
on Absolution. 'A new way seemed open to me ... and it
has failed me.' How then was she to trust her present
conclusions?

Newman sympathised with her distresses and urged her
forward. Pusey had bound her to a promise to remain
faithful to the English Church until that Christmas but she
was looking forward to the new year (1849), determined to
act independently of Pusey but still fearful. In February she
wrote again, asking for information on one point, on mira-
cles as a proof of the trust Church. Newman would not
answer this question and his letter, though civil was crusty.
Was she not becoming one who would ever be seeking and
so would never find?

She did become a Catholic that June and did not waver
again. Letters to Newman came to the Oratory occasionally
and she sent hangings for his Alcester Street chapel, but
generally she was content to live her life at Clifton without
direction from him. Her brother-in-law became a Catholic
and a dear niece, called Susan du Boulay. Miss Ward made
a late marriage to an Army man, also a Catholic convert,
called George Tylee. He died in 1865, only eight years after
the marriage, but she lived on, still in Clifton, almost to the
end of the century.

Another of the converts who could be described as a bird
of passage rather than a lifelong friend was a woman with a
very different background called Lavinia Wilson. She was

Sister Lavinia, a member of an Anglican sisterhood in
Oxford. It was called the Community of St Thomas-the-
Martyr, founded in 1857 by the Rector of the church of
that name. The sisters taught school children and visited
the poor, first under Sister Edith and then under Sister
Beatrice.

When Sister Lavinia wrote to Newman in 1864, from her
convent, she was already practically convinced that she
must become a Catholic and was, of course, in an anom-
alous position. Newman gave her clear guidelines for her
behaviour. She should wait about three months and do
nothing precipitately. Meanwhile she was to guard her
right to liberty of action but behave honourably about her
doubts to other sisters. This was clear and helpful but it did
not touch on matters of feeling – and Lavinia Wilson was in
distress at the sorrow she was causing her 'Spiritual
Mother.' Newman's next letter was short and full of
compassion. 'I seem to myself,' he said, 'so unkind but
what can I do?' He wrote a compassionate letter to her
Superior as well.

Round about Christmas she left the convent and went
home, though Newman suggested that she should stay with
the Sisters of Mercy in Handsworth, Birmingham. One
reason he offered for this suggestion was so that she should
see a nun's life at firsthand, which is curious since it is
unlikely that the routine of the Anglican religious house
was materially different from that in the Birmingham
convent. He advised her to study the catechism, which
could be bought from the Catholic publisher Burns for
sixpence, and to buy also two prayerbooks, *The Garden of the
Soul* and one called the *Golden Manual.* 'It is no sin', he
said, 'to feel it difficult to accommodate your mind to
certain things, and it is better not, in the way of devotions,
to force yourself at all.'[12] If she could, she would do well to
say the rosary. She was to be tactful with her relatives and
care for her own health. There was to be no fasting, even
in Lent, after the strain she had endured.

His instructions were all of this simple kind – she was not
concerned, as Miss Ward had been, to seek deep theological explanations. She was vulnerable, tender, very

courageous in leaving her chosen home in Oxford. At Easter time in 1865 she came to Birmingham, on Newman's instructions, and was received into the Church by him. Later her sister Fanny became a Catholic too and Lavinia Wilson entered a Catholic convent. When she was at home that Christmas, suspended as it were between her devout Anglican life and her new Catholic one, Newman bade her be cheerful and happy and the hope is she was so thereafter. But, as far as Newman was concerned, she vanished from the scene though probably not from his prayers because he was retentive of those he had known and kept detailed remembrances before him by means of notes and calendars.

The travel instructions and the charting of her coming to Birmingham are so minutely recorded in letters and Newman's diary that a little picture is made vivid that serves for her and for other ladies – the compressing of oneself, in a crinoline, into a railway carriage and then into a cab going to the Convent of the Sisters of Mercy, Hunter's Road, Handsworth and again into a cab to proceed to the Birmingham Oratory on the Hagley Road. Richer ladies presumably, after penning letters at an escritoire, would visit in a carriage and put up at the Plough and Harrow, just across the road from the Oratory.

Chapter Three

The Writers

*Harriett Mozley, Charlotte Mary Yonge, Lady
Georgiana Fullerton; Emily Bowles, Geraldine Penrose
Fitzgerald, Fanny Margaret Taylor; Lady Chatterton
and her circle*

In the early part of the nineteenth century there were few
opportunities for women to use their brains in the public
sphere and the best way they could express their views and
talents was to undertake the work that could be done at
home, that is by writing. When Newman was a child Jane
Austen was writing her famous novels, quietly creating
them in the midst of family life. Newman's best known
literary judgement is his comment on *Emma*, when he said
that he felt warmly towards the heroine, found Jane Fairfax
a dolt and thought Miss Austen's parsons vile creatures
created by a writer who had no dream of the high Catholic
ethos.

When Harriett Newman was married and living in
Cholderton she began to write for children, perhaps
because she was bored there or because, quite simply, an
urge to create forced her to take up her pen. Her first tale
(with a heroine called Grace) was called *The Fairy Bower*
and she followed this with a sequel which was published in
1841. *The Lost Brooch* carries on the story of the children in
the first book who have now become young adolescents.
Charlotte M. Yonge reviewed both books at a later date and
was not impressed, saying that these juvenile novels 'are a
curious study of antics and follies, enhanced by little
domesticities, as when the party, twenty in number, go and

return from Hastings in a stage coach. Tee-totalism is unknown, the young ladies walk about in long ringlets and smoothed hair is the token of being religious'.[1] Harriett herself was afraid her first publication was too deep for children, too shallow for grown-ups – just the unhappy medium.

She was too diffident about her writing. Her brother John was far more enthusiastic, found her story brilliant and sought out a publisher for her. A modern critic calls *The Fairy Bower* 'a neglected minor masterpiece'.[2] Where Charlotte M. Yonge had said of this book 'the distinctions of right and wrong, and the character drawing are a great deal too subtle for the childish mind', the same critic finds Harriett Newman's tracing of the mind of ten-year-old Grace an 'exquisite' searching of the child's moral dilemma.[3]

She brought out an adult novel, *Louisa,* in 1842, and her brother read it 'with great satisfaction'.[4] His only complaint was that the book was too short, characters could have been brought out more and situations expanded. 'It is so very good that I wish it better'. It was thought that one character in the book was inspired by Jemima and that Elizabeth Bowden was portrayed in another character. Lastly Harriet produced a little children's book called *Family Adventures,* where she and her brothers and sisters appear under other names. It is a tender and shrewd account of the Newmans' childhood.

Harriett Newman's books were not written to instruct nor to convert readers to a particular religious view but the didactic and religious novel often written by women, was also on the scene and amazingly popular. The best known of women writers in this genre was Charlotte Mary Yonge, who had been Harriett's reviewer. She spent all her life in the village of Otterbourne in Hampshire. John Keble had the parish of Hursley, very near, after he had married and resigned his Oriel fellowship, and he influenced her profoundly so that tractarian views colour all her many novels and children's tales but she wrote to entertain as well as to instruct and her books were read and are still read not so much for their religious content as for their

lively narratives, plentiful dialogue and the vivid pictures
they give of the different members of large families. The
moral tone of her books is pronounced and so it is in the
girls' magazine, *The Monthly Packet*, that she edited for
many years. Other women wrote in a still more didactic
vein, keen to convert not simply to Christianity but to a
particular kind of Christianity. There were Methodist
novels, Evangelical novels, Tractarian novels, novels explic-
itly written to warn against the corruptions and errors of
Rome and Roman Catholic novels calculated to convert to
Rome and warn against Protestantism. These books were
flourishing years before Charlotte M. Yonge published *The
Heir of Redclyffe*, her most popular novel, in 1864.

Perhaps the most distinguished Catholic woman writer,
distinguished both in her aristocratic birth and in her
talent was Lady Georgiana Fullerton. She was born in 1812,
Georgiana Leveson Gower, the daughter of Lord Granville
Leveson Gower. One grandfather was the Marquis of
Stafford and the other, on her mother's side, the Duke of
Devonshire. So elevated was her family that one of her
early recollections was of going to a ball given for young
aristocrats, sitting on George the Fourth's knee and telling
him she could not stay with him any longer in case she
missed a dance. Her father was ambassador at the Hague
and then in Paris and it was in Paris that she spent much of
her childhood and youth. Shortly after the family had
moved into the Embassy Georgiana and her sister were
taken to see the Duchess d'Angoulême, the daughter of
Louis XVI and Marie Antoinette, who seemed marked and
roughened by the sorrows of her life but who was still, the
monarchy having been restored, a person of some
grandeur. She complimented the Ambassador's wife in
words that were not wholly pleasing to British ears: 'Your
daughters are so well behaved, one might take them to be
French girls'.

For all these splendid connections, the two girls had a
dreary and straitened existence, shut up with a very strict
governess and kept on a plain and monotonous diet.
Georgiana was not allowed novels but she read a great deal
of history and delighted in poetry. She was bilingual and in

adolescence wrote a great many verses in French. Her talent for writing prose was to develop later. Her governess could not rule her inner imaginative life and as a young girl she had a secret passion for Lord Byron, some of whose poems she had read and admired (they were passages from *Childe Harold* and *The Corsair*, introduced to her by her mother). She said she scrupled to read all his poems and knew he had a bad reputation but she felt that if she had been his wife she would have done anything to convert him. The embargo on novel reading did not extend to a Protestant tale called *Father Clement* which she described as, 'written by a protestant of the evangelical school, and intended to expose the errors and corruptions of the Catholic religion, Jesuit intrigues and the like'.[5] The interesting fact here is that the tale had exactly the opposite effect on the young reader from what the author, a Presbyterian lady called Grace Kennedy, intended. Georgiana loved the descriptions of an old Popish castle, 'the chapel with its tall crucifix, pictures of saints and dim religious light'.[6] She wished she could go to confession to Father Clement and after reading the book, she knelt down and addressed a prayer to the Virgin Mary. Furthermore, she thought she would enter a convent when she grew up.

When the time did come for her to come out into society she had, not surprisingly, forgotten all about this pious plan and gladly exchanged the rigours of the schoolroom for the great world, enjoying visits to her English relations and staying at noble houses such as Chatsworth and Castle Howard. In 1833 her father was made Earl Granville and she became Lady Georgiana Leveson – but the best news the spring of that year brought was that her parents sanctioned her engagement to Alexander Fullerton. He was a young man in the Grenadier Guards, heir to estates in Ireland and England and was of unexceptionable character. The parents hesitated at first because his father's settlement on him was not as munificent as they had hoped. However, all was well; he left his regiment to become Attaché at the Paris Embassy and the pair were married in the summer of the same year, 1833. A son,

William Granville, was born in 1834.

It was during the first years of her happy marriage that Lady Georgiana began to work for the poor of Paris, encouraged by her mother. Though Lady Granville was a charitable woman it was the daughter who really caught fire and began to devote much of her time to charitable concerns. Both ladies were impressed when they met the great Quaker reformer, Elizabeth Fry, and her example spurred on Lady Georgiana. She was now spending considerable sums of money on those who needed help. It is difficult to assess wealth and, in an age that saw it as a duty to keep up the standards of aristocratic life, it was taken for granted that the young Fullertons should travel, make splendid provision for the baby Granville and live according to their rank. However, they pruned away excesses and gave away a great deal. Lady Georgiana sold a poem to a publisher and realised that she had a talent by which she could earn. This is what prompted her to begin her first novel, *Ellen Middleton*.

While she was abroad she was busy writing, at Nice, in Germany and then in Rome with her husband and her parents. All were Anglicans but the young pair had been affected by the Oxford Movement. Both visited Catholic Churches on the Continent and Lady Georgiana, who had a romantic strain in her, under a reserved manner, was always impressed by rituals of Roman liturgy. She read St Francis de Sales' *Introduction to the Devout Life*, valued it and pondered on it. If she was a romantic who was drawn to Latin chantings, candlelight in dim chapels and stained glass, she was also of serious mind and did not rest on the surface of things. It was not she, however, but Alexander Fullerton who became a Catholic in Rome in 1843. It seems extraordinary that he did not tell his wife what he was doing. In much of the narrative of their life together – and it was undoubtedly a happy marriage – Alexander Fullerton's role was often that of a consort: he was well-born but not as well-born as she and not rich enough to please her parents, he aided his wife in her charities but it was she who was the instigator, he achieved no fame whereas she became well known as a writer. Mr Fullerton must often have been referred to as the husband of Lady Georgiana. But in this matter of conversion to Rome he blazed the trail and with a determined silence and reserve that is amazing.

The next year (1844, a crucial year for Newman and one that marks the end of the first stage of the Oxford Movement) saw the publication of *Ellen Middleton*. It was widely read and widely praised. The Queen and Prince Albert read it and approved. The writer Harriet Martineau read it avidly and thought it a fine book and Gladstone admired it greatly, its religious and moral tone, its 'eloquence and pathos', its handling of human action and motive. It is a sizable novel with a complicated and melo-dramatic plot and it was likely to be popular because it was exciting and at the same time dealt with one of the reli-gious issues of the day. The pious could justly feel that they were reading an improving book and at the same time they could enjoy plenty of dramatic incident and feel moved by the tragic outcome of the plot. The religious issue at the centre of the novel is the necessity for sacramental absolu-tion and the question of whether Anglican clergy should hear confessions and absolve.

The heroine, Ellen Middleton, suffers all her life from an act committed as a girl when she slapped her half-sister, aged eight, and the child fell down stone steps to her death. She is sure she is a murderess, even though the slap was without thought or intention and she bears the burden of guilt, wishing she could find a clergyman who would hear her tale and absolve her. Once she finds a kindly priest but she cannot bring herself to confess and says, 'If the fatal barrier which habit and prejudice so often raise between the priest of God and the erring and overbur-dened souls committed to his charge, had not in my case existed; if from his lips I might have heard the injunction to forsake all and follow Jesus, and he had added 'Do this, and be forgiven,' it might have changed my life'.[7]

She marries a stern husband but she has had another suitor, a Byronic figure called Henry Lovell who is wild, passionate, full of verve one time and sunk in gloom at another. He saw Ellen's fatal act but she is hounded by another blackmailer and then finally expelled from her home by her husband who has construed Ellen and Henry's frequent intimate conferences as proof of infidelity. It is only when she is near death that she meets a clergyman to whom she can tell the story of her life and she dies absolved.

In summary the story is revealed as the melodrama that it is but an outline does not show the subtler strokes of the novelist particularly her power to delineate states of mind. Georgiana Fullerton was something of a psychologist, describing the complexities of the mind of young Ellen, teased by her half-sister, understandably jealous and so racked with guilt when she kills the child that she has really wanted to remove from her life. She also wrote some powerful passages that delineate the strange bond between Ellen and Henry and Ellen's mingled fear of and desire for confession. *Ellen Middleton* is really the work of a novelist, not a glorified tract.

Newman read the novel and commented: 'I hardly know whether I ought to have read it – it has distressed me so. I wish people would not write sad things – they only make ones head ache; there are sad things enough in the world'.[8] He was so struck with one passage that he copied it out to include it in a letter to Ambrose St John. It is about suffering – 'I have often wondered whether the sensation of moral suffering is as surely allied to physical pain in everyone else as in myself. The expression of an aching heart has always appeared to me to have a literal as well as a figurative sense; there is a sort of positive pain which accompanies certain kinds of mental suffering, different in its nature from the feeling of grief, even in its highest degree'.[9] He read the book eight years after its publication, encouraged to do so by having read other novels by Lady Georgiana. At another time he made a comment on her skills which is very apt, pointing out that character drawing is 'the position in which you excel ... and female character.'[10] He also referred to 'that peculiar refinement of feeling and complexity of motive and passion, which you delight to draw.'[11]

After the first novel, she had it in mind to write the life

of St Elizabeth of Hungary but drew back when she discovered how much the project distressed her father. He feared that his daughter would follow her husband into the Roman Church and she was painfully aware of his hurt, particularly since his health was failing. She was in fact received into the Church of Rome in 1846, after her father's death, receiving instruction from that useful and omnipresent Jesuit, Father Brownbill. She found him solid and reassuringly English since he did not wear foreign religious dress but looked like a gentleman farmer. Newman heard the news from Lady Georgiana herself and replied from Maryvale:

> My dear Madam,
>   I feel the kindness of the information with which you have entrusted me, and which has given me very great pleasure. It has filled me with gratitude too; for I assure you, I have ever remembered your Ladyship's name in my prayers, and have listened for news of you with great interest. Nor will I fail to do so still, as you wish me. And while so doing, I shall not and cannot doubt that the peace and confidence which others have felt who have taken the same important step, will be granted to you as to them.
>   With all good wishes and kind thoughts, I am, dear Madam,
>   your Ladyship's faithful servant,
>   John H Newman[12]

Harriett heard the news too and commented sourly, 'I quite expected Lady Georgiana Fullerton to become a Romanist, after I heard she had written her Tale to enforce the desirableness of confession ... it is just one of the fallacious and hollow arguments that would satisfy a Romanising mind.'

In 1847 Lady Georgiana's second novel came out. *Grantley Manor* could be described as a Catholic tale but is not a piece of direct propaganda. Its heroine a young Catholic girl called Ginevra Leslie, who has been brought up in Italy, comes to Grantley Manor where her widowed father lives with her half-sister. Ginevra meets much petty anti-Catholic prejudice from various relations and then encounters much more serious prejudice since she has secretly married a young man who is the son of a fierce anti-papist, a landowner in Northern Ireland. However, Lady Georgiana is not simply concerned to show such prejudice as a destructive and false cast of mind but to examine it in the round and to give due praise for sincerity. A character in the story, describing Neville, the anti-Catholic Irishman, is shown as one who tolerantly sees both sides of his obsession. 'She saw the fatal result of long standing prejudices and hereditary hatreds, and deeply lamented them; but she did not blush for one whose convictions had been sincere, and whose motives had been conscientious and pure'.[14]

There are passages in the book which describe Lady Georgiana's thoughts about charity to the poor, put into the mouth of Ginevra. She says that true Catholics 'respect the poor, and count it an honour and a blessing to "have them always with us" ... to cast aside out refinement, our sensitiveness, our delicacy and our false shame, and perform real offices of love to the poor, not as a matter of display, or effort but as the natural result of belief in Christ's words and our trust in his promises.'[15] She loves the poor people she visits and inveighs against arrogant people who think it is their right, in their works of charity, to lord it over the poor 'to invade their houses, to examine into their concerns, and to comment and animadvert on their conduct in a manner which we would not ourselves endure from our best friends.'[16]

Newman read the novel and greatly enjoyed it. When Mr Fullerton wrote near Christmas to invite him to visit them, he declined and then went on in his letter to comment in detail upon Lady Georgiana's book. 'It abounds in just ideas of character, and originality, that is, acuteness of observation. I only regret that she has not brought out sometimes, and completed her sketches. The character of Walter is most true, beautiful and touching – and it is fully done justice to in the best scene in the Tale – the courtship scene at Heron Castle. I fancy I understand the objects the

Authoress had in view in drawing the character of Ginevra, but I am too old to take as much pleasure as I ought in tragedy – and especially in the very good, suffering in mind very dreadfully, not simply for the truth, but for their venial faults ... Now I really do trust and think that Lady Georgiana will be more pleased at my taking interest in her work, than amused at the impertinence of my particular remarks'.[17]

Walter is the friend and mentor of Margaret, the heroine's half-sister and he becomes her suitor. These are the calmest and most cheerful scenes in the book. Evidently Newman found the suffering of Ginevra harrowing – and indeed she did suffer a great deal and her troubles are described at great length before the tale reaches its happy ending with the acknowledged marriage of Ginevra and Neville's son. However, the book, perhaps because of its sad passages rather than in spite of them, found general acclaim and was absorbing. The actress Fanny Kemble was so engrossed in reading it during a meal that she raised the mustard pot to her lips instead of her wine glass.

Lady Georgiana and her husband were not in Newman's first circle of friends, nor were they directly under his influence. The Fullertons had a house in the country but spent much time in London, using their London address as an office for the considerable business occasioned by the charity work. In London they could find plenty of priests to advise them and they sought out Jesuits or Father Faber at the London Oratory. However, they corresponded with Newman, over the years, and admired him. He for his part had regard for them and was ready to help when he was asked. Lady Georgiana wrote to him when the education of Granville was being discussed, asking for information about Oscott, which at that time educated boys who were not intended for the priesthood as well as acting as a seminary. Newman replied in detail, giving Oscott a good report but saying that he found it rather rough – and Granville was not sent there. At another time she wrote for help to familiarise herself with the historical background for a projected novel set in the time of the early Church.

He wrote back at length, giving her an impressive reading list but she never wrote the novel. It was popular amongst the Catholic novelists to write a historical tale and Newman himself wrote *Callista* but Lady Georgiana seemed to feel that, if she turned to history it must be to a period that was easier to grasp imaginatively.

There were other links with Newman through Catholics known to both of them. At some time she met Miss Giberne in Rome and they became friendly. She knew James Hope-Scott from his Anglican days and hers, when he was plain James Hope. She was related by marriage to Lord Acton (who corresponded with Newman) because her brother, a politician, married Lord Acton's widowed mother. The young Lord Acton played sometimes with Granville Fullerton for they were much of an age. The links, the friendships, the exchange of books and items of news of Catholic concerns all show the English Catholics inhabiting a little sphere of their own. Both Newman and Lady Georgiana, in their several ways and in different degrees, had an influence beyond that sphere as well as being luminaries in it, 'names' known in their co-religionists. Her influence through her novels, however, did not last beyond her own day.

After *Grantley Manor* she wrote a novel entitled *Ladybird* and published a volume of verses. These publications bring her writing history up to the eighteen fifties and she wrote a considerable amount after that. However, no consideration of her life and writings can ignore the year 1855 which lay across her path like a great boulder; it was the most dreadful time of her life and affected her profoundly, writings and all. Granville Fullerton, nearly twenty one and his parents' pride, had joined the army but was not considered in fit health enough to go to the war in Crimea. This at once relieved his mother's mind and worried her. Just before his coming of age he died suddenly, away from home. Dr Manning bore the news to his parents. Both were so stricken that they wore mourning clothes ever after. Newman wrote a letter of condolence when he heard the news, a letter that reveals his own afflictions and his stern view that God sends suffering to his people.

If I seem intrusive, you must excuse it on the ground of the interest which has always accompanied the thought of you in my mind, since the day you let me call on you years ago as you passed through Oxford. I have already being saying Mass for your intention ...

It would be presumptuous in me to speak to you and Mr Fullerton of submission. However, let me bear witness, not only as a matter of faith, which we all receive, but as a point, which the experience of life has ever been impressing on me, more and more deeply, from my early youth down to this day, that unusual afflictions, coming on religious persons, are proofs that they are objects, more than others, of the love of God. Those whom He singularly and specially loves, He pursues with His blows, sometimes on one and the same wound, till perhaps they are tempted to cry out for mercy.

He loves you in proportion to the trials He sends you. I am telling you no news; but a testimony, external to ones self, strengthens one's own; and perhaps my testimony may be given with greater energy and fervency of conviction than another's.

We are in his hands – and cannot be in better.

With every respectful and earnest feeling of sympathy with Mr Fullerton ...[18]

A later picture of Lady Georgiana shows her in a black shawl or cloak and wearing a black frilled cap. Her face is plain but pleasant and sensitive and it speaks of reserve. She had a passionate, feeling nature and a near-impregnable reserve so that she did not talk about her loss or her grief. Her biographer does not go into the question of the quality of the communication between her and her husband – did they both suffer behind a cloak of silence? – but relates that years later Lady Georgiana took a friend to visit Granville's grave and there broke down with passionate weeping. It was a rare and telling display.

The bereavement had a great effect on her religious practice, making her detached from pleasure and from reliance on what the world could offer. Her prayer increased and deepened and she became a Franciscan tertiary. All this might have made her seem forbidding but some affectionate and naive notes written by her niece, Susan, seem to disprove this view. 'One learnt more from her example than her words,' she wrote and added, 'her religion had nothing in it that was morose'.[19] She remembered her sitting writing in her study, in the house at Slindon near Arundel which was her favourite home, and then breaking off to take her visitors on excursions or to go with them to visit her great friend the Duchess of Norfolk and she recalled her pleasure in children, taking them a pocketful of penny toys since they liked quantity. This last anecdote is a moving one since children must have reminded her of Granville's childhood.

Her work for the poor increased and Alexander Fullerton, who managed the finances, was in fact managing an extensive business. Schemes were devised and put into action for helping abandoned Catholic children and orphans and large donations went off to a variety of charities. Lady Georgiana herself did not simply work at her charities from a desk, but continued her visiting, having a special care for the poor who were difficult to find and to help because they were too proud to beg. One of her most attractive qualities was her capacity for enjoying people and enjoying her work: she did not go among the poor just because she thought she ought to but because she was engrossed in what she was doing.

As the work grew she felt that it was not enough to have individuals working, organising and collecting and expending money. She was no leveller and it did not occur to her, any more than it occurred to most of her contemporaries, that some ills could only be cured by a great change in social structures, but she required help on a larger scale. Nuns in an active Congregation were the answer. In 1859 she, and two other charitable ladies, wrote to the Sisters of Charity in Paris to ask that three nuns might be sent to London. Expenses for the Sisters' house would be borne by the ladies for two years. The three came, to a small house in York Street, Westminster and Lady Georgiana personally showed them the more wretched areas of London. The sisterhood was established and their great winged headdresses were seen in a good many slums. Lady Georgiana was also instrumental in the establishing of the English Congregation devoted to the poor, The Poor Servants of the Mother of God.

All this, as well as her care for her husband and her ready response to any call on her personal sympathy (for her own sorrow had made her a great consoler) meant that her time had to be well organised. She seriously debated whether she should continue to write novels. The arguments went to and fro. Novels sold well – she reckoned a steady output of fiction would bring in £200 to £300 per annum ('How many orphans could be provided for and good works promoted with such a sum?')[20] If she wrote lives of saints she might do more good but the money would be less. If she devoted herself to literature she would have to give up a great deal of her personal work amongst the poor and she would also surrender a certain influence over other people that she was encouraging in the same charitable pursuits.

In fact, she turned to writing a great many religious works, lives of saints such as St Frances of Rome and, with more originality, the lives of holy people who had not been canonised, such as her biography of Elizabeth, Lady Falkland which was published at the end of her life. She translated the life of the Marchesa Falletti di Baroto from Italian and wrote two novels in French.

English novels appeared too, despite her doubts. One was set in the time of Henry VI and one was set in the sixteenth century, so that she had to manage an amount of background reading. All were more markedly religious in tone than her first books: her biographer puts it like this: 'in her later years she naturally wrote more or less with a distinctly religious purpose before her, and we may perhaps attribute the gradual lessening of her popularity with the public in general, at least in part, to this cause.'[21] The truth is that there was a falling off in quality, inevitably, for to write to earn money for good causes and in the hope of doing good to the minds and souls of others is no guarantee of a lively tale and Lady Georgiana had not the same interest in constructing plots and examining the minutiae of character development. A novel called *Mrs Gerald's Niece* is a kind of sequel to *Grantley Manor* since some characters reappear but there is much attention given to long discussions between two clergymen debating the respective merits of the Anglican and the Roman position – the tale, written more than twenty years after the first one, has more polemic and is less effective as a novel.

Lady Georgiana died in January 1885. Her friend Fanny Margaret Taylor (by then Sister Magdalen) intended to write about her and ask Newman's help. He replied that he had not seen Lady Georgiana many times nor had he exchanged many letters with her so that he could not offer help, only a blessing on the work which concerned someone he had admired and respected. A full biography was undertaken by Mrs Augustus Craven, a French lady who had also been a great friend of Lady Georgiana's. This was published in Paris and Father Coleridge S.J. translated it and edited it to make it more suitable for English readers. Mrs Craven asked that an earlier letter of Newman's, written when he heard she was starting on the memoir, should be printed at the beginning of her book, due to come out in 1888. The letter was used and it contained a tribute to Lady Georgiana Fullerton that expressed in felicitous language the kind of person she was and the life she led. He said, 'Since I have been a Catholic I have looked upon her with reverence and admiration for her saintly life. A character and mental history such as hers make her a fit representative of those ladies of rank and position in society who, during the last half century have thought it little to become Catholics by halves, and who have devoted their lives and all they were to their Lord's service'.[22]

Newman was ambivalent about the value of religious novels. In 1843, speaking of evangelical novelists, he said:

That they sometimes do good I am far from denying; – but do they do more harm than good? They do harm on

the whole; they lead men to cultivate their religious
affections separate from religious practice.[1]

This theme, the danger of unreality where people indulge
their religious emotions, is a recurring one in his sermons.
John Keble was of the same mind with regard to religious
tales, though from a different point of view: having reference to the tractarian doctrine of the necessity for reserve
in religious matters, he warned Charlotte Yonge against
too much discussion of church matters in her books,
particularly of church doctrine.

In *Loss and Gain* Newman mocks the fashion for quantities of religious books and their appeal to silly women. In
the scene in the bookshop where the hero encounters
Henry and his fiancée, the pair who had been devoted to
the idea of celibacy, Louisa is confused by choice.

> 'Oh, there's one book, I can't recall it; tell me what it is,
> Henry? I shall be so sorry not to have got it.' 'Was it the
> new work on Gregorian Chants?' asked he. 'Ah, it's true,
> I want it for the schoolchildren, but it's not that.' 'Is it
> the *Catholic Parsonage?*' he asked again; 'or, *Lays of the
> Apostles?* or, *The English Church older than the Roman?* or
> *Anglicanism of the Early Martyrs?* or, *Confessions of a Pervert?*
> or *Eustace Beville?* or, *Modified Celibacy?*' 'No, no, no,' said
> Louisa; 'dear me, it is so stupid.' 'Well, now really,
> Louisa,' he insisted, 'you must come another time; it
> won't do, dearest; it won't do.' 'Oh, I recollect,' she said,
> 'I recollect – *Abbeys and Abbots*; I want to get some hints
> for improving the rectory windows for when we get
> home; and our church wants, you know, a porch for the
> people. The book is full of designs.' The book was found
> and added to the rest, which had already been taken to
> the carriage.[2]

In this wonderful list of Anglo-Catholic books (where
Newman mocks himself amongst others since he was the
main contributor to the *Lyra Apostolica*, much like *Lays of
the Apostles*, and he had used 'Gregorians' for the
Littlemore schoolchildren) there is surely one novel:

Eustace Beville is a perfect title for the kind of novel he was thinking about.

However, he encouraged the women he knew when they turned to writing and collected quantities of their works, mostly novels, since they always sent him a copy when the book came out. He read them with care and usually sent some comments to the author, as he did with the first two novels of Lady Georgiana Fullerton. When the Birmingham Oratorians acquired their country house at Rednal, the novels were kept on his shelves there since novel-reading was best done on rest days out of the city.

There was a case for writing what might be called counter-novels, not so much Roman novels opposed to Puseyite or Protestant ones as stories that could be set against ridiculous publications. In 1847 a novel called *Oxford to Rome* was published by Elizabeth F.S. Harris. Newman found it 'wantonly and preposterously fanciful,' and his own *Loss and Gain* was a reply. He said in the advertisement to the sixth edition of his own novel that Miss Harris's story had called for the production of a second tale; 'drawn up with stricter regard to truth and probability ... showing as in a specimen, that those who were smitten with love of the Catholic Church, were nevertheless able to write common-sense prose as other men.'[5]

There was also a case for producing novels that showed Catholics as real people, living, thinking, worshipping, with their distinct views on religious matters but recognisably men and women like others. Anti-Catholic bigotry and ignorance of Catholics and Catholic practices could make them seem monsters or creatures with no personal conviction who were manoeuvred by cunning priests. The novel that had influenced the young Miss Bowles, Miss Agnew's *Geraldine*, has an air of the documentary about it. There is something unlikely in the constant high degree of fervour in the characters but still there is a sense of reality in the story's simple structures: it tells how Catholics worship and sets out what they believe.

Of all Newman's close friends Miss Bowles was herself the person to be considered pre-eminently as a writer. She published before she entered the convent, she used her writing skills there and during the rest of her life she divided her time between works of charity and her books. She wrote several novels, much shorter ones than Lady Georgiana's three-deckers and all with some religious and proselytising element. Two of them may be taken as representative of her writing in this genre.

One called *St Martha's Home* or *Work for Women* was published in 1864. It is really a collection of little stories set in London, loosely linked by having characters in each one that have something to do with St Martha's Home, or a Catholic Guild for pious ladies who go out to visit, nurse, instruct and help the poor. None of the stories has much in the way of a plot and no character is fully developed but if the work is weak as a novel it is marvellously interesting as a social document. It really exists to preach the virtues of Catholic practices and to serve as a handbook for those who want to help the London slum-dwellers. It give information on the general habits and plight of the poor: some are upright, pious and thrifty, managing to keep a reasonably decent home with pitifully small resources, but in general they are ignorant and shiftless, hating soap and water and closing the windows of their noisome dwellings against any inrush of fresh air. There is an attempt in one chapter, when a group of poor women gathers for a practical discussion on shopping and cooking with one of the 'Sisters', to present information and suggestions from the women themselves, but in general the book is a manual of instructions given by the visitors from St Martha's.

Detailed information can be gathered from the narrative or the reader may turn to an appendix to the book which has tips for nursing and many recipes. So one may learn how to nurse a patient with smallpox, how to minister to a badly burnt child, how to apply a leech (one should first select a leech that seems lively), a blister and a poultice. There are instructions on how to make smooth gruel and sago pudding and many recipes for those who should be making nourishing but cheap dinners for their families: it is recommended that stews should be made from cowheel and root vegetables or a pudding made from oatmeal, bound and seasoned with dripping, rather than feeding husband and children on tea and bread and butter or buying bacon, which is considered easy and tasty but is expensive. There is another appendix on the value of co-operative societies. In other words, the book is severely practical and based on a day to day experience of visiting the poor.

It is also hortatory in tone. One sets out the duties of a housewife, another describes a good Catholic middle class lady who takes in a poor maidservant who is very young and carefully trains her in household work rather than leaving her to find out by trial and error. Another tale is of a good, poor wife whose husband drinks until he suffers from delirium tremens: her patience and her Catholic example rescue him, as one might gather from the title, *The Wife's Victory*. Nelly, aged sixteen, in another story, falls ill and, though she is devotedly nursed by one of the St Martha's Sisters, dies, but repentant after some years of wickedness and loss of faith. The good doctor and the priest appear in several tales, called in by the ladies when their professional help is necessary.

There is pietistic *naiveté* in the book and the air of condescension implicit in the instructresses' care for the poor is on every page, but *St Martha's Home* cannot simply be dismissed with a laugh. It has plenty of commonsense in it and there is more practical advice than airy theorising or pious platitudes. Many of the religious biographies of the day refer to the good works done by ladies but in general terms: they helped, they visited, they distributed alms. What exactly did they do? Miss Bowles fills out the details.

It is a little book but it has many resonances. The voice of Emily Bowles herself is heard in it, pious, brisk and managing. There are echoes heard of the sensitive tones of Lady Georgiana Fullerton who warned against intrusion into the homes of the poor or commenting on their conduct in an impertinent way. The reader longs to hear more from the poor themselves. Did they simply resent the help offered, the moral exhortations and the condescension? Or, more positively, did those women, who were being shown how to do better by themselves and their families, respect the tenacity and the goodwill of those well-to-do Catholics who bothered to feed, nurse and instruct others, braving the tenements that smelled of dirt and disease?

Another of Miss Bowles' books is more of a novel and indeed, in a dim kind of way, is a love story. This is *In the Carmargue*, published in 1873. The setting can be gathered from the title and the author fills in the details of the French farms, rather in the manner of a travelogue. The heroine, Noël, is sixteen years old, beautiful and with a mind of her own. Her father intends she shall marry a local man, Rambert, but she is courted by an English painter, Leopold Morland, and falls in love with him. It is made clear early on that their love is doomed. Strangely enough, given the author's ironclad convictions, it is not Noël's loyalty to her Catholic faith that is challenged: it is made clear that Morland may marry her, given certain conditions. It is his selfish and weak character that stands in the way and the fact that there is a young Englishwoman at home who means to have him. Her name is Car Chetwynd. Emily Bowles leaves the reader in no doubt of the outcome as she apostrophises the heroine:

> Ah! Noël, as you stood in your pure, single high-souled love, under the old, fretted church porch at Aignes Mortes, did a shadow of this 'false Isolte' fall on you with a death-like chill? Did an icy revealing freeze your heart as to what a man's love can be?[4]

There is some high drama when Rambert sacrifices his own life to save his rival and then, inevitably, Morland goes back to England and Noël must lose him. It is a customary device in many Victorian novels to contrast the character or the fortunes of two girls. Thackeray did this most memorably in *Vanity Fair* and Lady Georgiana Fullerton used the same plan, for instance in *Grantley Manor*. Morland has a sister called Anne and a good friend called Nasmyth and their love has a happy outcome. Another contrast is worked out, less mechanically, and this is between the French characters and most of the English ones. The English (except Anne Morland and Nasmyth) are shallow creatures but convinced that they are socially superior to the French in the Carmargue. The French are more primitive, more genuine and possessed of great dignity. They love the land, their toil amongst the beasts, their families, and their faith is bound up with the earth, their work and their history. This part of the book is convincingly done and without too much recourse to high-flown sentimental language.

Noël (like Trollope's heroines) cannot love twice and she devotes herself and her considerable inheritance to the care of the sick and poor, setting up a hospice. As in *St Martha's Home*, the ideal is presented of the dedicated lay woman and Miss Bowles does not let her heroines go into convents. It is as though these dear children of her imagination cannot be allowed to succeed where she had failed.

Besides novels she wrote many different kinds of nonfiction – in fact there is an astonishing spread. She wrote amongst other things a life of St Jane Frances de Chantal, a history textbook for Irish children, translated a long religious work in French, written by Mrs Augustus Craven, and published a volume of poetry. One poem that Newman admired was a Wordsworthian one about bluebells – perhaps its author had the woods at Rednal in mind, a famous place for bluebells.

The books arrived at the Birmingham Oratory promptly on their publication, bearing an inscription on the fly leaf. The translated work, *The Story of a Soul*, written by Mrs Craven, has 'with loving gratitude from E.B. August 1875' inside Newman's copy. He read her books attentively, enjoying the life of St Jane Frances, which he read a little at a time, and rejoicing, like a good friend, when favourable reviews appeared. *In the Carmargue* was praised by a reviewer in the *Guardian* and Newman wrote to say she had been 'righteously puffed'[5] in that paper and that was 'a sort of reparation for having wronged you by some offhand ill natured criticisms at other times.'

He had written his own puff on the novel in a detailed criticism sent in January 1874, a letter that shows how carefully he read the books he had been sent.

My Dear Child

I have read with great pleasure your Tale. First let me express pleasure that Smith and Elder have taken it – for, if they take one, perhaps they will take another, which I hope you will write. Next of course I take for granted he (Smith etc) buys the Edition from you – it is a shame, if he does not pay you for it. Having thus cleared my ground I come to the book itself.

The greatest fault I find in it, is, that it is too short; and this *is* a fault. It shows a wonderful knowledge of the district in which the scene is laid and of its peculiarities. And that knowledge is imparted to the reader in the easiest, liveliest and most engaging manner. But from its being too consecutive, it is somewhat wearisome. The whole Tale is an excitement from beginning to end – and needs more incidents. The Muselade and Ferrade [ie the muzzling and branding of cattle] are too much of the same kind. The death of Rambert is abrupt.

Now all this arises from the one fault, the shortness of the Tale. This is the reason, I think why skilful novelists like Trollope have underplots. Such a contrivance obliged events to go more slowly – also it gives opportunity for variety and *repose.* Of course in London scenes do something in this way for the volume – but they too are somewhat abrupt on their side.

Car's character is too much *told* instead of being naturally acted out. I don't think you are happy in the speeches of the Abbess. Leopold's unconscious escape from the bull upon Rambert's horn is a violent expedient.

I can't think of any more criticisms. You may be sure I should not set them down unless I was *much* pleased with the Tale. It is brilliant, interesting and graphic – few Tales, that I have read, equal it. I do hope you will go on writing, that is, if you can get paid for it. There is just enough Catholicism in it – not too much, tho' I was surprised Smith & Elder took so much. In a word, I admire it very much.

Yours affly, John H Newman[6]

It was praise indeed to have a novel described as brilliant and interesting by a writer of Newman's calibre – but Miss Bowles' novels have not lived on and she will be remembered, not for the books she wrote, but for the letters she caused to be written. Of course Newman confided in other correspondents, men and women, but his letters to Emily Bowles include some remarkably outspoken ones that give his mind on topics that are still relevant and deeply interesting, especially to Catholics. He was constantly grateful that he had joined the Church of Rome and unfailingly loyal, but he knew that loyalty did not demand an uncritical acceptance of injustice and lack of wisdom on the part of the church authorities. It was often in letters to her that he uttered what he called 'growls'.

She was the recipient of growls for two reasons. Firstly, the friendship between them was very cordial, though there was no over-familiarity. She said that Newman always had a certain reserve with women and she set him so high on a priestly pedestal that there was no chance that she would even dream of the faintest impropriety. Secondly, he was prompted to be frank and explanatory because from time to time she wrote in a forthright way to stir him up to be more of a public figure, to do this or that or fight his corner. For instance, when the Bishops decreed in 1865 that no Catholic College should be set up in Oxford, thus overturning all Newman's plans, he thought the Bishops had acted under orders from Propaganda in Rome. So did Miss Bowles and she told him in no uncertain terms what he should do. She wrote in March: 'If I had been ... a man with a name known wherever English is known ... I would have gone to Rome and opened people's eyes'.[7] He replied to her 'dear enthusiastic letter', indicating that she did not know the half of the difficulties and adding a trenchant account of the Roman way of making decisions without consulting the people most concerned. It would achieve nothing to go to Rome. 'No – we are in a transition time – and must wait patiently – though of course the tempest will last through our day'.[8]

Miss Bowles needed to stir her friend to fight, to stand forth as the great man he was. This was partly because she

was immensely proud of him and it was also an expression
of her own needs. She led a busy and most useful life and
was known through her writings but still she was in some
measure frustrated. Had she lived at a later time she would
probably have been a professional woman of standing. She
could have run some enterprise or institution and it is not
at all surprising that she saw herself, when she was a Holy
Child nun, as one about to found and run a college of
education. Had she had work and status of this kind,
however, she would still have been in danger of balks and
frustrations for her temperament was not an easy one. Her
instinct for power and her veneration for Newman
combined to make her his champion and his goad. If she
could not be powerful as a woman she could urge this
genius who was her mentor and friend to make himself
more of a force on the English Catholic scene. Later generations can be grateful that he was induced to utter his
growls.

It was to Miss Bowles that he spoke concerning the attitude of powerful ecclesiastics to the laity.

> A great Prelate said to me years ago, when I said that the
> laity needed instruction, guidance, tenderness, consider-
> ation etc. etc., 'you do not know them, Dr N. Our laity
> are a peaceable body – they are peaceable'. I understood
> him to mean 'They are grossly ignorant and unintellec-
> tual – and we need not consult or consult for them at
> all'. Don't repeat this – and at Rome they treat them
> according to the tradition of the Middle Ages, as, in
> *Harold the Dauntless*, the Abbot of Durham, treated
> Count Wittikin. Well, facts alone will slowly make them
> recognise the fact of what a laity must be in the nine-
> teenth century, even if it is not, if it is to cope with
> Protestantism.[9]

Harold the Dauntless is a poem by one of Newman's
favourite authors, Scott, in which Count Wittikin outwardly
renounced heathenism and became the Church's
defender in return for gifts of land. The comparison
underlines the severity of Newman's criticism of Roman

attitudes and methods. The phrase – 'don't repeat this' or 'don't tell' appears in these outbursts – and he relied on Emily Bowles to obey the injunction. There is no evidence that she did tell.

Another growl, a long letter written in May 1863, was also in answer to Miss Bowle's entreaties. She said 'I have had a good deal of talk with Sir John Acton lately – and he does so lament – he does so fully *appreciate* – what we all lose in your silence. Why should you be out there, so far away from us all?' According to her, he should have been in London, in the thick of things, entering into all the religious controversies of the day. He replied, giving an account of work he had undertaken and the snubs he had had from Rome in consequence. He went on:

> Don't you see that this, if nothing else, puts a great obex to my writing? This age of the church is peculiar – in former times, primitive and medieval, there was not the extreme centralization which is now in use. If a private theologian said any thing free, another answered him. If the controversy grew, then it went to a Bishop, a theological faculty, or to some foreign University. The Holy See was but the court of ultimate appeal. *Now*, if I, as a private priest, put any thing into print, *Propaganda* answers me at once. How can I fight with such a chain on my arm? It is like the Persians driven on to fight *under the lash*. There was true private judgement in the primitive and medieval schools – there are no schools now, no private judgement (in the religious sense of the phrase) no freedom that is, of opinion. That is, no exercise of the intellect. No, the system goes on by the tradition of the intellect of former times. This is a way of things which, in God's own time, will work its own cure, of necessity ...[10]

He ended by calling to mind the experiences of holy men in former times, including his own St Philip who suffered at the hands of Roman authorities, being much misunderstood. He then added to the letter, ten days later, weighing up his own mixed feelings: he was content to live a retired life and in fact had more than enough to do at his own Oratory – yet he wondered if he should not be out and active and controversial, especially when others urged him, 'and then, since I think I could do a great deal, if I were let to do it, I become uneasy'.[11] This long explanation tells much of Newman's experiences and his reflections on them, and his general disquisition on Church centralization and the curbing of legitimate intellectual probing has echoes in the thoughts of many Catholics more than a century later. This, as he said, was a freer letter than he had ever sent to anyone before. Here was Emily Bowles' great prize – that she was the recipient of such important explanations and musings.

Sometimes Newman asked his friend Miss Bowles to befriend some woman convert or enquirer who happened to be in London. One of these was a girl from a Protestant family in Ireland: she was Geraldine Penrose Fitzgerald, born in Corkbeg, Cork, in 1846. She worshipped with the High Anglicans but, despite her family's fear of Rome, she was turning her thoughts there. As a very old lady she set out in a long letter to a Jesuit friend the story of her reading Newman's *Apologia*:

> When I was a young girl I used to read his *Apologia* sitting on the top of a ladder in my cousin Willy Cumbleton's library ... when Willy found me doing this he took it away and locked it up and said – 'There's been enough of that' but it had set me off on the road to Popery; I longed to read more, but it was a dear book. I had but little pocket money, I used to stand gazing at a shop that had it in the window; finally I pawned a valuable gold and ruby brooch one of my Aunts had given me and bought it ... Finally I was praying in the chapel he built in Stephen's Green when the truth of the Catholic Church came over me like a thunderclap: but I would not join, I was afraid of being turned out of the house.[12]

When she was twenty one she began to write to Newman and he described her letters as striking in their simplicity and frankness and showing too, he thought, that her conversion to Rome was inevitable, despite her relatives' attempts to divert her. At some time (as she mentioned to Francis Brown S.J. in the letter written years later) Newman heard from her the story of her acquiring the cherished copy of the *Apologia* and he sent her copies of many of his older books with 'from the author' written in them.

When Geraldine Fitzgerald came to London to live, with her mother and sister, Newman asked Miss Bowles to help her and she, old enough to be the young woman's mother, was most willing to help her on her path to the Roman Catholic Church but found her a handful. She had it in mind to introduce her to the Jesuits in Farm Street, near where she herself lived, but 'that provoking child, Geraldine Fitzgerald' (to quote Miss Bowles) had gone with another friend to Father Knox at the London Oratory and she was received there. Her own story of the matter was that it was Newman who advised her to go to the Jesuits and she thought that his letters to her on the matter had better not be published lest the wrath of the London Oratorians be roused.

> Now a very strange thing happened: I wrote to Newman to ask him who he would advise me to go to, to be received into the church, he said 'go to *Jesuits* not to the Oratorians' (and yet he was an Oratorian and Head of the Birmingham Oratory) and then he said a still stranger thing, 'Father Knox is hard and wooden ...' Newman added, 'the Jesuits though severe to themselves are wonderfully kind and gentle and considerate to their penitents.'[13]

Miss Bowles thought the new convert's side-stepping of the Farm Street arrangement was 'not nice'. Miss Fitzgerald, wondering what the London Oratory years later, would think of Newman's advice, imagined that they would kick up: 'pistols and coffee before breakfast, wigs on the green, Vesuvius not in it.'[14]

She always got the maximum of drama out of a situation, though she was perfectly sincere in her religious beliefs.

Three years after she was received into the church, Newman was writing to Emily Bowles to say that he had had a letter from Miss Fitzgerald saying that she was going to be a nun 'and that some Revd Mother in London was going to smuggle her to Dublin without her Mother's knowledge.'[15] His speedy note to the young convert said very simply, 'You seem to be acting very hastily and to run away from your Mother in that way is shocking.'[16] She was no child but a young woman of twenty five but her proposed action was both precipitous and unkind.

Mrs Fitzgerald took her daughter's conversion hard and she and her other daughter worked on Geraldine in the first days of her new Church life: 'they used every means to bring me back.'[17] However, matters changed in time and in retrospect Geraldine Fitzgerald was full of memories of her mother's kindness: 'not only did my mother not turn me out but was marvellously kind to me, always had fish for me on Fridays, always sent for the priest when I was ill and would not allow a word to be said against my religion before my face.'[18]

Newman had something to do with the softening of her mother's and sister's attitude. He visited them in their London house, took lunch there and impressed them with his simplicity of manner and his capacity for a joke. 'My mother and sister were just simply enchanted with him; it is impossible to describe his fascination of voice and manner, I have never seen anything the least like it.'[19] After this lunch he sent Mrs Fitzgerald a copy of his own volume of verses and the sister had a volume of poems by Father Edward Caswall of the Birmingham Oratory: he had told them, laughing, that Father Caswall, who had since published more weighty works, had once written 'The Art of Pluck' and had never written anything so good since.

Nothing came of Geraldine Fitzgerald's plans to become a nun, nor did she ever marry. She busied herself writing novels. They ran to two or three volumes apiece, some published under her own name and some under the *nom-de-plume* 'Naseby'. Her first novel was called *Ereighda Castle*. The second one, *Only Three Weeks*, came out early in 1872. Newman received a copy and read it with interest. His letter of thanks gave her a detailed critique:

It shows the experience you have gained from writing your first. It is in every respect better. I don't complain of little plot, but of bad plot and unnatural plot – there is nothing to find fault with in yours. I don't see there need be any plot – but, if there is one, it should be good of its kind. Characters seem to me far important – but often they cannot be brought out without plot.

Your two principals, hero and heroine, are very well conceived. They are original and true. This combination is a great praise. And in part they are well drawn out – and well play upon each other. I mean there are scenes ' and dialogues which do them justice. But I think you might have developed them more. The lady is too young certainly. I don't see why you should not have put her at twenty. Then again as to a hero, no-one but a man can draw a man such as he. You would have got into great difficulty, if you had attempted it – but for all that there is that need. Then again, you sometimes, just a little, *preach*. For instance you say 'Nora was not religious'. This was loading your gun in sight. She *evidently* was *not* – and you might have brought this out still more fully.[20]

This is an interesting piece of criticism, though it fills a reader's mind with questions about the plot of a novel – for what on earth could Newman mean by the statement that there need be no plot? His assertion that characters are more important causes no difficulty, characters seen in action and interaction. It is in the interplay of realistic characters that the Catholic novel would do its work, not in preaching directly. Again and again he warned, in his letters of literary criticism, against loading one's gun in sight, a prevalent fault among the Catholic ladies when zeal outran literary tact. He wrote to one lady: '... as far as your writing a good work goes I think if you informed your plan without reference to religion and only let religious feeling show itself in that spontaneous way in which religious people can't help showing it, you would write in a higher style of art'.[21]

Miss Fitzgerald had trouble finding a publisher in 1875 and Newman told her that probably the market was over-

stocked 'and that makes publishers high and mighty'.[22]
Her literary career continued, however, and in 1882 her
novel writing occasioned an interesting exchange of letters
between her and Newman on the subject of Ireland. She
belonged to a well-to-do Anglo-Irish family and was much
incensed at Parnell and the Land League: her mother
(who had succoured the poor and sick on their Irish property) and her brothers where losing rents and the brothers,
who still lived in Ireland, one as a landlord and one as a
land agent, lived in fear. She was engaged in writing a
novel which would bring out the difference in the English
and the Irish character (depicting the Irish as a people
with no idea of truthfulness) and she was intending to
satirise Parnell as Snarlwell. Newman was sorry for the
satire – 'the Irish matter is so very grave that it does not
admit of what looks like a joke'[23] – and, though he was
sorry for her family's troubles, he took a very different
general line on the Irish situation. He told her gravely, 'It
seems as if at last a judgement was coming down on
England for its centuries of pride and self confidence.'[24]
Poor Geraldine Fitzgerald was torn between her respect for
Newman's opinion (she modified her novel, removing her
passages on Parnell) and her family feeling, and as a
Catholic she suffered a great deal 'when I see the priests
about our neighbourhood in Cork stirring up the people
to revolution.'[25]

In 1885 she published a novel called *Oaks and Birches*.
Newman, then well advanced in age, did not try to read it
but he noted with pleasure that it had a good review in the
Saturday Review where it was described as a 'really brilliant
novel' and 'an unusually clever book, though it must be
read for the characters rather than the story.'[26] It would
seem that she had followed Newman's earlier prescription.

His short literary critiques of ladies' books were
numerous, for the simple reason that so many were busy
writing them. Some tried but never made the grade. Miss
Giberne wrote a religious tale in her youth and in her tractarian days. It was for children and was called *Little Mary*.
This was the product of much trouble because she wrote it
on her knees and Newman had a laborious time seeing it

through the press. *Little Mary* did not captivate the minds of the young and that was the end of her literary career. Miss Holmes entered the lists but could not get her writings published: in fact she is described in a modern biography of her friend Anthony Trollope as 'an unsuccessful writer'.[27] Newman thought she showed talent in her letters but doubted whether she could manage a sustained work between her teaching duties. His remarks about her potential as a writer are interesting in a general way.

> As to writing about what one knows and what one does not, as e.g. I have written in *Loss and Gain* of persons and things that I knew – but if I were to attempt a fashionable novel, I should make a fool of myself, because I do not know men of fashion, and should have to draw on imagination or on books. As to yourself, I would not trust you, if you attempted to describe a Common Room, or a Seminary, or the Chinese court at Pekin; but I think you capital in the sketches of persons and things which from time to time you have written to me, according to the place you have been in. It is not to the purpose whether they are correct or not, as representations of fact (about which I can know nothing) but they are clear, consistent, and persuasive, as pictures.[28]

This was sound encouragement and she had the same help from Trollope with regard to her literary aspirations, but it all came to nothing. Perhaps she could not sustain the labour of a book any more than she could bear to stay in one place, and she had no protracted leisure. Publishers did not encourage her.

Some ladies who were not novelists and indeed not professional writers at all brought out devotional books. Elizabeth Bowden, proficient in French, translated *Thoughts on Some Passages of Holy Scriptures by a Layman* in 1872. Newman received a copy when it was published and was pleased to learn from it that Catholics abroad made use of the Bible. Many Catholics in France and Italy, he feared, gave up religion because 'they have not impressed upon their hearts the life of our Lord and Saviour as given

us in the Evangelists'.[29] Later she translated and published
Mère de Chaugy's book, *The Lives of the First Religious of the
Visitation*, a topic that would be dear to her because of
Marianne's vocation.[30] Emily Bowden employed herself
(and was very well employed, according to Newman) trans-
lating from German *Lives of the Fathers of the Desert* by the
Countess Hahn-Hahn.[31] Her translation had a preface by
Father Dalgairns of the London Oratory.

It was not obligatory to write or translate a whole book in
an age when the magazine or periodical was flourishing,
having its boom time in the eighteen sixties. Ladies could
have their say and assist the Catholic cause by writing articles for the serious Catholic periodicals that were coming
out. An enterprising lady in this field was a convert called
Fanny Margaret Taylor who took on the editorship of two
Catholic magazines, the *Lamp* and the *Month*. This took
much time and labour and one of her tasks was to interest
important patrons in what she was doing and so assure
possible readers that the magazines were orthodox and
worthwhile. She hoped that Dr. Newman would contribute
an article to the *Lamp*, but he did not give her much
encouragement. She took on this periodical in 1862 and
sent him a circular about it: its object would be 'to supply
Catholics with papers of general interest which they can
read without fear of meeting with objectionable passages.
At the same time as controversy does not enter into its
scheme, there is nothing to prevent non-Catholics from
seeking information and recreation in its pages.'[32]
Newman, being very busy, made no reply, so in March 1864
Miss Taylor wrote to a Mr Formby, a convert priest of a
literary turn who was known to Newman and was then
staying at the Birmingham Oratory. Perhaps he would
speak to Newman on her behalf and assure him that the
Lamp was doing well, its circulation having increased, but
that she wished to see it improved and hoped that Newman
would contribute. She had the support of Wiseman,
Manning, Bishop Amherst and of an influential Jesuit,
Father Gallwey. Newman did write to her but said he could
hold out no expectations. He was as busy as ever and,
moreover, he distrusted a kind of journalism that offered

its readers a series of theological opinions. She had chosen her intermediary unwisely because Formby was exactly such a writer, an extremist who offered his views as if they were dogma. Newman made his point with clarity and at length.

> When a writer puts forward an opinion of his own though it be a true one, as vital, he seems to me to be committing a great offence against the Catholic faith itself. Now really I am not alluding to anything in particular in the Lamp – and it seems almost cruel to say these things to a lady, whose privilege it is to be a woman, and to believe and to be devout without entering into controversies, but there is a spirit afloat, not less now than at other times, on the surface of society, in publications of the day, and in public transactions, with which I wish to have nothing to do – a spirit of arbitrary assumption in matters on which the church has determined nothing.[33]

However, he did not, in his own mind, rule out the possibility that he would write for the magazine because he put a note on her letter to Formby saying that he would not write if ecclesiastical politics came in or controversy in theological opinion but adding that he would like to know if the publication was Miss Taylor's for if the financial gain was to be hers and not the publisher's he would write without expecting payment. She replied that she was going to attempt a second magazine 'a monthly magazine for the educated and keeping the *Lamp* for the poor and middle class readers.'[34] This new magazine was the *Month* and its first number came out in July that year, 1864. It has had a long and distinguished history. Miss Taylor kept it going for a year and then the Jesuits, who had helped with its inception, took it over and it continues to this day. The *Lamp* remained, as Miss Taylor's publication, until 1871.

Although Catholic periodicals came crowding in – a Miss Maling was anxious to start one and Newman's friend, William Monsell, had it in mind to start another – Newman was determined to oblige Miss Taylor with some article or articles for the *Month*. He looked through his papers and wondered if some of the letters between himself and Miss Holmes might be the basis for a piece but decided that this would not serve. He contributed two poems about his sister Mary and then sent in *Saints of the Desert*, short sayings of the Fathers selected by him. This series was parodied, thought not unkindly, in *Punch* as 'Sayings of the Fathers of the Dessert, (Dedicated with feeling of the greatest possible respect to an eminent contributor to the *Month*).' He obliged Miss Taylor, rather than Monsell and Miss Maling, for a reason that was not wholly complimentary to her and her magazine. He said to Monsell, 'I could send anything, however old and trivial, to the Month, and I told Miss T. as much – but I could not write for you without trouble to myself. I could send Miss T. a sermon – but to write for such a magazine as you or Miss M. propose, I must dress myself out full fig; and this I have no stomach for doing.'[35]

Miss Taylor, however, was glad of his help and pleased to use his distinguished name. She wrote of the *Month* with disarming modesty years later, even disclaiming her own work in initiating it, maintaining that Father Gallwey S.J. was its real progenitor and she was only an *avant-courier*. She added that Father Coleridge wrote for each number and Newman took it up from the first and called on her that summer (1864) about it.

It was Miss Taylor, however, who netted a piece for the *Month* that was neither old nor trivial. Newman gave her the text of the *Dream of Gerontius*, his most sustained poem, written at speed and produced as it were from the strains and fears of the time when he was writing the *Apologia* so that his exhaustion led to thoughts of death and thence to a vision of the life to come. There is a legend that he took the crumpled pages from his wastepaper basket to give Miss Taylor something for her magazine, but this is an unlikely story. Newman was a hoarder of writings, not one to cast a long poem away. He wrote it in January 1865 and told a friend that he really could not say how it came into his head and that he wrote on till it was finished, on small bits of paper. It was published in the May and June

numbers of the *Month,* in 1865, and received instant approbation. The students training as teachers with the Notre
Dame nuns in Liverpool acted *Gerontius,* though it seems
an unlikely text for dramatic representation. Bishop Brown
of Newport loved the poem when he first read it and used
it as a meditation book thereafter. When staying at the
Benedictine Priory at Colwich in the summer of '65, he
read the poem to the nuns and he and many of his
listeners wept before he had finished it. A Lady Charles
Thynne, among others, wrote to express her approbation
and he replied: 'I am as much pleased, and half-surprised
that you and others should like the *Dream of Gerontius.* It
was written by accident – and it was published by accident.'[36] This latter phrase does not corroborate the story
of the wastepaper basket but perhaps it shows how the idea
originated: Newman did not think of publishing his poem
but had the sudden notion of handing it over to Miss
Taylor. By the end of the year he published it by itself.

Emily Bowles amongst other women writers, contributed
many articles to various journals, including the *Lamp,* so
that Newman, writing to thank her in 1863 for a whole
parcel of *Lamps,* commented that he was very glad to see
them 'and your own contributions to its luminousness'.[37]

Why did so many of these Catholic women turn to
writing? It is clear that one reason that it was uppermost in
their minds was the importance of published books and
articles for the Catholic cause. Also, if they wished to have
their say, exercise their talents and perhaps make some
money for themselves there was very little else they could
do. Trollope expressed it exactly when he said in a story
called *Mrs Brumby* that authorship 'seems to be the only
desirable harbour to which a female captain can steer her
vessel with much hope of success'.

Trollope probably had in mind his own mother who
started writing when she was over fifty, worked with
amazing industry and produced more than forty books.
Fanny Trollope, however, is a generation back from
Newman's friends and she began her late literary career in
the eighteen thirties. It is easy to see that Harriett
Newman, marooned at Cholderton in the forties, would

have no other way of occupying her mind and making her mark than by writing. As the century progressed, however, should not that small but vigorous Catholic society in England have produced women who were exercising their talents in many ways?

This, after all, was the age of female emancipation. Political choice, educational opportunity, freedom to manage one's own property and money and the possibility of entering the professions were all on the horizon for women. Women's suffrage was not to come in until the next century but it was already being advocated, notably by the reformer, John Stuart Mill. The Married Women's Property Act was passed in 1870. The days of the governess like Mary Holmes were numbered: good boarding and day schools were being set up by pioneers like the redoubtable Miss Beale and Miss Buss and by 1890 women were going up to Oxford and Cambridge. Teachers were being trained (the nuns had seen the necessity for this quite early on) and two women doctors were practising in England in the eighteen sixties.

There are no references to these events in Newman's letters and he took no part in the campaign for the emancipation of women: it would be fair to say that he had enough to do with his pastoral work, his writing and the causes he did espouse, the defence of Catholicism in Protestant England and the building up of the Catholic body by means of education. Moreover, he was constitutionally conservative in his attitude to social institutions and was not likely to view the movement for women's emancipation with enthusiasm. Yet his friendships with women were open enough for him to see the necessity for greater opportunities for them and, when an old man, he said once that the century in which he had lived, a century when England had steadily deteriorated in that it had become more irreligious, had as one of its best points 'that it has made so many openings for the activity of women'.[38] That is as far as his active support went.

Newman could be a fierce satirist when engaged in religious controversy but in his personal relationships he was a notably courteous man. It was natural to him, both from the customs he learned in his youth and from his own disposition, to adopt a chivalrous tone. Chivalry, for all its graciousness, can mask reality, and he seemed to forget sometimes something he really knew very well, that women can be tough. He could not bear to think of the tender creatures suffering when he read Lady Georgiana's novels and his early experience, when he was the support, the bread-winner and the organiser for his sisters and his widowed mother, led him to think of women as creatures to be protected. He did not expect them to be active politically, to seek the vote or an education that was on a par with the opportunities enjoyed by men.

Not one of the Catholic women converts known to Newman espoused the cause of women's emancipation. It was not that they were interested but were discouraged by him or by some other spiritual adviser – they simply did not see this as a cause to be supported. They all had it in them to take an independent line and to fight against prejudice and the prevailing philosophy which was anti-Catholic, and some of them had fought a hard battle. Elizabeth Bowden had had to contend with her late husband's family, Maria Rosina Giberne and others had had trouble enough with their own. Catherine Froude perhaps had the hardest task of all, asserting her rights and duties in conscience against the wishes of a dearly loved partner.

When they had fought their personal battle and become Catholics they adopted one cause, that of the Church, and when they entered that hierarchically ordered community they seemed to accept the hierarchic structures of secular society. This was true, even of Geraldine Fitzgerald, a spirited and intelligent woman who was living and writing in the seventies and eighties when the movement for emancipation of women was well on the way. It never occurred to her to campaign for the vote nor did she wish to join the movement for the higher education of women, though she spent time at Somerville College, Oxford (presumably enrolling for some short course) in 1881. This college was early in the field, working for degrees for women, but Geraldine Fitzgerald was detached from its aims and its ethos. Oxford was to her the place where her dear Father

Newman had once held sway and where his own battle had been fought. Her letter to Newman on the subject makes her viewpoint very clear.

> I have come up as a student to Oxford to the Ladies' college under Miss Shaw le Fevre to keep one term. In reality what I wanted to do was to make a sort of pilgrimage to a spot which must always be linked in my mind with you, to whom I owe my soul also. Every stone here seems to speak of you. I cannot tell you the dream of delight I am living in. I have got the *Apologia* and *Loss and Gain* and I am going over every spot with a veneration which is the greatest happiness I have ever felt. Today I have been to St Mary's where you have preached those sermons which have become the classics for all time. I cannot describe the feelings which came over me as first I went in, the virginia creeper is crimson outside and the whole building looks poetic and most beautiful. Dr Percival of Trinity preached the University sermon, it was a great feat of intellectual skill but it was broad church and wanted that full strong depth which only belief in dogma can give. At any rate all my thoughts all the time were with the face and form that once held entranced all that multitude of young eager faces ...[39]

Many of the undergraduates listening to Dr Percival yawned and lolled or fell asleep, unlike the young men of that earlier time when Newman preached to them. As for the new students, the girls at Somerville, Miss Fitzgerald thought them 'extraordinarily clever, but very liberal and freethinking.'[40] When she crossed herself, saying grace before and after dinner, they gave a polite quiet smile. However, she did note down for admiration the intellectual exploits of a Miss Seeward: she was only eighteen but had come sixth in an examination with several hundred men, the examination covering History, Ancient and Modern, Euclid, Latin and Greek, French and German, Geometry, Geology, Botany, Biology, Astronomy and Modern and Ancient Literature.

Geraldine Fitzgerald had no wish to stay, once her

pilgrimage was done, and returned to her novel writing. Like the Catholic women who had preceded her, authorship continued to be the safe harbour to which she could steer her vessel.

∽◌⃝◌∾

There was one other noted novelist who became a Catholic and who was received into the Church by Newman and corresponded with him thereafter. Her story cannot be separated from that of her second husband, her niece and her husband, nor from the house where this serious-minded and eccentric quartet lived. This is Baddesley Clinton, an attractive country house on the Warwick side of Birmingham. It is moated, its grey stone and tall redbrick chimneys reflected in the water. In the spring there are daffodils all about it and a little later the hedges are thick with Queen Anne's lace on the approaches. This old Warwickshire house which looks as though it holds a hundred tales of the past and is so remote and lovely in its country setting amongst the trees of the old Arden forest seems many miles away from the smoky centre of the Birmingham in Newman's time. But one of the house's stories is of nineteenth century Catholic converts and how they came to live there. There is a portrait of Newman as a cardinal still hung there, prompting the visitor to ask how he was connected with Baddesley Clinton.

In 1863 Newman received letters from a Lady Chatterton, asking questions about Roman doctrine and practices. She was known to him as a novelist, though at that time he had not read any of her books. She raised objections to the claims of the Roman church but it was clear that a deep interest had prompted her questions. Practices she had observed abroad had disgusted her especially the setting up of what she called tawdry and doll-like figures of the Blessed Virgin and she found signs of superstition and a deplorable lack of taste. Newman replied that Christianity was intended for whole populations, not for a refined élite, and was bound to have extravagance, ignorance and bad taste within its system. 'There are far more important things in religion, than to decide whether the Blessed Virgin should be painted by Rafaelle or a sign painter, should be arrayed mediaevally or in modern millinery.'[1] To her more serious charge, that of corruption within the Church, he replied at length, remarking that Christ himself had spoken of wheat and weeds growing together. 'One out of his twelve Apostles fell, and one of the seven deacons. Thus a church, such as we behold, is bound up with the very idea of Christianity.'[2]

Lady Chatterton was born Georgiana Iremonger (in full, Henrietta Georgiana Marcia Lascelles Iremonger), the daughter of a Prebendary of Winchester Cathedral. She married an Irish baronet, Sir William Chatterton, who lost all his rents and revenues in the Irish famine and died a disappointed man in 1855. His wife published her first book, *Aunt Dorothy's Tales* in 1837 and then a popular account of travels in Ireland in the following year. Other novels and verses followed and also translations from Plato, – and she continued to be known as Lady Chatterton, presumably because that name was known in literary circles, when she re-married in 1859.

Her second husband was Edward Heneage Dering, a cultured man and an officer in the Coldstream Guards, twenty years younger than she was. An unlikely story was told about the match, that he called to ask to pay his addresses to Lady Chatterton's niece who lived with her, the elder lady did not hear him correctly and accepted the proposal which she thought he had made her. He was too polite to disabuse her and so they were married. It soon became clear in the correspondence with Newman that Mr Dering too was debating the claims of Rome and that he greatly admired Newman. He asked his wife to send to the Oratory a volume of poems he had written, wishing to dedicate them to Newman, thus, as he said, to ask shelter for a dwarf in a giant's house. The courteous letters went to and fro and it seemed clear to Newman that Dering had made up his mind and was sufficiently informed about Catholic doctrine. He said that he himself would journey to Finchden in Kent, where they lived, having armed himself with faculties from the Bishop of Southwark to receive this convert into the church. When he got there he found three converts waiting for him, Dering, Lady Chatterton and her niece, Rebecca Dulcibella Orpen. He duly received the three of them and the bishop, who providentially had given Newman faculties for the reception of converts while he was in that diocese, not merely of Dering, sent his congratulations.

Dering had an older friend who had also been in the army, one Marmion Edward Ferrers. He was the squire of Baddesley Clinton, the house where the Ferrers family had lived for generations and often paid fines as recusants for they were Catholics. The house was steeped in Catholic history: in the 1590's the house was let to two sisters of the name of Vaux who sheltered priests, providing at least three hiding places within the walls. A room known as the library or Solar was alway haunted with whisperings – and there is a hide beneath the floorboards. Marmion Edward Ferrers' mother 'suppressed all ghostly traditions and forbade her children to name them,'[3] which is not to say that they never mentioned them out of her hearing. He inherited an impoverished property and after school at Oscott and a time in the army, lived a plain bachelor existence with the lovely old house heavily mortgaged and in need of having money spent on it. As squire he was popular locally since he was a no-nonsense man with a good heart who would rather cuff a poacher himself than turn him over to the justices.

In 1867 he married Rebecca Dulcibella Orpen who, like him, had a distinguished family tree but no money. However, her aunt and his friend also moved to Baddesley Clinton and with Dering's money and Lady Chatterton's force of character, the house took on a new life. Lady Chatterton was described as a person who not only 'possessed an acute and far seeing intellect, which gave her an almost masculine grasp of any subject that might engage her attention: she shone equally in the elegant accomplishments, or in the midst of society, and the mind which was habitually engrossed with the deep problems of faith and religion could unbend in an appreciation of humour, or concentrate itself upon the ordinary duties of everyday life.'[4]

She was extremely talented, being an amateur artist as well as a writer, particularly good at sketching. The prolific and keen painter from the group, however, was Rebecca Dulcibella Ferrers. She filled Baddesley Clinton with pictures of her husband, her aunt and her husband, pictures of the house itself. One of the glories of Baddesley Clinton is its old armorial glass and she added much more heraldry, painting shields. Furniture and stained glass bore further witness to family history. She and Lady Chatterton set up their easels in the bay window of the Great Parlour while Edward Heneage Dering studied or wrote and Marmion Edward Ferrers walked his estate. The characters of the two men are set out in two portraits called 'The Squire's Morning Walk' and 'The Philosopher's Evening Walk'. One of her most interesting pictures is of the quartet in the Great Hall, which they used as their living room: Rebecca Dulcibella herself is standing, the others sit with their books.

All four of them gloried in history, seen romantically and in connection with their families and the house they were living in. The men often wore an archaic costume with the kneebreeches of Stuart times. The ladies retained a Victorian style, though it was not so far removed, with its sweeping skirts and decorative lace, from the seventeenth century mode. All four had a penchant for black velvet. Catholicism must have appealed to them partly because of their belief in the values and glories of antiquity – indeed Marmion Ferrers, the most downright among them, could not have separated his attachment to his faith from his thoughts about his family, the Ferrers, who had remained true to the old religion over the centuries.

In the Solar or 'ghost room', where in mediaeval times one Nicholas Brome murdered the Baddesley chaplain whom he caught 'chockinge his wife under ye chinne' (and where there is a stain by the fireplace, said to be of blood that cannot be expunged) the family set up great bookcases for the old books that had been in the house for generations, genealogical tomes, books on the topography of the area. Nowadays the books by Lady Chatterton and the many books written by her husband are ranged there –

for Edward Heneage Dering emulated his wife and took to his pen. He wrote Catholic novels of great tediousness and soon lost his readers. After his death, a priest who preached in the Catholic church at Warwick praised Edward Dering for his evangelising works: 'he would write a novel and let the heroes and heroines speak Catholic Doctrine. His books were at first well received; but as soon as the general public realised his aim they resented his teaching'.[5] The general public could not really be blamed for their reaction. At home he was a staunch Tory of the most old fashioned kind and when he spoke in his novels of political matters abroad he allied himself with the kind of Catholic who thought much of the iniquities of Freemasons, Italian insurgents against the Pope and dangerous freethinkers.

His wife corresponded with Newman on the subject of the publication of novels and of poetry. She wrote in complaint, early in 1865, saying that there was 'such a strong feeling in the public and particularly in the period- ical press against all writing which tends to indicate any good or high religious or even moral principles.'[6] She made it clear to him how strongly she felt that it was a good work to supply literature that would elevate and, since the public were hungry for novels, in book form or serialised in the periodicals, they must be given novels to counterbal- ance the sensational ones.

At this time she seemed to have difficulty finding a review that would publish her poems or serialise her tales, but in general over her writing life she certainly found publishers and a public. To her novels, travel books, poems, short stories and translations she added essays, one play and a memoir of her uncle, Admiral Gambier. Newman read the books she sent him with great attention, commenting in detail on a poem called *Lady May* and enjoying the novels. He commented for instance, on her three volume novel *The Lost Bride*, published in 1872, written with an ease and fluency that he admired and envied, written indeed 'with the joyousness of riding or driving through green lanes or in a wild wood.'[7] However, he took her to task for what he described as a tendency in the book to 'an indifferentism between creeds and parties.' She had depicted Italians who clearly had less faith than some English people but she had not averted to the great fact, 'that Catholicism is true, and Protestantism is false.' He added an exculpatory clause to his objection, speaking of an impression of indifferentism 'which you cannot mean.' He probably did not read her mind correctly.

When corresponding, she or her husband often invited him to visit them at Baddesley but he would not be lured to country houses: 'it requires siege guns and naval artillery to dislodge me from home.'[8] He did visit at least once, however, going on the train (presumably to the little station at Lapworth nearby) and returning the same day, and the whole party of four visited him at Edgbaston where he could renew acquaintance with his three converts and meet Mr Ferrers.

Life went on tranquilly at Baddesley as the countryside bloomed around it and as the waters rippled in its moat. They seem, the two couples, removed from the ordinary bustle of life, enclosed in their old fashioned ways. Their very names, so distinctive and lengthy, set them apart – and it is a relief to know that the two ladies had pet names, amongst their dearest friends, Rebecca Dulcibella being 'Pysie' and Lady Chatterton being 'Gintle'. There was one inner disturbance to mar their seclusion. Lady Chatterton was not at all happy with her new faith and she wrote to Newman in great perturbation of spirit. The devotion to Mary and the belief in the real presence of Christ in the Eucharist – central to Catholic beliefs and practices – brought her doubts and distress. Newman replied to her long letter at Easter 1866:

> To me it is wonderful that you should speak as you do. Why, what exercise of devotion is there, which equals that going before the Blessed Sacrament, before our Lord Jesus really present, though unseen? ... And so, far from the teaching of the Church concerning the Blessed Virgin being a burden, it seems to me the greatest of privileges and honours to be admitted into the very family of God ...[9]

There was a great outpouring here: to cheer and strengthen this sad convert Newman set forth what had made him deeply happy for the twenty years he had been a Roman Catholic. Lady Chatterton had also complained of feelings of alienation at Catholic services, to which he replied that converts came as strangers who travelled from their homes: 'Abraham doubtless found his life in Canaan not so pleasant to him as his native Mesopotamia.' She found the idea of purgatory unpleasant, which did not prove, said Newman, that it was untrue. He could have said more on this subject for, when he wrote imaginatively on purgatory in *The Dream of Gerontius* he did it in a spirit of solemn joy – but Lady Chatterton would find no joy in any practice of her religion until God had made her generally happy in it. Newman did not argue further.

Lady Chatterton had one other trouble. The emphasis on family history at Baddesley was no help to her for her family were not the recusant Ferrers. She was haunted, not by the ghosts of Tudor priests or the murdered chaplain, but by the shade of Prebendary Iremonger and his forebears. They seemed to tell her that she had betrayed her family in her new adherence to a foreign religion. Newman understood her plight, saying her suffering grieved him deeply, and that he knew how much it would distress her niece and husband to differ from her and how this distressed her too. One thing that comes out clearly in their letters is the deep affection that bound the three converts together. The squire kept apart from this correspondence with Newman – he was not his convert – and heaven knows what he thought of the difficulties poor Gintle raised. Perhaps he was amazed at the troubles converts could have.

In 1870, the year of the definition of Papal Infallibility during the first Vatican Council, Newman corresponded with Lady Chatterton to explain and encourage, for she was one of those much disturbed by the definition. So he was well advised of all her intellectual and emotional difficulties. All the same, he was shocked when he was informed by Mrs Ferrers in 1873 that her aunt had left the Church. He said to her that he loved her aunt so much 'from the sweet composure and tenderness of her mind'[10] that he would not willingly pain and he knew her health was not good – all the same he could not agree with what she was doing and no priest could absolve her from her religious duty. He wrote to Lady Chatterton herself, 'I do sincerely trust that by prayer, on your part and on our part, you will see that God has called you to a great blessing, and will thank Him for having done so.'[11] And there he left it.

In September 1875 Newman received a letter he must have hoped for: 'I have, thank God,' wrote Lady Chatterton, 'been able gradually to see that I was wrong.'[12] He replied, 'You will be rewarded abundantly, do not doubt it, for the pain, anxiety and weariness you have gone through in arriving at the safe ground and sure home of peace where you now are. I congratulate, with all my heart, the dear friends who surround you upon so happy a termination of their own anxieties and prayers.'[13]

She had been corresponding with her bishop, Ullathorne, who had helped her resolve her doubts and it was he who reconciled her with the Church. Her husband always referred to this event as the time when she became a Catholic. He described her character, her thoughts and religious doubts and her final spell of peace in a memoir published after her death, a curious document that ignored the fact that she had been received into the church with him in 1865. Edward Dering was a very conformist convert, the last person one would expect to take a line contrary to that of priests and theologians and certainly not one to oppose Newman whom he revered as priest, guide and literary giant. Yet in this matter he took his own line, either because of his chivalrous love for his wife who must be described as one who had set her hand to the plough and then turned back, or because he could not believe that someone could properly be described as a Catholic when unhappy with its doctrines. However, by anyone's reckoning, Lady Chatterton was a practising and devout Catholic in the last months of her life.

There was another reason for rejoicing at Baddesley at this time – the chapel was restored and they were allowed to have Mass said there. Lady Chatterton provided embossed leather hangings, dating from the mid eighteenth century and Mrs Ferrers painted panels and the reredos. The chapel stands now as it did then – lovingly overdecorated and unmistakably Victorian, though the worshippers in the seventies must have thought much of the return to the past, to the days when the Latin prayers were said in secret and in courageous defiance of persecution.

Lady Chatterton died in February 1876 and Newman wrote feeling letters both to Edward Dering and Marmion Ferrers who invited him to the funeral – which Newman could not attend. Lady Chatterton's last literary work was *The Consolation of the Devout Soul*, translated from the Italian of Joseph Frassinetti; Mrs Ferrers sent Newman a copy and he saw there a preface in it by the widower explaining that this translation was the fruit of her Catholic conviction which she had lately gained.

Edward Dering's *Memoirs of Georgiana Lady Chatterton* soon followed and Bishop Ullathorne wrote to Newman in some anxiety because the book made it clear that she had found Newman's rebuke in 1873 (when she left the Church) distressing and Ullathorne's comments were published verbatim. Those comments were discreet and reasonable and Newman could find no fault with them.

In 1875 Ullathorne had written, 'I know Dr Newman's vigorous way. Depend upon it, my dear friend, it was not want of sympathy, but from strong sympathy restrained, that he wrote. He wished to give you an electric shock ...'[14] Newman did not say that he could have done no other than remonstrate at the time and it seems that he was simply glad that Ullathorne had succeeded as a counsellor. He never commented on the *Memoirs* themselves and the line taken by Edward Dering, though the reference to the quotations from the Bishop's letters shows that he read them. Lady Georgiana had 'passed the awful stream which we all have to ford and is safe'[15] and, as he said to Marmion Ferrers, 'you have much to thank God for on the retrospect and we all have.'[16] There was no more to say.

Correspondence between Newman and his converts at Baddesley Clinton petered out after Lady Chatterton's death but when he had been made a Cardinal in 1879 Rebecca Dulcibella wished to make a portrait of him. He granted her one sitting and otherwise she worked from photographs. This was one of her most ambitious works and not her most successful but there it still hangs, recalling the link between him and the family.

Marmion Ferrers died in 1884. The next year she and the widowed Edward Heneage Dering were married, making no great show of the event but setting off quietly one day in a carriage, dressed in black velvet, for the nearest Catholic church. Dering lived seven years more. His second wife lived on well into the next century as the chatelaine of Baddesley Clinton, managing the house and adhering to old customs as her dearly loved aunt had done before her. The servants wore quaint liveries and had to forswear all modern inventions which might have lightened their work, but felt themselves to be treasured members of the household. In this feudal and Catholic setting, old Mrs Dering, handsome, clad in black, prayed, welcomed guests with graciousness and busied herself with works of charity.

The house and estate passed to a great-nephew of Marmion Ferrers and in time it became the property of the National Trust. The Victorian portion of its history is displayed very clearly to modern visitors because of Rebecca Dulcibella's many pictures. The house also holds the many books written by Edward Heneage Dering and by that interesting woman, his wife Georgiana, talented, powerful, deeply religious and often troubled.

Chapter Four

The Nuns

Sophy Ryder, Marianne Bowden; The Foundresses –
Fanny Margaret Taylor, Catherine Ann Bathurst,
Margaret Hallahan (with Maria Ruscombe Poole);
Maria Rosina Giberne.

One of the defects of Protestantism, according to Newman,
was that it had opposed the Religious life and thus had
affected women adversely. He said in an essay, written in
his Anglican days:

> I know not any more distressing development of the
> cruel temper of Protestantism than the determined,
> bitter, and scoffing spirit in which it has set itself against
> institutions which give dignity and independence to the
> position of women in society. As matters stand, marriage
> is almost the only shelter which a defenceless portion of
> the community has against the rude world ...[1]

This last sentence, describing both marriage and conventual life as havens, providing a thick carapace for the
tender females to shelter in, does not do justice to his
thinking on the matter. He certainly thought Religious life
would provide a way of using female gifts and talents, a
settled, dignified, useful way – hence his wish that the restless Mary Holmes might consider the possibility of a
Religious vocation. At the same time he saw it as a particular vocation and a high one – its usefulness to society or
to the individual did not constitute its whole raison d'être.
It was a gift, a precious means by which a woman might

171

unite herself to Christ Himself.

Many of the converts from Anglicanism, Newman's friends or the daughters and sisters of his friends, entered Religious life and they made up a notable part of the band of women who made convents part of the English scene again in the nineteenth century. One of the first to consult him about a Religious vocation, after his conversion to Rome and her own, was Sophy Ryder, the sister of his old friend, George Ryder. Somewhat confusingly, George Ryder's mother, his wife and his sister were all named Sophia. The Ryders, George, his wife, his sister and his children all became Catholics in 1846 and Newman was impressed with the ladies' settled, happy air. 'It is impossible to see Mrs and still more Miss Ryder, without seeing how firmly they are Catholics, and that excitement has had nothing to do with their conversion.'[2] The whole family was in Rome that year. When they returned to England Sophy Ryder lived for a time with her mother but she was already considering a religious vocation and wrote to Newman, particularly to ask his advice about what congregation of nuns she should choose. Her recollection of the extent of his influence does not accord with his statements on the matter and unfortunately the correspondence has not survived. She wrote to the new Superior of the Birmingham Oratory, after Newman's death, to explain to him (he was her own nephew, Henry Ignatius Dudley Ryder) why there was such a dearth of letters.

> I am very sorry that I have no more letters that I can send you ... I had so many before I became a nun and then I was so afraid that I liked them too much that I burnt them. There was a sentence in one I think you would like; it was at the time I was thinking I would prefer the Carmelites as I had a very great admiration for Saint Theresa. I used to write and ask Father Newman what he thought of the different contemplative Orders, but to my dismay he put doubts and obstacles in my way, so at last I thought I would ask what he thought of the Good Shepherd, devoutly hoping that *he would not think of it*, when to my dismay he wrote me a long letter

with nothing but praise and admiration, concluding with these words

> 'The Order of the Good Shepherd is *nearest* to the *Priesthood*, the *dearest* to the Heart of Jesus; and it will last to the end of the world as it will be needed.'

> So you may think I felt I ought to try and overcome my dislike and enter as soon as I could tho' your beloved Mother and Father were much against my going anywhere – however I entered on the Feast of S. Peter and S. Paul in the year 1849. Dear Fr Newman came to my clothing on the following August.[3]

The special work of the French Congregation of the Good Shepherd was the rehabilitation of female penitents, women who had been prostitutes. Sophy Ryder entered their convent at Hammersmith and Newman, before she entered there, wrote to George Ryder to express his good opinion of the nuns but disclaiming any particular influence on her choice. He wrote in February 1849:

> I don't think anything of the reports you mention about the Good Shepherd – on the contrary, all I hear shows that a remarkable blessing and success has attended the Institution. And it is one with so heavenly an object that I cannot but think that other ladies will be joining it. I should not have *mentioned* it to your sister, not liking to bias her considering the peculiar work which it pursues – but I rejoice to find it has been brought before her and that she has been arrested by it.[4]

It would seem that Miss Ryder raised the matter of the Good Shepherd vocation, was struck by the warm praise that Newman wrote and acted on that prompting, though he did not think that it was his recommendation that had motivated her. She was the first English novice to be received and trained in England: before then any English postulants were sent to the Mother House in Angers. It was hoped that she would be useful when new houses were set up in England for with her good connections she could smooth the path for this French Congregation and she could act as secretary when English letters were exchanged. However, it was not surprising that Sophy Ryder's mother, an English lady not in favour of Catholics or of nuns, and even her brother George would flinch at the thought of her being immured with French nuns and with women and girls from the very lowest stratum of society. She was, in the event, both useful and happy in the life, though she found the enclosure hard at first.

The Ryders had a portrait of Sophy, done before her entry into the convent at Hammersmith, and in due time had her nun's wimple and black veil painted in. It shows a small, vivacious face with large dark eyes, a high-bridged and rather beaky nose, and an air of nervous brightness. She was not unlike Harriett Newman in physical type, hyper-active, prone to headaches, impetuous. Her nature was sweeter than Harriett's, however, and she was loved for her cheerfulness.

Newman attended the clothing ceremony and her profession and must have noted with satisfaction that George Ryder became fully supportive of his sister's vocation. She was called Sister Mary of the Sacred Heart, though Newman always referred to her as 'Miss Ryder', addressing her in rare letters as 'My Dear Child'.

She worked extremely hard, partly from religious zeal and partly, no doubt, because of her active temperament. Moreover, she soon found herself in positions of responsibility, having to make decisions about finance and management, not simply enduring poverty or sharing the extra tasks that poverty laid on the household or coping with the disturbed and coarse behaviour of the girls she was caring for. She worked, early on in her Religious life, at Arno's Vale in Bristol. When she was there Newman wrote to another hard-working woman, saying that he knew how one's occupation could be a trial in itself. 'Poor Miss Ryder,' he told her, 'in addition to it all, has good part of the management of the House, and is sorely straitened for money to live by.'[5] In another letter he said that the nuns in Bristol were 'as poor as rats.'[6]

This same convent, in Sister Mary Ryder's time there, closed their home for penitents and opened a reformatory for girls instead. The younger age of their charges did nothing to ease the lives of the nuns. Newman wrote to Miss Giberne in 1856:

Do you know that Miss Ryder's convent is turned into a Reformatory, and is already attracting the attention of Protestants by the businesslike way in which the Nuns go to work? She describes the children, all of whom are under sixteen, as terrific. They seem to think nothing of, if so be, killing a person, when they are in a rage – and would not mind if it were a nun. I am always anxious lest the strain upon her body and mind should be too much for her – but she is wonderfully supported. You must say some prayers for her.[7]

It was at Bristol that she suffered the worst strain of her life because of a terrible accident. Before the reformatory came into being it was one of Sister Mary of the Sacred Heart's duties to administer medicines to sick penitents. One girl, called Melanie, required a medicine to be taken internally and a lotion. The medicine was to be given early in the morning, the light was poor, it was not then obligatory to label poisons clearly. Sister Mary of the Sacred Heart was overworked, quick in all she did, had no nurse's training. The lotion was given Melanie to drink and she died later that day.

This death and this responsibility was anguish enough but more trouble came for the unfortunate nuns and for Sister Mary Ryder in particular with the subsequent enquiry which lasted six days. Terrible stories went around, of cruelty and murderous nuns, though as the investigation proceeded the atmosphere became less threatening. An early biographer gave one reason for the change, though presumably the nuns themselves and the way they gave their testimony must have made it clear that Sister Mary of the Sacred Heart was no murderess. 'The coroner,' according to the account, 'had used the words "that female," meaning poor Sister Mary of the Sacred Heart.

Hearing this, one of her friends, who happened to be present, stood forward and said: "That female is Lord Harrowby's cousin."[8] It transpired also that she was related to the Protestant Bishop of Lichfield, who was well known and much respected in Bristol, 'having resided in the neighbourhood when occupying the See of Gloucester.' She was cautioned, not imprisoned, but she was ill after it all and perhaps never quite recovered from such a trial.

She was sent to be Prioress in Malta until the climate affected her health and then exchanged the heat there for northern cold, going to Liverpool and Glasgow. Wherever she went she was known for her active, self-sacrificing spirit and a certain lightness of touch and brightness in her contacts with her charges. She liked to sketch and paint in her youthful days (and when in Rome had inadvertently set up her easel in a monastery's enclosed grounds until she was chased out by an enraged monk) and she would decorate rooms for Christmas, paint little gifts or deck a Christmas tree. Her Religious superiors had always thought she would be useful to new houses in England but they had not reckoned with one of her talents, which was to draw plans when a house was to be altered to be more suitable as a convent and a refuge. Perhaps if she had been a man and seeking a secular profession she would have been an architect.

She went for a short time to a new convent in Cardiff, having first sketched plans for it, and then went back to Arno's Vale. She was an old lady then, thin and becoming frail, but she worked in the garden zealously. This was one of her favourite jobs and she did not simply plant, weed and tidy but set about landscaping the whole. The habit of a Good Shepherd nun was white and she protected it by two aprons and she wore clogs when at her outdoor work. The details conjure up a vivid picture of a slight, birdlike figure, busy beyond her strength. 'Rest?' she would say 'I shall rest in heaven.'

A closer tie bound Newman to another candidate for the Religious life, Marianne Bowden, the elder daughter of John and Elizabeth Bowden. He had christened her, in his

Anglican days and though, as a Catholic priest, he doubted that all Anglican baptisms were validly administered (it was the custom until recently to give conditional baptism to converts), he believed that this time every care had been taken. It was 15 April 1831 when he took the child in his arms and, as he told her years later. 'I baptized you with water in the name of the Three Divine Persons and signed you with the sign of the cross .... I fully believe that from that moment you were rescued from the power of Satan, and made the subject of God's supernatural promises and supernatural graces. From your very infancy then God has chosen you, and claimed you as his own.'[10]

The glimpses we have of her as a child and as a girl are of a quiet, devout, good creature. Her father said when she was a child that he thought she would grow up to be a nun. She was well-behaved in Elizabeth Bowden's schoolroom, gentle and gracious as she stood on the stairs to bid Mr Newman goodbye so that he wished it had been the Anglican custom to give her a blessing as he went. Newman watched her narrowly because of the love he bore her parents and noted her manners and her ways. She was not a child to give pain to her relatives or friend except that her health caused worry. She was often ill and the Bowdens, like the Froudes, had to watch for signs of tuberculosis. Would Marianne go the same way as her father?

When she was seventeen she announced that she wanted to be a nun, not seeking some active work of charity but simply wanting a life of dedication and prayer. Her mother and Newman (who was very like a caring uncle to a fatherless girl) were not surprised but were anxious. Newman took endless trouble to try to find the best place for this delicate girl. He probably considered the contemplative Orders, like the Carmelites, far too severe for her, and certainly he wished that Marianne would turn her mind to an active life. Taken with his advice to Sophy Ryder, his leanings seemed to have been towards the active congregations for women when the vocations of his young friends were in question. Eventually he suggested the Convent of the Visitation, then at Westbury, near Bristol. The Order of the Visitation, founded by St Francis de Sales and St Jane

Frances Chantal, was enclosed and contemplative but had always admitted widows, older women and delicate women. It did not go in for physical austerities such as long fasts. Newman heard very good things of this particular convent and its grounds were spacious, the air of Westbury good. Marianne might find her heart's desire there and still be cared for and live for years.

He looked into every detail and outlined to Mrs Bowden what seemed to him some signal disadvantages of this convent. They had some very depressing customs. There was an embargo on music – no musical instruments in the house, little singing in church, even at Mass, and the office was chanted on two high notes. Newman was musical and he recoiled from all this as he had from the mode of chanting in the convents of the Good Shepherd which he described as a bad imitation of French Latin through the nose. In the Visitation's chapel a veil hung between the Sanctuary and the nuns' stalls; another depressing feature. He observed too that their admitting delicate women meant that Marianne would have the company of some invalidish people and this 'must ever *tend* to want of elasticity and a want of life.'[11] The absence of a practical object too 'must, except when persons are very devout, create dullness and apathy.' However, the Westbury nuns *were* devout and, moreover, were ladies by birth and education. Marianne had been gently reared and would find rough manners a great trial.

All these disadvantages and advantages had to be weighed because Newman was always against anyone's precipitous entry into the Church or into a convent, going on a wave of ill-informed enthusiasm. He put the Westbury convent's negative aspects in strong, clear outline because he thought he should act as an Advocatus Diaboli in the matter. Marianne was not deterred and entered the convent in August 1852. When she had been there a little while she wrote to Newman the kind of letter one might send to a concerned uncle.

My Dear Father Newman,

I would not write to you until I had been here a week and had recovered from the grief and the novelty which oppressed me at first. I am beginning to feel very happy and like everything very much. As far as I can judge the spirit of this Institute suits me for it is very simple and seems to consist in doing small things well. The great subdivision of time is a rest at first though it will probably become a mortification. Mortification of this sort seems necessary for there are no austerities. I am getting quite fond of the chapel in spite of the veil which is only drawn back on Christmas night. The office seems extremely slow. They tell me that when I join in the ceremonies it will appear less monotonous. I am learning to sing it but I have no idea of music. This is an advantage to me for it prevents me from feeling the want of it so much. The schoolchildren sing at the Mass on Sundays and the nuns sing the Litany of our B. Lady in parts. The extreme affection the nuns show to each other is very nice. I have been treated as a child and not a stranger from the first moment of my coming. Our Mistress of novices is a very superior and nice person, she has been Mistress of Novices or Superioress for a long time. Her name is Vaughan, she has a brother a Jesuit and another a Redemptorist. I like my companions in the noviceship very much, Miss Walmesley and Miss Robinson are novices and Miss Buckle is a postulant. We expect another, a Miss Mason, a convert. They say that half the community have been converts and more than half of the last comers. I feel the happiness of the religious life more every day and I ought to pray for you because you sent me here, if for no other reason. I have had as comfortable letters as could be expected from Mamma and Emily. They have had the trial of going back alone to the old places. I am exceedingly thankful for your saying Mass for us – I shall be sorry when the Nativity comes, only I am not afraid of your forgetting us. I hope you have not had quite so much work lately.

> Believe me
> Ever your affect.
> M. J. Bowden[12]

Presumably Newman had promised special Masses for Marianne and her family until the feast of Our Lady's Nativity (8 September). He thought very tenderly of the wrench the parting would be to these three women. Marianne was twenty two and had been in the company of Mamma and Emily all her life. Mamma was teacher, guide, companion, in a closer relationship than would be customary now. Trollope described some such situation when he wrote of the Dales of Allington at the Small House. Newman wrote a message of great sympathy to Mrs Bowden and kept them all in mind.

Marianne was clothed as a novice in January 1853, taking the Religious name of Sister Mary Francis Dominica. Newman was away in Scotland and so he did not attend the ceremony but in the November of that year he was staying at Clifton and went over to Westbury to see her. On 12 January the next year she was to take her vows, with her companions (was this the shadowy but amiable Miss Buckle[13] and Miss Mason?). Newman did attend this time and preached a lengthy sermon on the subject of vowed virginity – leaving Marianne a wonderful reminder of her profession day and giving, incidentlly, a full, considered account of his thinking on the subject of the celibate vocation. Some such thoughts had been with him for years, though whether he had worked out such a whole theory and philosophy on the single, dedicated life when he was disappointed years before at Henry Wilberforce's marriage, when he discussed the high calling of virginity with Hurrell Froude, when he chose the celibate life when he was an Anglican, we do not know. The sermon tells us a great deal of his ideals, for himself and for the women he knew who were nuns.

He outlined first a view of marriage, presenting it as divinely ordained, meant for the happiness and perfection of the partners:

> It is by the law of our nature, the happiness of everyone,
> man and women, to have one central and supreme
> attachment, to which none other can be compared. An
> affection, one, mutual, sovereign, unalterable, is earthly
> happiness and his earthly strength. Two mortal crea-
> tures of God, placed in this rough world, exposed to its
> many fortunes, destined to suffering and death, join
> hands, and give the faith to each other that each of them
> will love the other wholly until death. Henceforth each
> is made for the other – each has possession of the affec-
> tions of the other in a transcendent way; each loves the
> other better than anything else in the way; each is all in
> all to the other; each can confide in the other unre-
> servedly, each is the others irreversibly. There is but one
> mind, one aim, one course, one happiness, between two.
> Each is reflected in the other; each reads his own
> thought in the other's face; each feels for the other
> more than for himself. Such is the fountain head of
> human society and the continual provision of the
> human race: such is the beginning of civilisation, the
> guardian of religion, and the norm of philanthropy ...[14]

This is a very idealised picture of the married state –
perhaps it is not meant to be a description of the marriages
Newman had observed (though he had in his sights some
very good marriages, that of his parents, of William and
Catherine Froude, and of Marianne Bowden's parents) but
of marriage as God intended it to be. He then went on to
set beside it the Gospel call to the celibate life, noting that
there was a way of living the single life that had nothing of
the love and blessedness of the Gospel call about it.

> There is a state of celibacy recommended by philoso-
> phers, exemplified in religious teaching, which does but
> harden the heart, which is of that forlorn, haughty and
> repulsive nature – as it has been imaged and extolled in
> the pages of heathen writers or in the teaching of false
> religions... There have been those among false religions

who have actually observed the state of celibacy, and that on the ground that it was higher than the common life of man. To make a single life its own end, to adopt it simply and solely for its own sake, I do not know whether such a state of life is more melancholy or more unamiable, melancholy from its unrequited desolateness and unamiable from the pride and self-esteem on which it is based.

At this point Newman's rhetoric became exalted, as he praised virginity seen as marriage to Christ. The union of the soul with God is a reality but the idea of commitment to Christ as marriage, with illustrations from the poetry of the *Song of Songs,* is of course a metaphor and to extend this metaphor and to descant upon it is only apropriate when applied to dedicated women. The occasion of Sister Dominica's profession provided Newman with the opportunity to speak with lyrical freedom on a matter close to his heart. First he distinguished Christian virginity from the cold celibacy he had spoken of before.

This is not the Virginity of the Gospel – it is not a state of independence or isolation, or dreary pride, or barren indolence, or crushed affections; man is made for sympathy, for the interchange of love, for self-denial for the sake of another dearer to him than himself. The Virginity of the Christian soul is a marriage with Christ. Hence the words, 'I have espoused you to one husband, that I may present you as a chaste virgin to Christ.' O surprising love and wisdom, that has thus allowed us to aim at being Angels without ceasing to be men. O transcending condescension that He should stoop to be ours in the tenderest and most endearing way – ours to love, ours to consult, ours to minister to, ours to converse with, ours to joy in. Ours so fully that it is as if He had none to think of but each of us personally. The very idea of matrimony is possession – whole possession – the husband is the wife's and no other's, and the wife is the husband's and none but his. This is to enter into the marriage bond, this is the force of the marriage vow, this

The young J. H. Newman

Harriet & Mary Newman

Family group: Francis, Mrs Newman, Jemima, John & Harriet

The young Emily Bowles

Maria Rosina Giberne: a self-portrait

Elena and Vincenzo

Mrs Willliam Froude

Lady Chatterton

Lady Georgiana Fullerton

Fanny Taylor

Mother Mary Imelda Poole

Sister Maria Pia
(M. R. Giberne)

Mother Margaret Hallahan

Left: Jemima Mozley

Right: Anne Mozley

Left: Mrs Wootton

is the lesson of the marriage ring. And this it is to be married to Jesus. It is to have Him, ours wholly, henceforth and for ever – it is to be united to Him by an indissoluble tie – it is to be His, while He is ours – it is to partake of that wonderful sacrament which unites Him to His Blessed Mother on high – Dilectus meus mihi, et ego illi, qui pascitur inter lilias. Such has the Highest deigned to be to His elect; to all of them in the world to come, as the text tells us, and to those of them in their degree by earnest or by anticipation who are called to follow the Lamb whithersoever He goes, to those who are called to the holy orders or to the monastic state – to those especially the Spouses of Christ, those dear children of grace, who leave the earth and its allurements and its enjoyments, for Him alone, all of them ineffably united to Him, (you know it far better than I can tell you, my sisters) some of them ascending so high along the ladder of mystical devotion as actually already to forestall that perfect solemnity which will be the portion of all the saints in the world to come.

Sister Dominica lived out her Religious life faithfully, gently and obscurely. In time her convent moved from Westbury to Saffron Walden in Essex but that was the only major break in the quiet monotony of her days. Her life was rather dull without but precious within. She was busy in several employments, illuminating cards and texts, helping in the infirmary, especially with the handing out of medicines, and at times acting as secretary to the Reverend Mother. The nuns were much concerned with Newman's plans to set up an Oratory in Oxford and wrote to him to assure him of their prayers. Also he had, from time to time, a little letter from Sister Dominica asking for prayers for a nun who had just died, enclosing what was called, in a depressing phrase, a mortuary billet.

She had said in her first letter to him from the convent that she felt at home with the spirit of the Visitation because 'it is very simple and seems to consist in doing small things well'. It is impossible not to think of Newman's own exhortations to perfection and his recipe

It is the saying of holy men that, if we wish to be perfect, we have nothing more to do than to perform the ordinary duties of the day well. A short road to perfection – short, not because easy, but because pertinent and intelligible. There are no short ways to perfection, but there are sure ones ...

We must bear in mind what is meant by perfection. It does not mean any extraordinary service, anythig out of the way, or especially heroic – not all have the opportunity of heroic acts, of sufferings – but it means what the word perfection ordinarily means. By perfect we mean that which has no flaw in it, that which is complete, that which is consistent, that which is sound – we mean the opposite to imperfect. As we know well what *im*perfection in religious service means, we know by the contrast what is meant by perfection. He then is perfect who does the work of the day perfectly, and we need not go beyond this to seek for perfection. You need not go out of the *round* of the day.[15]

It is also impossible not to move one's thoughts thirty or forty years on and to Lisieux in France where another nun was working out her 'Little Way'. Like Theresa of Lisieux, Marianne Bowden did not spend long years in her convent. The almost inevitable happened and, as her father had done, she contracted tuberculosis. Unlike the French saint, she was always well looked after by the other nuns. Nor did she suffer intense desolation though she was much oppressed by what she described as languor, so that at one point she seemed not to care whether she lived or died. Later, on a more positive note, she said with her customary sweetness that she had been happy to live and would be happy to die for she knew that God loved her. She once wrote to Newman expressing her puzzlement at the fact that whenever special prayers were said for her recovery she seemed thereafter to get worse. A gentle letter came in answer, addressed to 'My dear Child'.

It is no want of faith in you to put yourself simply into

the hands of our dear Lord, that He may do with you what He will. He must not be supposed to turn a deaf ear to prayer, because He answers it in His own way. It is impossible that a blessing should not come to you in consequence of so many prayers made for you – and if He does not give the very favour asked for, it is because He has it in purpose to give you a greater. Any how, you are His – and prayer will make you more fully His....[16]

This was sent in May 1867 and it was clear that she would not recover. She worked at her small tasks, such as her illuminating, throughout her illness and spent a great deal of time in the garden when the weather was good. When she could not reach the garden she sat in an armchair in the convent infirmary, looking out on the quadrangle and the field, and carefully sent out short messages, trying to keep up Mamma's spirits, telling Father Newman that she was 'most happy to go'. She said that she felt freedom was approaching.

The Victorians thought much on deathbeds and talked about them, sometimes frightening each other. Marianne Bowden did not pretend to heroism and she feared her approaching death agony. However, as the nun who wrote to Newman in October 1867 reported, there was no last agony. She had slipped away gently on the tenth of that month, aged thirty six. 'May we all die such deaths, and leave such memories behind us',[17] Newman wrote to Mrs Bowden. He prayed for the family and for Marianne though he thought he had more need of her prayers than she had of his.

As for Emily Bowden, she too thought of becoming a nun. Newman would not encourage her at first and vetoed her suggestion that she should make a retreat within the enclosure of the Visitation convent, believing that the consciousness of her sister's presence within those walls would be too powerful a lure. When she remained firm in her resolve he changed tack, believing that her steadfastness, despite the cold water he had cast on the idea, indicated a true Religious vocation. Perhaps the discouragement had, temporarily, made her determined to go on

and Newman's strategy had not taken note of the tendency
of the young to pull back as their elders urge advance and
tug forwards when advice is on the side of caution. At any
rate, the moment Father Newman said that she had a
Religious vocation Emily ceased to press on. She did not
enter a convent, nor did she marry. It looked at times as if
the widowed Mrs Bowden would be quite alone for
Marianne departed, John became an Oratorian and
Charles too, though he first announced that he would join
the Dominicans in Malta. Emily stayed on at home,
companion to Mamma. It was the destiny of many
Victorian girls and perhaps she saw this as her duty. Her
motives and her character remain obscure to us – it is
Marianne, Sister Dominica, who emerges from the letters
as a rounded personality, not outstandingly intelligent or
talented, but gently and attractively good. Newman loved
all the Bowden children, but perhaps Marianne most of all.

⌒◌⌒

There were women converts who did not simply join an
existing Religious Congregation but who founded a new
one. They were devoted and strong-minded to an extraordinary degree because their task was a hard one,
forming a body of nuns to do a particular work of charity,
finding a suitable rule to live by, building convents and
financing them and (like Cornelia Connelly) often having
difficulties with ecclesiastical authority. The degree to
which priests and bishops controlled and shaped the lives
of Religious women is remarkable – after all, the women
themselves were setting about their tasks with clear notions
of what they wished to do and what they could do and
had no thought of taking up extremist positions or oper-
ating as mavericks within the church. They could well have
been given more independence.

Newman had no part in the formation of new Religious
Institutes but he knew some of the foundresses. One was
Fanny Margaret Taylor. She was not a close friend of
Newman's and her correspondence with him about her
journals pre-dates the years when she was setting about

establishing her Congregation, The Poor Servants of the Mother of God. She does, however, illustrate the remarkable fact that there were very few women converts of note in England who did not correspond with Newman at one time or another. Her story is an interesting one.

She was born in 1832, the tenth child of Henry and Louisa Taylor. Her father was the Rector of Stoke Rochford in Lincolnshire and it was he who educated his daughters. Fanny did not have long to profit from his instructions for he died of tuberculosis when she was ten and the family moved to London. When still a girl Fanny joined her elder sisters, Emma and Charlotte, in attending a church which favoured the doctrines and liturgy of the Tractarians, even though their father had not been persuaded by the Movement. Emma Taylor became a sister in an Anglican convent under the direction of Dr Pusey; this was a convent of the Society of the Sisters of Mercy of the Holy Trinity, working in schools and orphanages and founded by Miss Priscilla Lydia Sellon. Fanny, although she was only sixteen, joined the Sisterhood too. She did not stay long but two ideas rooted in her mind, that the poor needed help urgently and that Religious Sisters lived nobly and charitably. Back at home, she tried to work for the London poor, opening a school for boys off the streets, visiting homes in the slums.

When Fanny was twenty-two she joined the volunteers rounded up by Florence Nightingale to go out to nurse in the Crimea, traveling with the second contingent that went out there. There were nine ladies, twenty two paid nurses and fifteen Roman Catholic Sisters of Mercy, warned by Sidney Herbert, the Secretary of War, to expect 'many hardships and discomforts, and to be prepared to witness many scenes of horror'.[1] A uniform was provided, except for the nuns, a plain, thick dress and a round cap. There is a portrait of Fanny Taylor in this costume; she has a round, sweet face under the cap and smooth hair and she is clearly tall and well built.

In the Crimea there were certainly hardships and scenes of horror and also delays and muddles and the difficulties of having three classes of volunteers, the nuns, the professional nurses who were not properly trained but who had experience, and the ladies who had little experience and a refined horror of the rough ways of their nurse companions who sometimes resembled Dickens' Mrs Gamp and had a propensity for drinking gin. Fanny worked first at Scutari and observed Miss Nightingale carrying her lantern, and then she was at a hospital in Koulali, five miles away. All through her journey to the Crimea and during her working time she watched and admired the Irish nuns and the ladies' first superintendent, Mary Stanley, who was a convert to Rome. She herself was received into the Catholic Church at Easter, 1855.

When back at home she resumed her work among the London poor this time under the direction of the parish priest at Bayswater, Dr Manning. She also wrote a book, *Eastern Hospials and English Nurses: the Narrative of Twelve Months Experience in the Hospitals of Koulali and Scutari by a Lady Volunteer*. After the publication of this work she turned to novel writing and published *Tyborne and Who Went Thither in the Days of Queen Elizabeth*. This came out in 1857 and in the early sixties she also published a compilation of prose and poetry by various writers called *Offerings for Orphans* (the proceeds were to go to a fund for orphans and destitute children) and a book of short sketches of Religious Congregations for women.

This little book shows the way her thoughts were tending. She wanted to become a nun herself and after a friend of hers had joined the Sisters of Charity in their great convent in the Rue du Bac in Paris she visited the place to see if that should be her destination too. However, she did not feel that she could leave home; her writing brought in some money, which was needed, and her mother craved her company. Louisa Taylor once wrote to her daughter, 'It is so selfish of me to keep you from a devoted life, for I begin to see that you are more likely to be happy in a convent than at home, but it is such a struggle to say: 'Yes, go – I think I can never say so'.[2]

Miss Taylor had another occasion when she needed to write to Newman, not about Catholic journalism but about her sister who was an Anglican nun. Emma Taylor was

Sister Phoebe of Miss Sellon's Sisterhood and seemed to have vanished from her convent, to the distress of Mrs Taylor. She had gone to the Sandwich Islands but no word had come to her mother or sister. Fanny wrote to Newman to ask that letters should be sent on via Dr Pusey who had directed Miss Sellon's congregation. Pusey obliged but made it clear that he thought he should not be used as a channel of communication between one of Miss Sellon's nuns and her family. Newman agreed that the arrangement had been 'very cruel' but he thought that Pusey did not wield the power over his convents which the Taylors attributed to him. Sister Phoebe was tracked down and was well and content with her work and her location, so that her mother's anxieties were allayed. Her sister was angered by the incident and must have noted for future reference how important a charge the foundress of a Sisterhood must bear: she was responsible for her nuns and had to keep a balance between preserving the necessary separation between daughter and family and observing ordinary decency and kindness.

It was about this time (1867) that Fanny Taylor was setting about founding a Congregation of nuns herself, an Institute to have as its work the care of the poor. She was admirably suited for the task. Not only was she sincerely devout, ready to give herself totally to God and his poor, she was intelligent and capable. Also she was courageous: she had gone out to Koulali, facing its hazards, and when she wrote her book about her experiences she had not minced her words but set out fully the dreadful state of the hospitals in the Crimea. In small matters she had spirit and a mind to persevere – hence her repeated application to Newman for his help in her journalistic endeavours.

It was Dr Manning who favoured the idea of a Congregation of active nuns who would devote themselves to the poor but the person who was to be the prime mover in the affair was Lady Georgiana Fullerton. She and Miss Taylor had been friends for some time; there was a great difference between them socially and a difference in age, Lady Georgiana being the elder by twenty years, but they had much in common too, with their writing, their piety and their charitable work. There might have been some difficulty in having so distinguished a lady as a kind of co-foundress – power struggles were not unknown in new congregations – but it says much for the goodness and good sense of both ladies that all worked out well. Fanny Taylor had her times of self-doubt (and she would have been unusually conceited if this had not been the case) but she did not shirk her responsibility as Mother Foundress.

In 1868 she sent Newman her translation of some meditations from a French text and he gave her his volume of verses in return, saying he hoped her plans were going well. These were the plans for her order which was to be called The Poor Servants of the Mother of God. In the February of the next year Louisa Taylor died and Newman sent her daughter a comforting letter, which she badly needed. She had hoped her mother would become a Catholic and her sorrow at the bereavement was increased by this disappointment and was perhaps compounded with guilt, for she had after all, left home to begin her real life's work and her mother had always made great emotional demands on her. Thereafter she did not correspond with Newman but turned to nearer advisors when she needed to. She had long had friends and directors among the Jesuits and her order was to be guided by them and to adopt Ignatian spirituality. One Jesuit in particular guided the new community, a Father Dignam. In later years Fanny Taylor, now Mother Magdalen, wrote tributes to both the people who had been such a powerful force in helping her set up her congregation. She wrote a *Memoir of Father Dignam* and a book called *The Inner Life of Lady Georgiana Fullerton*. She wrote them towards the end of her life, when she was not so burdened with labours and travels, but it is remarkable that she accomplished some more literary work. Earlier in 1875, in the very midst of her activities, she wrote three stories with religious themes, to be published together in one volume.

As well as taking help from individuals, Mother Magdalen looked to other Congregations of nuns abroad in order to learn from their lives and their work. Her own Sisters first tried to make a living by needlework and then decided to run a laundry, work that needed great organisation and, in those days of elaborate starching and ironing, very specific skills. The Servants of the Sacred Heart of Jesus and Mary in Antwerp were already succeeding with laundry work and she sought their advice and teaching for two sisters who went to Antwerp to become proficient in specialised ironing. The laundries that were set up in England made the sisters self-supporting, exactly Mother Magdalen's aim: although they had wealthy patrons who had been interested in the new congregation by Lady Georgiana, they were to be independent. Moreover, they were not required to bring a dowry when they entered the convent. The Poor Servants took in working-class girls who had a religious vocation and there was one class of sister, not, as in some Congregations, choir nuns and lay sisters. The very first little group who had rented rooms in Tower Hill had consisted of Fanny Taylor herself and three working-class women. As for the poor they served, the foundress made the splendid statement that they were not merely people to be helped but were 'a striking image of Jesus himself.'

The Congregation that provided the model for the new Institute in its inception was a Polish one called the Little Servants of Mary. In 1867 Lady Georgiana obtained their rule and suggested that it would serve the English aspirants well and in 1869 Miss Taylor (who had not yet taken vows and a Religious name) journeyed to Posen in Poland. She had her difficulties, knowing French but no German, let alone Polish, but she visited the convent she sought and got back despite misunderstandings, poor trains and the temporary loss of her carpetbag. She was as intrepid as Miss Giberne. The Polish Congregation ministered to rural poor people, not to the urban poor, and Miss Taylor was right to set up her own Institute rather than to affiliate with a distant foreign one.

Her new Congregation soon grew and developed, with good relationships with bishops in several dioceses. Houses were first set up in London, where a laundry was attached to such institutions as orphanages and refuges for women. There were also smaller convents in districts such as Soho, whence the sisters visited the poor in their houses. One account of the spread of Mother Magdalen's convents gives a summary that shows how amazingly rapid was the growth, and how extensive their work.

> By 1900, the year of Mother Magdalen's death, they had women's refuges in Streatham, Soho, Brentford and Liverpool; orphanages in Roehampton and Brentford; charge of a home for the elderly in Dublin and Rathdown Union Workhouse; a hostel for working girls in Paris; schools in Rome and Cork and, their most ambitious undertaking, a free industrial hospital in St. Helen's, staffed by the sisters.[3]

Mother Magdalen was delighted to found convents in Ireland because its people had been dear to her from the time that she had observed the Irish nuns and the Irish soldiers in the hospitals in the Crimea and had been encouraged by their example to become a Catholic herself. She wrote essays on Ireland and the Irish that show her esteem for that country, she sent her nuns in England to care for their emigrants and she established a network of contacts in Ireland to recruit postulants. Newman would have sympathised with her feelings for, despite the shabby treatment meted out to him by some bishops in the matter of the Irish University, he enjoyed his visits to that country and gave it as his considered opinion to Gerard Manley Hopkins (when the latter was harried and wretched, teaching in Dublin) that if he, Newman, were an Irishman he would be in heart a rebel. Mother Magdalen Taylor thought the English had treated the Irish ill and set out to redress the injustice. Newman added in his letter to Father Hopkins that the English and Irish characters were very different. Fanny Taylor, born and reared in that very English setting, a parsonage, had found any differences no trouble at all. She had a natural affinity with all things Irish.

A photograph of the foundress in age shows a very large woman, tall and bulky. Her size makes her look formidable but in fact she was not a grim matriarch, but was extremely sympathetic with her nuns. Many were very young, unlettered, needing encouragement as well as training and Mother Magdalen gave them unstinting personal concern. She watched their health, fostered their talents, looked to the details such as the need for young girls from England or Ireland who were toiling in the laundry or at the housework to have snacks of bread and butter between meals. Convents were then strictly hierarchical and the model for the Superior, still more for the Foundress, was that of a mother who was provider and a kind of gentle but all-powerful ruler. Mother Magdalen was 'Mother' not only in name.

The spirituality that she fostered was very direct and appealing. The centre of her vocation was her faith in the Incarnation. As Mary made her assent at the Annunciation and then gave the incarnate Word to the world so she sought to let Christ be born in her heart and to give him in the works of love. This is what she taught her nuns and it was not in the number of the laundries and refugees and hospitals that the congregation would succeed but in the quality of their hearts' response. Fanny Margaret Taylor was a remarkable woman both in her achievements and in her spiritual insights.

Newman had much more to do with another foundress, called Catherine Ann Bathurst. His friendship with her and his correspondence lasted over many years. The two women offer a study in contrast. There were times in Fanny Taylor's life when she must have thought that she did not know where she was going – in the time she tried the Anglican Sisterhood when she was very young, when she felt caught in her duties at home and when her spirit quailed at the problems before her as she began her foundation. In general, however, her life proceeded steadily and was all of a piece. She knew she would be a nun and that her work lay with the poor and every piece of training and experience that came her way proved to be useful. Lady Georgiana appeared as a friend at the right time, her literary endeavours made her influential and provided money, both writing and working for the poor made her known to priests who could and did assist her. Catherine Bathurst wanted to be a nun, from her girlhood, but she spent years not knowing exactly where her niche was. She was a worrier by nature and she needed steady affectionate counselling to be able to possess her soul in patience.

She was the daughter of General Sir James Bathurst, the son of the Bishop of Norwich, and of Caroline Stuart who was of aristocratic birth. She had one sister and three brothers who all became clergymen. One brother, Stuart Eyre Bathurst, ten years older than Catherine and a powerful influence on her, went up to Christ Church in 1834 and then became a Fellow of Merton College. In 1845, the year of Newman's conversion to Rome, he took the living of Kibworth Beauchamp in Leicestershire and was appointed Registrar of the diocese of Norwich. It was clear that a distinguished career in the Church of England was opening up for him but in 1850 he was received into the Church of Rome at the Birmingham Oratory and entered there as a novice the following year. His sister Catherine also became a Catholic in 1850, at the age of twenty five, received in London by Father Brownbill. It was through Stuart that she was introduced to Newman and their long friendship began.

She found it difficult to be at home because her sister harried her about her religious beliefs and Newman undertook the task of soothing her agitation and trying at the same time to prevent a total rift between the sisters. This pattern, of letters sent to cheer and support a very sensitive and scrupulous person, was to continue for years. Miss Bathurst came to Birmingham, where Newman and his first Oratorians were established at their first Oratory house in Alcester Street and started a parish school for girls. This is the other side of Catherine Bathurst – in work for young people she was extremely efficient, cared for them tirelessly and had an excellent head for management. Outwardly she was more than ordinarily competent and inwardly she was very tender. Her brother made one false start: he decided after a year that he had no vocation to the Oratory and left to be a secular priest. He became the parish priest at Stone, in Staffordshire, and a Canon of Birmingham.

His sister was to find it harder to find her place in the

Church. She left Birmingham to join a group of convert ladies who were forming a conventual Community round a Miss Elizabeth Lockhart. This was at that time not a Religious Congregation properly speaking and Newman felt that such a community was what his 'child', Catherine Bathurst needed. It would lead her to 'higher things' but was a 'gentle and kindly support'.[4] He also said, speaking of Miss Lockhart's community and of Miss Bathurst's suggestion that she should try her vocation at Loughborough with the Rosminian Sisters that it was not unreasonable to think that there should be communities of women like the Oratorians 'whose bond and principle of action is, not *mere* obedience, but personal attachment'. 'I think', he told her, 'you are equal to this – I doubt whether you are equal to a simple Religious rule'.[5] She did, however, go off to Loughborough but she did not find her vocation with the Rosminians and she returned to Miss Lockhart.

Her community was in Greenwich, called the Sisters of Charity of the Precious Blood, and were invited by Dr Manning to move from there to Bayswater; Sister Mary Philip Bathurst, with one or two companions, was sent back to Birmingham to help with the girls' parish school. A formal letter went from Newman to Bishop Ullathorne in December 1856.

We hope in the course of the next half year to apply for the Government aid for our Girls' School. The certificated teacher whom we think of employing is our friend Miss Bathurst who knows the Oratory so well – sister to Mr Bathurst at Stone, but, as she appears to belong to Dr Manning's Greenwich Convent, I feel it is necessary to apprise your Lordship of the arrangement we are making with her before concluding it.[6]

Her help was invaluable in the big Oratory parish, full of organisations for the support of the needy in Birmingham. Sister Mary Philip in fact started the orphanage there and got it on a good footing. However, again she moved, this time to try her vocation with the Third Order Dominican nuns at Stone. She must have known them initially through her brother Stuart. Her health was not good at the time she entered at Stone and her stability and peace of mind were shaken when she was there by hearing of the death of her sister by suicide. Newman wrote at length, having read her sister's last letter which Catherine sent him, giving it as his considered opinion that the dead woman had suffered some derangement of mind. Catherine, orthodox, deeply devout, shaken, was not to think that she was to contemplate eternal life without her sister Caroline, but the grave event should deepen her sense of detachment as she entered on her Religious life. She was not to stay at Stone, however, for her health broke down. Her next move was to Ghent in Belgium. There she retained her allegiance to the Dominicans by becoming a tertiary of that Order and in time she gathered other tertiaries round her, started a school for girls and began a conventual Third Order community. As Sister Mary Catherine – her baptismal name was that of the great Dominican St Catherine – and wearing her white habit, she visited England and came to Birmingham again to see Newman. Eventually her nuns came and settled in Harrow, running a girls' school as they had done abroad.

These are her outward moves, her real vocation declaring itself after years of searching. Newman had little to do with her convent foundation in Ghent, except that he advised her on the necessity of careful financing, getting his rich friend Hope-Scott to send her some money, but he was her best prop as she faltered sometimes along the way. He would not direct her life as a nun, bidding her seek counsel from her Religious superiors. She was a little like Mary Holmes, clinging to him when she had other counsellors at hand, but he was less severe with her on this score, partly because the mature Newman was less severe and rigid than his young self, and partly because Miss Bathurst really needed the comfort of a familiar guide whereas Miss Holmes was prone to assiduous demanding of advice when she had little intention of following it.

The guidance, in general terms, was always at hand. He was patient with her troubles but brisk when her conscience was over-tender. Doubts came to her, he once said, because she was yielding to imagination. At another time he told her to eat up her scruples with her breakfast bread and butter. At the same time, he was not dismissive or discouraging. He treated her as one who was sincerely set on the ways of spiritual perfection, potentially a high flyer. It is typical of his counsel to her that when he thought it best for her to stay with Miss Lockhart's familiar Community he indicated that this Community would lead her on to higher things. He made it clear too that set backs and false starts did not mean that God had abandoned her or that she was to think of herself as unsuccessful in the spiritual life. His letter sent when she had to leave the convent in Stone is typical of his sensitive counsel. He said:

> You sent me some time ago a Litany of resignation to the Will of God – and you know well that you, being you, can glorify that Blessed Will more by accepting it heartily, than by having fulfilled ever so strictly and excellently duties which were the abiding inspiration of your own will. You need not tell me how grievous the trial must be to you: still at all times and under all circumstances it is less grievous (at least so I feel myself) to know God's Blessed Will than to be in suspense about it.
>
> One thing I am sure of, that, tho' you might have been possibly happier in your own feelings, if you had obtained that state of life for which you have so long been praying, yet more useful you were not likely to be than you have already been during those years in which you served God out of that state.[7]

It says much for Newman that he did not try to keep her in Birmingham when she was so useful to the parish schools and the orphanage. In a later time when her school was prospering in Ghent (for she seemed able to build up an institution successfully, whenever she set her hand to such work), she nevertheless felt personally downcast. A letter came to cheer her, at Christmas time, with copious news of people she knew connected with the Oratory parish, some of it news of illness and death, as though Newman would remind her that she was not alone in that she was remembered and was not alone in suffering some trials. At another time, he paralleled his own life and sense of failure with hers. There is some self pity in this letter but also a deliberate setting out of a pattern of shared experience. Sometimes, writing to these ladies who tended to see him as an all-wise guide, protected from the self-doubts they felt in themselves, he reminded them that they were pilgrims journeying together.

> If we attain to the Life to come, it will be a joyful contemplation to understand how all our failures, borne well, tended to God's glory and our own salvation. I assure you, those persons like yourself, whom I know best, whom I have known longest, who have been most faithful to me and open with me, are so driven to and fro, that there seems a sort of law in Providence bringing it about. I do not mean simply locally driven, but in their aims, in their work, in their prospects. I feel it intensely of myself – my life seems wasted in attempting many things and doing nothing.[8]

The friendship between Newman and another founder of a congregation of Third Order Dominican sisters is the strangest of all his many friendships because of the difference in his background and hers.

Margaret Hallahan was born of Catholic and Irish parents in the East End of London, a year after Newman was born, also in London but in a very different household. Her father was amiable but shiftless and her mother, worn by poverty, ill health and irritation at her husband's inability to provide for her and their one child, vented her frustrations on Margaret, beating her frequently. Both parents died when she was a child and she went to an orphanage which did not offer much in the way of schooling and cast her on the world when she was only ten, the authorities believing that she had other means of subsistence. She then became a servant, first in the household of a Madame Caulier, the wife of a French emigré. When Newman was at school, proceeding to Trinity

College, establishing himself as a brilliant Fellow at Oriel, she was labouring in other people's houses, often beaten and bullied and made a general drudge. Newman's family was not always prosperous but an account of the early lives of these two could be used to demonstrate England's division into two nations.

Margaret Hallahan was a remarkably powerful character with plenty of fire and passion in her. She was deeply religious, from her cradle, and her beginnings in such poverty and neglect did not make her cross-grained or resentful but inspired her to be splendidly charitable. When she earned money as a servant she spent it on those who were poorer than she was and she impressed people, as she grew up, not only by her piety and generosity but by her style. Madame Caulier (who on the whole was cruel to her) said she was 'queenly and more fitted to command than to obey'. She was born to make her mark in the world.

Later on she had some employers called Thompson who were also capable of great insensitivity and at times downright cruelty to the young woman who worked for them. They moved to Belgium, to Bruges, and took 'Peggy' with them. She was then twenty four and convinced that she should dedicate her life wholly to God: one day she would be a nun but where she should go was not clear to her and her confessor, the Abbé Versavel, was a strict man who counselled waiting and patience. She made a private vow of chastity, kneeling on a kitchen chair amongst the cooking utensils at a time when she was alone and keenly conscious as she prayed that this was what she should do, and in 1835 she made her profession as a Dominican tertiary.

As an outward sign of her dedication she took to wearing a black dress, a Belgian close cap, and for the streets a large cloak with a hood. In this costume (much like that of the Little Sisters of the Poor) she became well known in Bruges as 'Margarita' she prayed in the church of St Jacques and who used all her spare time to visit the sick and the poor. Active, always going about and meeting people, she was fundamentally a most solitary person and, although she was known for her warm and caring manner and for ready speech in her own racy idiom, she was also a

woman of deep reserve. Later on she was to adopt as a
motto the phrase 'God Alone' and this was wholly appropriate. She had been left in childhood with very little
human love and her harsh circumstances made her seek
love at its source.

Eventually Father Versavel felt he knew where Margaret
Hallahan could serve best – back in her native England.
She had feared the move to Belgium and then she feared
the return to the country she now thought of as alien and
deeply antagonistic to her Catholic faith, but she went in
1842 encouraged and helped by an English lady and found
work in the industrial Midlands.

She brought with her very litle except a statue of Our Lady,
Flemish in style, which was her one dearly loved possession
and sought out Dr Ullathorne, then in charge of the
Benedictine mission at Coventry, who was looking for a
devout woman to be in charge of the girls in the parish
school and to help with parish visiting. They speedily liked
and trusted one another. He was one of the outstanding
priests of his day, honest, downright, a good friend and counsellor. He said afterwards that he was instantly impressed by
Margaret Hallahan's dignified and modest appearance. She
was tall and well built, with a massive head and fine features
and she was possessed of a good, expressive voice. When he
knew the person wthin her he had an admiration bordering
on reverence for the depth of her spritual life and the
breadth of her charity. When she looked back on those first
days in Coventry her recollection was of her initial surprise at
the idleness of some of the priests – there was so much work
to do among the sick and distressed in the slums there but
she met some of their pastors who were as she put it, content
to sit with their feet on the fender.

In time she gathered three companions who also
became Dominican tertiaries and the idea grew that they
might form the nucleus of a Religious Congregation. Dr
Ullathorne was ready to house them and to instruct and
the Dominican friars at Hinckley and Leicester were also
supportive. As in London and Bruges, Sister Margaret was
known for her devoted work especially amongst the most
needy and there were certainly admirers of this little

Sisterhood in Coventry. There were also those who took a snobbish line; when the little band of four had made their religious profession it was said by some that 'those lassies' were making as much fuss as if they were nuns and they were not respectable, there was not a lady amongst them. They continued, however, despite criticisms and despite the poverty and uncertainty that attended the venture. So the Congregation of Saint Catherine of Siena came into being. Then a further difficulty came their way when their guide Dr Ullathorne, was appointed Vicar Apostolic for the Western District and would leave Coventry for Bristol. In June 1846 he was consecrated as a bishop and Newman, a new convert then living at Maryvale and not yet gone to Rome to prepare for the priesthood, came to the ceremony with Ambrose St John and it was there that he met Margaret Hallahan. She had followed the story of his conversion with interest and gave him her prayers – what was more remarkable was that he engaged her sympathy and she felt she understood him. She would never have entered fully into his intellectual explorations, his doubts and his subtle reasonings but she had an intuitive grasp of the mind and character of the man.

The newly formed Congregation moved to Clifton to be near their guide, Ullathorne, receiving a great deal of help and hospitality on the way from established Communities of nuns, Dominican contemplatives at Atherstone, Benedictines at Colwich and the Visitation nuns at Westbury. Despite being dogged by poverty, Mother Margaret was set on building a proper convent, not buying a house and adapting it but seeing a conventual building rise with square cloisters, a public church and a cemetery. That she should take such a decision shows the power she now wielded and the responsibilities she now carried, for the establishment of her community, for housing, training and inspiring her sisters, and for setting up schemes to help the poor. uneducated and infirm in Bristol.

Of her many responsibilities she said, 'This is the way I see it, that Almighty God would do the work himself, and so he chose out the lowest instrument he could find, that no one else should have any part in it. You see he chose a sinful woman, a sickly woman, a woman without family, without friends, without education and without reputation. If he could have chosen anything viler he would, but he could not; so the work is his from beginning to end'.[9]

The one surprising adjective here is 'sickly' because every description of Margaret depicts her as powerfully built and having amazing unflagging energy. She had her afflictions though, trouble with her back since she injured it in her servant days carrying a heavy stove and a persistent skin condition that she could hide from others since it did not show on her face and hands. She added physical penances to these ills, actually wearing a hair shirt on her inflamed skin. Yet she radiated an energetic cheerfulness.

Once the Clifton convent was built Mother Margaret yearned for more postulants and in particular for educated young women. Since the Community was Dominican and traditions go back for centuries, retaining some monastic features such as daily recitation of the office in choir, she needed, as she said, 'Someone to see to the Latins and music'. With splendid irony, the snobbish critics in Coventry had their answer as the Community grew because there was an influx of well-educated and cultured convert ladies, many of them known to Newman.

The most important of these was Maria Spencer Ruscombe Poole (Minnie in the family), the daughter of a solicitor in Bridgewater, part of a large family who lost their mother early and whose father died when most of them were young adults. Her sister Elizabeth, who was intelligent and had a lively pen, left a short memoir of Minnie and described her as a bookish girl who read Greek and admired Homer's heroes. In order to strengthen her own muscles and to be more like the heroes she did gymnastics on her four-poster bed. She liked riding and reading more than ladylike pursuits and was known for torn flounces and untidy hair. Although she was a blue-stocking and somewhat of a tomboy, Elizabeth said that when the sisters were of age to receive attentions from young men, Minnie had more proposals than any of them. Elizabeth herself married a university professor, Joseph Anstice, and was very early widowed.

She returned home and she with Minnie and another sister, Lucy, became earnest Tractarians, reading the Tracts and Newman's sermons. They put themselves under the spiritual direction of Dr Pusey who, with the highest motives, gave them a very hard time: he was in a state of depression himself, preached austerity and disseminated gloom. Minnie looking back at her time as a Tractarian, wrote an account of her steps towards the Roman Church, *The Modern Pilgrim's Progess or the History of Puseyism in a Dream* which was published in the *Rambler* in 1853. Newman, referring to Miss Maria Poole as 'a gifted and deeply earnest lady,' quoted in the *Apologia* a passage from her article which describes the puzzlement felt by Tractarians when he was in the state of feeling unable to lead them as he had done and yet could not see his way to accepting the claims of Rome. 'All my fears and disquiets were speedily renewed by seeing the most daring of our leaders (the same who had forced his way through the palisade, and in whose courage and sagacity we all put implicit trust,) suddenly stop short, and declare that he would go on no further. He did not, however, take the leap at once, but quietly sat down on the top of the fence with his feet hanging towards the road as if he meant to take his time about it, and let himself down easily.'[10]

To continue her metaphor, she with her two sisters jumped the fence Romewards a short time before Newman himself. They then lived more cheerfully than before so that their aunt said she preferred their new religion to their old one. Lucy, perhaps weakened by the austerites she had undertaken under Pusey's regime, began to show the symptoms of tuberculosis, so the sisters went out to Rome for two years, for the warmer climate. Their path crossed that of Newman again, for he was in Rome preparing for ordination at the same time. So a long friendship with him began and another link was forged by Newman's friendship with one James Spencer Northcote. He was an Oxford graduate and a Tractarian who became curate at Ilfracombe where the Pooles lived. He married another sister, Susannah, and he and his wife became Catholics a short time after her sisters' reception.

When they came back from Rome, Minnie declared her intention of joining Mother Margaret's community at Clifton, having heard of it from Dr Ullathorne, and to everyone's surprise Lucy Poole (who was not cured) said that she too would enter the convent. They were impressed with their first meeting with Mother Margaret, and she felt she was gaining two earnest postulants, tall young women, with a standing and an education that would make them very useful to the Community. The accounts of the first meeting indicate that there was a certain awe on both sides; the Mother Foundress was half surprised at her new recruits and they were clearly in the presence of a holy and forceful Religious superior. Minnie became Sister Mary Imelda and Lucy took the name Mary Columba.

Sister Mary Columba did not look as if she was dying: she seemed to have a good physique and she had the bright complexion of the consumptive. However, she lasted only a year. Mother Margaret said to her once that she was sorry she should have to suffer illness and decline without the comforts of her home but the young Sister replied that she was so happy to be in the convent that she sometimes stretched out her hands to touch its walls.

Sister Mary Imelda did not have an easy time especially in her first years in Religious life. She was not stricken with disease like her sister but she had the kind of constitution that needed rest and sleep enough, and this was hard to come by. Also she found the Dominican fasts difficult, Mother Margaret was all for penance and fasting but she was realistic enough to see to it that the main meal was ample and moreover she knew about cooking and could see that the convent cook was up to the mark. Sister Mary Imelda, unfortunately, was one of those who simply cannot take a large meal. All the while she was bearing these physical trials she was working very hard: Mother Margaret tried her in various offices and behaved as though she did not quite trust her in the responsibilities she laid on her. This was really because she wanted to make sure this young woman was not acting out of affection for herself. Sister Mary Imelda was too single minded to be deflected from her obedient path and in time she became the foundress's right hand. There was something heroic about Minnie Poole, though she did not resemble in appearance the Greek heroes she admired since she peered shortsightedly through spectacles. There was genuine love between these two women, different as they were in background (Mother Margaret expressing amazement that anyone should have a partiality for 'those old heathen') and chastened as they were by the thoughts of the dangers of too close and selfish a friendship.

The Pooles were not the only recruits who were educated converts and acquaintances of Newman. There was Susan du Boulay who lived at Clifton with her aunt, Catherine Ward, and who was received into the Church by Newman in 1850. She had a friend, also a convert, called Augusta Theodosia Drane, a person whose stately christian names were not matched by her surname. This young woman was both devout and very clever, with more of a literary turn of mind than the clever Minnie Poole whose talents were for music, philosophy and Latin. The two friends entered the Clifton convent together in 1852, Susan becoming Sister Mary Gabriel and her friend Sister Frances Raphael. Another young woman known to Newman had entered the year before. This was Elizabeth Moore, the sister of John Moore who became the President of Oscott; she was described by Mother Margaret as an Oratorian since she was directed to the convent by Newman's Oratorians. A sister from another Congregation who met her said she was 'a little creature of great sanctity and splendid views.'[11] Her Religious name was Sister Agnes Philip. All these women were marked out from the start as likely candidates for important offices in the new Congregation. Education and brains were of no account without religious fervour but these sisters were clearly useful additions to Mother Margaret's flock on every count. There was a generous spirit in the Community that welcomed talents and did not think it favouritism when someone like Sister Mary Imelda was early taken up and loaded with responsibility.

These educated recruits admired the foundress, especially for what was described as 'her noble liberality and boundless benevolence'. She loved them but occasionally found them, educated as they were in the mores of the upper middle class, finicky and bothered about trifles. There is an echo of this in a story about a visit to the Benedictines at Colwich in Staffordshire where the Abbess was celebrating her Jubilee. A decorous little concert was given and at the end of it Mother Margaret was asked to sing. She took a favourite hymn, one to Mary, from her pocket book and one of her own nuns, anxious that all should go well, offered to pitch the note. She received a little push and the reply, 'Get along with you, I'll sing to my Mother by myself.'

On another occasion, visiting the Westbury convent, she shared a half hour of spiritual reading with her hosts. They were accustomed to do this reading together and then expressed their thoughts on the passage. Mother Margaret listened to each well-bred utterance but when she was asked to say what had brought her profit, she surprised the Visitandines with the reply, 'La, Mother, just no profit at all.' She was very reserved about her prayer, very simple and direct. She did not understand the recommendation given in books to place oneself in the presence of God, saying that she was always in His presence and she said of making a 'composition of place,' for instance when making a meditation on the Annunciation, that she would rather do some useful praying for the souls in purgatory than bother about where she would put a flower-pot in the picture.

Newman corresponded regularly with the Dominican sisters he knew, particularly with Sister Mary Imelda Poole and Sister Mary Gabriel du Boulay and he liked everything he heard about the community at Clifton. He wrote to one of his protégées, Miss Munro, in December 1851: 'It is a really good community and a sure gate to heaven.'

He did have direct contact with Mother Margaret too. He started to write to her when troubled with the protracted worry of the Achilli case and began by writing to Sister Imelda to ask the prayers of her 'good Mother'.[13] Mother Margaret responded with enthusiasm and combined prayer with action, having her favourite Belgian statue of Mary carried in procession for three days. Her personal prayer was simple and she was reserved about it but for public prayer she gloried in processions, singing, outward shows. She found English Catholicism shy and cold and longed too to gather in all the poor she laboured amongst to services and processions that would colour and warm their lives and increase their faith. She and Newman sent letters, he claiming that it was too much to ask for an acquittal and he could only ask for a moral victory and she scolding him for his lack of confidence in the Mother of God. He was to promise to go to Clifton to carry her statue in procession and preach if he was acquitted and to all this he replied humbly, 'I know well I am an unbelieving old beast and so perhaps in this instance.'[14] In the event they were both right: he was not acquitted but he did gain a moral victory and was not sent to prison, and for these mercies he could thank those who had prayed so earnestly on his behalf. He would not go to Clifton to carry the image in procession since the original conditions, set out by Mother Margaret, had not been fulfilled. He was not, however, rude about her dear Belgian statue, as was Father Dalgairns of the Oratory, who told the owner plainly that it was ugly.

She went on urging Newman to visit them at Clifton and meanwhile she had done him a signal favour by talking about him to Ullathorne. A suspicion of converts was not uncommon and Ullathorne distrusted Newman, believing that as an Anglican he had resisted the bishops. A brilliant, successful, fighting Anglican who had come over to Rome was surely a dubious Catholic. Mother Margaret held a very different view of Newman. She wrote once, 'I am so sorry for Dr Newman, it seems as if he could not do right, do what he will. It will all be known when he is dead.'[15] She also used the word 'submissive' of him. All this she conveyed to Ullathorne, speaking with her usual force, and he respected her opinion. It was important to Newman to have this distrust of himself removed: Ullathorne came back to the Midlands in 1848 and became the first Bishop of Birmingham two years later, so that he was Newman's bishop. Newman acknowledged Mother Margaret's intervention and Ullathorne endorsed her opinion more and more as he came to know the man he had distrusted. There was a general move to the Midlands. The Dominican Community first opened a house at Longton in the Potteries, so dismal a manufacturing area that Mother Margaret called it the fag-end of the world. When Sister Frances Raphael who, like Minnie Poole, had had plenty of exercise as a girl complained of the confinement of space at Clifton and said she yearned for a rat-hunt, Mother Margaret said she would find plenty of rats at Longton, in the cellars of their convent. Later they moved to Stoke, but set up their main house at Stone, near Stafford. Father Ambrose St John visited them in the earliest days at Stone and urged Newman, who was then in Dublin, to visit the Community as he had promised to do or disappoint Mother Margaret greatly.

> She is very wrath against you, says you have more to do with her convent than any others, that they have all prayed their knees off for you, and you have not kept your promise, and she wont pray any more till you come. You are to be sure to be at the opening of their new church at Stone, and that you are to stay for two days at least. I let her say what she liked about you, for she is a regular old brick. I am quite in love with the old lady.[16]

Newman promised to preach at the opening of the church, 'though I have to come from Connemara or the Giant's Causeway'[17] and he did come over specially from Ireland for the ceremony on 3 May 1854. Ullathorne presided and Newman preached. Mother Margaret did not feel she had seen him enough on the great day and urged a further visit, but he was not to be drawn, not even for the professions of more Oratorians.

Their correspondence continued; it was spasmodic but always cordial. Letters from the two of them laid side by side present a study in friendship and a contrast in style: his are in the scratchy, neat hand of a scholar and hers are ill spelt, curiously punctuated and in a sprawling hand that fills the paper and looks as though it will spill off it. He always asked her prayers and those of her nuns, especially when he was in trouble, and she responded by sharing financial anxieties: 'Excuse all this but I feel and think I am writing to a father and true friend who knows what anxieties are.'[18] She was delighted when the first parts of the *Apologia* came out and sent her congratulations to 'Dear Respected Dr Newman,' pleased 'that you are humbling that very vain man.'[19]

Meantime her Congregation was being ever more firmly established. She wanted it to be a real part of the great Dominican Order with its Rule acknowledged as fully Dominican and this involved a long legal process; it involved discussions with the Fathers of the English Dominican province, a visit to Rome by Margaret Hallahan herself and much paper work. The Poole sisters helped initially by translating the Rule of the Second Order Dominicans, the enclosed and contemplative nuns, from French and from Latin. Sister Mary Imelda and other sisters helped later with much translating of Latin documents.

One result of the affiliation was the granting of the privilege of reciting the Divine Office every day in choir and this applied to the whole Community since Mother Margaret did not separate her Sisters into choir nuns and lay sisters. Even with the influx of educated women it must have been difficult to set up the recitation of the Office in Latin, and it must have been done in part with love and reverence but without total understanding.

There was no lack of candidates and other women known to Newman joined Mother Margaret's Dominicans. One was Lavinia Wilson, the convert who had been an Anglican nun. Another was Catherine Bowden, one of the daughters of Henry Bowden. She entered at Stone in 1868 and became Sister Mary Alban. Newman was invited to her clothing ceremony and said, 'if anything would carry me away from my "*nido*" here, it would be the claim which you and yours have on me for every the most affectionate manifestation of my interest in you and anxiety for your welfare,'[20] but he could say Mass for her at Birmingham and that was the greatest thing he could do for her. 'Katie

Bowden clothed' is the entry in his diary for 15 December. She was professed and spent nearly all her prayerful zealous life at Stone, living to the age of ninety six.

More Sisters meant new foundations and convents were set up at St Marychurch in Devon and at Bow in London; it was deprived Bow that pleased Mother Margaret more than a house near the sea and the pleasant, enervating, seductive Devon countryside. New foundations of course meant building and her plans for this have an interestingly double edged quality. When she wanted room for more poor, sick or orphaned unfortunates she would, to use Sister Mary Imelda's phrasing, stretch their gutta percha accommodation to the absolute limits. In time, and when she could, she planned big churches and solid convents. The mother house at Stone is large and imposing. This was part of her plan to make Catholicism visible in England, to give glory to God by public services. Like many Victorians, she set great store by buildings and was determined to have convents that looked like convents and churches that would impress by their size, their furniture, vestments and plate.

The Sisters' work was consolidated too. Stories of Mother Margaret's dealings with the poor she served are often about individual cases. The most famous is an anecdote about her conversation with a workman when she asked him what he did for his soul. The man was found later thoughtful and touched to the heart: he said he had never before met anyone who cared whether he had a soul. The work for the poor in time led to the setting up of institutions: for instance at Stone there was a home for women who were old and ill and also an orphanage.

With less enthusiasm Mother Margaret instituted a girls' school at Stone. She was not in favour of the higher education of girls and women and she feared that schools would mean incursions by state inspectors. Like many Catholics of the time she saw the state as the enemy of all that devout teachers wished to achieve – it was not an unnatural reaction from those who had known anti-Catholic suppression – and she did not glimpse Newman's vision of a Catholic laity who would influence public life at every level. With an endearing inconsistency, however, she once said that she would be so pleased if inspectors would find the Sisters' schools to be the very best.

In earlier days Elizabeth Anstice's little girl did not enjoy being taught by her Aunt Minnie: she found her strict and over pious. Aunt Minnie, having become a nun, had found her place in the world and did not need to be so rigid. She was acclaimed as a very good teacher indeed when she was employed in the convent school.

The evidence is thin for Newman's views on the education of girls. He did write a significant short letter to Catherine Bathurst, who had at that time set up her girls' school at Harrow, and it is tantalising that he did not expand on the ideas contained in this note, far more tantalising that the brevity of his critiques on some ladies' novels in that the subject is immeasurably more important.

He said: 'I cannot but be anxious about the issues of this tip top education of girls. Of course, as you are used to say, that high education excludes a number of evils, which else abound, but we may find ourselves out of the frying pan into the fire.'[21] The date of this is 1884 when the education of girls was advancing. It was not so relevant a topic when he was writing, in the fifties, the lectures on university education which were to make up the great, seminal book *The Idea of a University* which was published later. However, it is startling to contemplate the fact that this great educator expressed his theories solely in the context of education for young men. It is also a curious fact, given his interest in education, that he was not in touch with Religious Congregations of women whose sole work was education, though he took a personal interest in Catherine Bathurst and fleetingly met (and disliked) Mother Connelly who was an educator and an innovator. His dearest convent, Stone, did not consider education the main work for its nuns though, given the personalities and intellect of some of them, the Stone convent school must have achieved quality.

The foundation of this Dominican Congregation was a large work and it wore out Margaret Hallahan. In her last years she suffered every day: she was corpulent and very

weary, her back was painful and her skin broke into open
sores. Her last illness lasted six months and the pain in her
back was so acute that her nurses made her straps by which
she could rise in bed, her outstretched arms reminding
them that she was indeed on a cross. She died in May 1868.
Newman wrote to Sister Mary Gabriel du Boulay:

My dear Child,
What can I say to console you better than what you
must be saying to yourself, that your long sorrow is over,
and that now after her intense sufferings, your dear
Mother is at rest, or rather in heaven.
If ever there were persons who had cause to rejoice
and whose joy is but intermeddled with, not increased by
the words of a third person, you are they.
What can you all desire more than that your
Communities should receive so special a consecration as
is granted to you in the agony and triumph of such a
mother?
It is a thought to raise you and encourage you while
you live, and is the augury of many holy and happy
deaths.
Pray for an old man and believe me.
Ever Yrs affectly in XT
John H. Newman of the Oratory.[22]

It was Sister Mary Imelda Poole who succeeded to the
office of Mother Provincial, a person very different from
the foundress but, like Newman, one who could leap the
constricting bounds of class and culture to reverence a
woman who had no worldly advantages but who had
achieved a great work in God. The new Superior had made
her own sacrifices. Her sister said 'her love of demonstra-
tion and the rules of right reason had to be mortified when
she entered Religion and was considerably mortified.'[23]
She would have said, however, that she gained far more
than she suffered: she was thoroughly happy to be a
Dominican nun and she ever counted it an inestimable
blessing to have lived for years in close proximity to
Margaret Hallahan. She did not say that it was to live with,

talk to a saint, but her account adds up to that as her deeply felt opinion. Clever, quiet and disciplined she took up the burden of office. She wrote to Newman to say that she knew that Mother Margaret's regard for him was 'something special. She instinctively felt that you understood her, and as many did not understand her – she felt a freedom of soul with those who did – and could show her genuine self to them. You were one of those for whom she most constantly prayed and she took the most lively interest as you know in all that concerned you.'[24]

Sister Frances Raphael Drane had already published books of a religious kind and she was literary in her tastes and skills, far more imaginative than Sister Mary Imelda Poole. The two of them, very different in the tenor of their minds, were friends – for despite the general embargo on particular friendships, friendship like cheerfulness would keep breaking in. It was entirely appropriate that Sister Frances Raphael should undertake the writing of a biography of the foundress. The *Life of Mother Margaret Mary Hallahan*, published in 1869, is typical of Victorian biographies in that it is weighty and prolix and imparts more hagiography than biography. It is also skilfully done, giving a rounded, human picture of the woman it describes. Newman disliked books on holy people that cut them into morsels to describe them by separate virtues. The nearer one could get to the living person, the nearer to his or her living voice (as in letters) the more profitable the reading would be. The book fits his requirements. Mother Mary Imelda wrote at the end of the year it was published to say that it had already reached a second edition and that she was surprised, given its general popularity, that it did not effect more conversions. A letter came back from Newman to Sister Mary Gabriel which is in part an answer to Mother Imelda's (for letters and news were obviously shared, as Newman's friendship with the nuns was shared by the other Oratorians). His remarks on religious books are wise little treatise on writing for the purpose of evangelisation.

... there are two reasons for writing quite distinct from

conversion, and, considering all things, I prefer them to any other reason – the one is to edify Catholics. Catholics are so often *raw*. Many do not know their religion – many do not know the reasons for it. And there is in a day like this, a vast deal of semi-doubting. There are those who only wish to convert, and then leave the poor converts to shift for themselves, as far as knowledge *of their religion* goes. The other end which is so important, is what I call levelling up. If we are to convert souls savingly they must have the due preparation of heart, and if England is to be converted, there must be a great more of the national mind to a better sort of religious sentiment. Wesleyans, Anglicans, Congregationalists, Unitarians, must be raised to one and the same (what we used to call at Oxford) 'ethos'. That is the same moral and intellectual state of mind.... We cannot begin from the top, we must begin with the foundations.[25]

This life of Mother Margaret might well effect conversions but it was, judging by the accounts of the responses to the book, certainly levelling up.

He continued to keep in close contact with his friends at Stone. They made a point of remembering him on St John's day, just after Christmas. He wrote to Mother Provincial on this day in 1870 to say that he had sung the High Mass remembering 'all who should pray for me today, knowing you and yours were foremost in this charitable work.'[26]

∽๑๑๑∾

In 1857 Miss Giberne made a visit to England, stayed for a time in Birmingham and made other visits to old friends. Newman thought, from something she said, that she would call on his sister and he warned Jemima not to give her letters, pictures, samples of his handwriting or anything at all which would help in the compiling of biographical information. 'I can't help having the suspicion,' he said, 'that she means, if she lives longer than I, to write some account of me – which I should not know indeed then, but the prospect of which I cannot endure.'[1] Having thus, as usual, made her friends glad and also caused some irritation, she went back to Rome. She was now in her fifties, had a bad leg, and was as independent as ever, choosing her own way of life, painting, travelling as she chose. The last thing those friends would expect to hear was that she now intended to try her vocation as a nun.

However, she returned two years later with just such an announcement. Newman heard that she was coming and prudently warned Father Flanagan, one of the Oratorians, who was in Italy, saying, 'Miss Giberne will be coming to England, and perhaps will want you to chaperon her.'[2] Father Flanagan was to say that he could not promise to accompany her because the Father had not yet told him where to go and what to do. Then Miss Giberne wrote to the Birmingham Oratory with her great news that, as she had been praying at the Shrine of Galloro near Rome, she had a vivid intimation that Our Lady wanted her to be a nun and that her intention was to seek out a convent in England. She had an audience with the Pope who was very kind, promised to pray for her and advised her to try the Visitation Order.

She applied, however, to some Benedictine nuns in Rugley, in Staffordshire and to a similar convent at Atherstone, choosing them because they had perpetual adoration of the Blessed Sacrament. They would not take a lady of fifty seven who would find it hard to climb the stairs to the novices' cells at the top of the house. Pious and indomitable as ever, she hoped that she would cure her knee at St. Winifred's Well in North Wales. She next made an application to some Franciscan nuns in Taunton in Somerset but they too rejected her. Newman sent her sensible advice at this point. She had tried hard, to 'fulfil your sense of what is due to your belief that the Madonna bade you try to be a nun.'[3] She had, therefore, done all she could and would have the merit of making the sacrifice, even though it had not been accepted. The best thing would be to settle for another form of devout life. She might perhaps lodge in a convent or, if this did not suit her, there was an alternative.

> My own present idea is that you should try to get
> someone to live with you, and should live in a house,
> and paint and pray. If you put yourself near a church,
> you could be as often in it as you pleased. You ought to
> have a room for painting. In this way you would be of
> great use. You would not all at once find a person
> perhaps, who would suit you – but in time you would get
> a person who would really be attached to you; and who
> would be more and more so, year after year. You should
> spend all your money on yourself. I think you could be
> useful in this way, as well as comfortable. And you might
> give yourself a rule of life, if you choose. But I say all this
> of course, merely as throwing out ideas to you.[4]

This letter shows his knowledge of her – her need for an
affectionate woman friend, her propensity for not looking
after herself (she should live in a house, not a garret or some
rented rooms, have a room for painting and spend all her
modest income on herself). The last sentence is written by a
friend who knows that advice may well be rejected.

In fact she bethought her of the Pope's recommendation, applied to the Visitation convent at Westbury and was
accepted. She was to enter on the thirteenth of January
1860, and stayed in Birmingham for a time prior to this
solemn day. When visiting Newman just after Christmas
she spoke of intending to 'floor' her Superior when she
reached Westbury. Perhaps she had an attack of nerves and
spoke half in jest – she never could be moderate in speech,
whether she was enthusing, remonstrating, expressing her
likes or dislikes. Newman meant to interview her but he
had lost his voice so he followed up her visit with one of
the most severe letters he ever wrote. It was guaranteed to
pull up Miss Giberne sharply and shows his views on religious obedience.

> Written words are harsher than spoken, so you must
> made allowances as you read on. Please to bear what will
> give you pain; and invoke the Blessed Virgin.

The truth is, your conversation the other day about Westbury quite frightens me. your dispositions towards the place are not the right ones. Change them, or do not attempt what will infallibly be a failure, entailing pain on yourself and others.

St Philip tells us that the razionale is the source of all evil. Now, that you should fancy yourself interrogating and flooring your Mother Superior, is portentous. I think you must clean wipe out from your heart, as a sin, any intention to allow yourself even in *inward* criticism, or you had better not go.

I think deliberately, that, as a Catholic represses thoughts against *faith*, so a novice represses all *criticism*, if she be a good and true novice. As you would not allow yourself to tax our Lord with inconsistency, after the manner of unbelievers, so neither must you consent to any mental questionings of the acts of those, under whom you are voluntarily placing yourself. You must put down every such thought, every such imagination, by an act of the will.

Such strict and stern repression of criticism is as much involved in the vow of obedience, as is the extermination of all light thoughts by the vow of chastity. It would be more wicked indeed, but not more inconsistent, for a profligate unbelieving woman, some French novelist, or Italian red-republicaness to go to the Visitation, than for you as you showed your feeling the other day.

I think it is your duty to promise this mortification of your natural reason to our Lord, and to go to communion upon the promise, or not to attempt to be a nun....[5]

She should not be like Ananias or Sapphira, promising a whole gift and keeping back part. As for the severity of the letter, he said that sometimes charity is greatest in severity and promised to say Mass for her the next morning. She was stricken to repentance by this letter but not so stricken that she confined her reply to a humble admittance of guilt and a promise of repentance: her letter asked that she should look round the Oratory before she departed since she thought a book of hers was lodged on its library shelves. Newman replied that she could not go to the library but could be accompanied to the refectory and recreation room. He also reported that Frank had written to say that he had heard of Miss Giberne's plans, from her, and he expressed some annoyance. That Frank, the old flame, should be made aware that her faith and devotion had led to her present resolve might do him good – but she had better not write again.

She departed for Westbury and Father Neville at the Oratory said, 'She retired in full sail and tearless'. Did she, in her time at Westbury, have anything to do with the young professed nun, Sister Dominica Bowden? The two of them were as different in temperament as can be imagined, though in the same place and seeking the same goal. Miss Giberne's time there was not very long for by the spring the Superior, Mother Margaret Mary Weld, had said that she saw no sign of a Religious vocation in her. Newman, seeing that her heart was set on the Religious life, suggested that she should ask Reverend Mother where she had gone wrong, and perhaps draw from her a detailed response by putting certain questions. The questions that he drew up for her again show a most detailed knowledge of his old friend's character.

> Is it that I am too passionately fond of things, instead of being resigned – too absorbed in enjoyment, instead of denying myself spiritual consolations? Am I not prone to make particular friendships? Is my love deficient in reverence and obedience, and thus too human for the Religious state? Have I unintentionally put myself forward too much? Sung too loudly, read with too much emphasis, or in some way or another annoyed others? Have I shown an over desire for the joy of Holy Communion? Have I, from my love of you, Reverend Mother, got in your way, and thought of my own gratification rather than of your convenience?[6]

Perhaps Miss Giberne at Westbury was like a bird with coloured plumage, given to loud song and flapping wings but shut in a dovecote with much more sober-spirited birds. Obviously she had not been tempted to floor Reverend Mother but had developed an intense affection for her. Newman answered a letter from Mother Margaret Mary Weld and apologised for the anxiety she had been caused over the case of Miss Giberne. He had hoped that the Visitation, which was accustomed to take in elderly postulants, might suit and enable his friend to shake off habits she had acquired in her long years of independence in the world. The Pope himself had encouraged her and she had been 'so determined to submit herself'.[7] Poor Miss Giberne left, very discouraged, and stayed for a time with the Dominican nuns at Clifton.

This, however, was not the end of the matter. Casting about rather wildly, she thought of becoming a lay sister with the Carmelites and also considered the Assumption nuns, a Congregation founded in France in 1839. She then turned again to the Visitation nuns and entered a French convent at Paray-le-Monial, the very place where St Margaret Mary had had her visions of the Sacred Heart. Newman had his doubts and told Jemima he thought she would return to Rome, not staying either in England or in France. She did in fact receive the Religious habit at Paray and took the name of Sister Maria Pia, presumably because of her regard for Pio Nono. Newman was amused and began one letter, 'My dear Sister M.P., Not Member of Parliament, or much presented, or miserably placed, but Maria Pia'.[8]

When her novitiate was coming to an end she encountered further trouble and the letters from the Birmingham Oratory contained no more jokes and there was no bantering tone but much sympathy from her old friend and measured encouragement. The nuns were not anxious to admit her to profession, the Bishop made enquiries and poor Sister Maria Pia was subjected to a grilling: when Newman said she must submit to such a searching process because she was attempting a great thing she wrote on the letter, 'That is true it was terrible',[9] a brief and heartfelt comment, lacking punctuation. She stayed on at Paray for some months, not as a professed nun, and then transferred to the Visitation convent at Autun in 1863. Newman wrote with warm congratulations on Christmas day because at last she was coming into harbour: the nuns at Autun would allow her to stay and make her final vows.

Newman said to Jemima that he would still be anxious about Miss Giberne, so long had she been struggling and was so unlikely a candidate for the Religious life, had not he been impressed by her perseverance so that he felt that God's grace would keep her in peace. One Dr Northcote who knew both Newman and Miss Giberne had sworn he would become a Capuchin friar the day she was professed – the ecclesiastical equivalent of saying that he would eat his hat. The joke was on Dr Northcote. Newman also reported to Jemima that the Autun convent, although enclosed, had a girls' school attached to it so that their friend's talent could come into play.

The Birmingham Oratory behaved like Miss Giberne's family and promised to send out anything she needed, remedies for her rheumatism, paint and canvas, a stove. They had charge of her money and were in some doubt about directions: 'as to the £100', went one message, 'we have kept it back, because none of us can make head or tail of your letter and its directions. It is a mixture of Mr Wilberforce, Lady Georgiana, lace, francs, and I don't know what beside'.[10] They were to despatch money for her dowry. Had Newman had his way, she would have paid the convent less of her capital in one go so that the Oratory could have plenty in hand to send out what she needed and even despatch money from time to time to pay for extras. 'The truth is', he said, 'abroad they do not understand our mode of living – and they serve up dabs of meat, which are a mockery'.[11] However, she was set on giving a larger sum and Newman wondered if this would make her a more influential person in the convent. It is a curious comment on a Religious house where all were vowed to poverty and common life but where, obviously, background, friends, contacts and the size of the dowry determined standing.

Letters continued to her, full of news, sometimes by Father Ambrose St John or other members of the Oratory.

On the whole, Newman did not treat of spiritual matters ('I fancied you had sufficient advice where you are, and because I am so unfitted to give it')[12] but when he did he wrote as one getting on in years to a friend who was the same age and experiencing the same difficulties. 'What you say of your own difficulty in meditation, is quite what I should say of myself, if that is any comfort to you. I think the mind is weakened as one gets old, and cannot *hold* an idea any more than the muscles can hold a heavy weight. And then again, as the eyes get dim and the hearing dull, so in like manner the affections do not act on sensible emotions as they do when people are young. All this is very painful and unsatisfactory – but I trust it is not a sign of falling back. What I try to do is to live more in the sight of God, and to try to be acting to His glory. But you must pray for me that I do not get into a bad way – and that I may not do anything that may mislead you'.[13]

Practical help and suggestions abounded. He was sure she needed flannel for underclothes, to keep out the damp, and once a parcel of flannel went from the Oratory to someone at the house of the Oblates of Mary Immaculate in Tower Hill who was going out to Autun, all done by the complicated arrangements common to good Religious who want to save money. Newman distrusted the French climate as he did French cuisine and perhaps it was partly her foreign location that caused him to comment admiringly on Sister Maria Pia's spirit of penance as she lived on resolutely in her convent. He commented once on the solitariness of the Religious life, particular friendships being discouraged so that each person stood alone and he recognised her need for affection. However, despite loneliness and rhematism, she was cheerful and once, writing to Gerard Manley Hopkins (who was related to her) Newman said that 'Miss Giberne is very happy, I find at Autun'.[14] Her nuns, remembering her after her death, thought of her as vivacious and jolly.

She went on with her painting, sending pictures still to the Birmingham Oratory, and wrote to them regularly. Sometimes her letters upset the more sensitive because she indulged in what Newman called 'skits and gibes'. Father

William Neville was distressed by one of her effusions, which she clearly meant to be harmless and amusing, for she wrote, apropos of Newman's comment on the offending letter that it had caused him to start as if a gnat had stung him, 'I cannot think what he means I wrote an easy friendly letter and nothing more'.[15]

It was somehow inevitable that Sister Maria Pia did not stay forever praying quietly in her enclosure. She was made to enter into situations of turmoil and history caught up with her. In 1870 Garibaldi's troops over-ran Autun and drove the Visitation nuns temporarily from their convent, in Newman's phrase, 'frightening them out of their skins'.[16] It was Sister Maria Pia who was so shaken by events that she had a breakdown. Newman, seriously alarmed for her, wrote to Monsignor Place, the Bishop of Marseilles, a friend to both of them, to ask what could be done for her. Perhaps she could be escorted to Marseilles or to Geneva, provided with funds, and come on to England; in any event, Newman would bear the expense. In fact the Reverend Mother at Autun got her to a Visitation convent in Fribourg in Switzerland where she recovered her health. There was some talk of her visiting England before she went back to Autun where peace had been restored but this did not happen. Newman said he did not know whether to wish it or not. 'I thought it would be so great a wrench for you, when you were summoned back'.[17] Jemima Mozley was interested and anxious about her old acquaintance over the time of doubt and danger and, had Sister Pia come to England, she could have stayed in Derby at Jemima's house or with her sisters-in-law, Anne and Elizabeth Mozley who had a pretty cottage at Barrow, not far from Derby. The chance of seeing old friends seemed to be there on the horizon, but it vanished again.

Five years later, when Newman lost his best friend, Ambrose St John, Sister Maria Pia, who also counted Father Ambrose among her friends, was one of the first to have the news. Newman wrote her a longer letter after a short time, sympathising with her solitariness: 'you have no partner nor confidant in your sorrow, and have no relief as having no outlet of it'.[18] The grief that Newman felt at this death has often been described but with his grief was a strong disposition to be positive, to thank God for all that Ambrose had been to him and to meditate gratefully on all friendships. He wrote to this old friend, so loyal and good, if at times maddening:

> What a faithful friend he has been to me for thirty-two years! Yet there are others as faithful. What a wonderful mercy it is to me that God has given me so many faithful friends! He has never left me without support at trying times. How much you did for me in the Achilli trial, (and at other times), and I have never thanked you, as I ought to have done. This sometimes oppresses me, as if I was very ungrateful. You truly say that you have been [seen?] my beginning, middle and end. Since his death, I have been reproaching myself for not expressing to *him* how much I felt *his* love – and I write this lest I should feel the same about you, should it be God's will that I should outlive you. I have above mentioned the Achilli matter, but that is only one specimen of the devotion, which by word and deed and prayer, you have been continually showing towards me most unworthy.

He ended, 'I hope I don't write too small for your eyes'.[19]

Chapter Five

The Nunnish Ladies

The Benefactresses – Elizabeth Bowden, Lady Herbert of Lea, The 'nunnish ladies' of the Oratory parish including Lady Olivia Acheson; Eleanor Bretherton; Frances Wootten

It remains to see what more pious women ('nunnish ladies' in Newman's phrase) could do if they did not have a vocation to the Religious life. The married ladies had plenty to do at home and might do charitable work besides. The single, like Emily Bowles, found plenty to their hands, and many, married and single, wrote copiously, as we have seen. The parish might be a focus for all sorts of activities and there was also the call to almsgiving. Women had certain restrictions on their handling of money – the Married Women's Property Act was not passed until 1870 – and they were constrained by custom and by psychological fears and ties as much as by law. The matter is slightly touched on in some Newman family letters when Jemima, a young married woman, was debating whether she was right to make a contribution to a fund to help penurious Aunt Betsey. This was not a matter of charity but of justice, as her elder brother pointed out, but Jemima was initially kept back by a fear that as a Mozley she should not act with such independence. Her brother was firm:

It is quite preposterous that a married woman should have nothing to spend but on herself. (I am taking the lowest ground, as if John were out of the question – though you are a Mozley, you are a Christian) Can any

husband, who is good for anything, like his wife only to
have so much as she spends on herself? and if you are
bound as a Christian to spend on others as well as yourself, who has claims before Aunt? must we not be just
before we are generous? is it not a case of justice? ...
And when a certain sum of money has come to you virtu-
ally, I cannot see any impropriety ... it comes to this –
are you to give nothing to God of what he has given you?
I think you are quite right.[1]

Despite their lack of freedom in financial affairs, Catholic
women as well as men were astonishingly generous in their
almsgiving throughout the century. Cynics might observe
that, in an ecclesiastical system which was strongly clerical
and gave limited scope for lay involvement (a fact which
Newman strongly and publicly deplored) there was never
any embargo on a lay person's giving of funds. And the
funds came in, for charity, for the support of priests, for
building. People like Mother Margaret Hallahan initiated
the building of churches and so of course did bishops and
priests but it was the laity who put up the money.

Elizabeth Bowden, who was comfortably off in her
widowhood, was one of those who gave generously. She
had a church built in Fulham, as a memorial to her
husband. The architect was Pugin, whose ideas on church
architecture were clearly defined and given out as though
they were derived from Holy Writ: he believed that Gothic
was the only style that could be called truly Catholic. Mrs
Bowden had much trouble with him because he started to
put up a screen between the sanctuary and the nave and,
since she did not want it, she had it taken down. Pugin was
so offended that he refused to come to the consecration of
the church, at which Newman preached.

Newman himself was not on the side of Augustus Welby
Pugin. He himself preferred the classical style and he felt
that, as a follower of St Philip, he was right to favour the
Renaissance architecture, based on the classical, which
dated from St Philip's time: he said that to adopt a thirteenth century style would be absurd for an Oratorian as to
put on a Dominican's cowl or adopt the tonsure of the

Carthusian. It was not a question, however, of favouring one style rather than another but of opposing Pugin's bigotry. It was bigotry to maintain that only one style was suitable for a Catholic church for ritual changes and architecture must change with it. Pugin's churches were not always convenient for celebrants or for congregations, as Newman made clear to Miss Giberne, after had had been to preach at the opening of Mrs Bowden's new church, which he thought very pretty, but having the faults of Pugin. 'In details Pugin is perfect but his altars are so small that you can't have a Pontifical High Mass at them, his tabernacles so low that you can scarce have exposition, his East windows so large that every thing else is hidden in the glare, and his skreens so heavy that you might as well have the function in Sacristy, for the seeing of it by the congregation.'[2] At any rate, Mrs Bowden had succeeded in the removal of the 'skreen'.

She was a benefactress in smaller matters too, ready to provide furniture, food and drink, all that was needed for the greater comfort of the Oratorians in London. Father Faber wrote of her when they first moved to London and were housed in King William Street, Strand: 'Mrs Bowden flits about the house, visits me in my bedroom, inundates us with floods of devout Irish charwomen, groans over the dirt and is a positive mother and St Elizabeth of our Chiesa Nuova.'[3] It has ever been a characteristic of religiously minded women to cosset priests and Newman, as well as suffering too much devotion from admirers at times, observed many examples of this phenomenon. He wrote to a Lady Campden in 1857 about an overworked priest '... one Sunday some weeks ago, a lady who lives near, observing him tired after his morning mass, obliged him to come to her house, forced on him a very substantial meal, and obliged him to put off a sermon he was to have preached – So you see he is in more potent hands than mine.'[4] There is laughter just under the surface of this anecdote and the spoiling of clerics by devout ladies has sometimes been a subject for humorists and satirists (Dickens tackled it, for instance in *Pickwick Papers*, where old Weller complains of his wife's partiality for the

Shepherd) but overworked priests could truly be needy and the Mrs Bowdens deserved gratitude.

It was the London Oratory, not the house in Birmingham, that she tended and both her sons were London Oratorians. Newman and Elizabeth Bowden never quarrelled but when there was division between the two Oratories she became in some degree alienated from her old friend. There was not the same amount of free communication between them as there had been in the forties.

Another great benefactress was a lady who was higher in the social scale, Lady Herbert of Lea, who was born Mary Elizabeth Ashe à Court. She married the famous Sidney Herbert, the son of the Earl of Pembroke who became a statesman, the Secretary of War at the outbreak of the Crimean War, the friend and the supporter of Florence Nightingale and the reformer of the Army's medical services. He was an affable, handsome man and his wife too was handsome, statuesque and dark-haired. He was made Baron Herbert of Lea towards the end of his brilliant, brief career – for he died at the age of fifty one, worn out and, as some said, harried by Miss Nightingale. He was an Oriel man, the pupil of Hurrell Froude so that he was acquainted with Newman and made a point of visiting him in Rome in 1847, with his wife. Newman liked and admired Sidney Herbert and was saddened when he heard that he was dying, thinking of him all day and praying for him. After her husband's death Lady Herbert became a Catholic. She was received into the church by Henry Manning and kept up a correspondence with him for some years, though she said of him that, when he became Archbishop of Westminster and then Cardinal 'he never seemed to care for me as before.'[5] Her abiding friendship was with another eminent priest who was eventually to succeed Manning at Westminster, Herbert Vaughan. Vaughan called her 'sister and mother' – she was twenty years his senior – and each guided and helped the other. His letters to her necessarily became more short and brisk as he took on greater responsibilities but he never lost his affection for her.

She was not, then, Newman's convert and she had priestly guidance in plenty, but she followed in the general path of the convert ladies in feeling that she must write to him at times. Her rank brought her sorrows, when she joined the Church of Rome, for her seven children, after much legal wrangling, were made wards in Chancery so that they should be kept from conversion to their mother's faith. One daughter, Mary, did become a Catholic, marrying the writer Baron Friedrich von Hügel. It was chiefly about her children that she consulted Newman, wanting prayers for her second son, another Sidney Herbert who was his father's living image and wanting to share her anxieties about her eldest, George, who became the 12th Earl of Pembroke. It was not simply that he did not share her religious views – she feared that the young man was a sceptic and a scoffer about Christianity in general. Both Newman and Vaughan urged her to prayer, reminding her of St Monica who sorrowed over and prayed for her son Augustine, but eventually Newman came out with a considered opinion and a practical policy in a letter that might give counsel to many a Christian parent.

Dearest Lady Herbert,
I have been thinking much about my best way, were I you to affect your dear Son, and to secure his restoration, and I feel strongly, though it may seem cruel, that it is decidedly the best treatment to leave him quite to himself. I take a great responsibility on me in saying this – for supposing this way did not succeed, I should be laying myself open to the charge of having my do-nothing policy brought about that sad result. But, you know, it frequently happens that medical men say of a patient – 'Leave him alone and give him no physic – let nature act.' Now I think controversy is Lord P's *food*. He is supported, as on crutches, on asking and urging difficulties on the one hand and demolishing answers on the other. The best hope of his changing lies in his having no one to combat with him. Especially no one whom he loves or knows about. There is no *substance* in his scepticism, and this is most likely to come home upon him, if

silence is offered to his restless activity of mind, and he has nothing brought before him to make him think that he is an object of anxiety to others. I doubt whether he would like to have his own way. Excuse this, but I feel it strongly – it gives him the best chance.[6]

Lady Herbert followed other convert ladies in another respect, that she busied herself with a great deal of religious writing. She wrote one novel, called *Edith*, which Herbert Vaughan read and stigmatised as too autobiographical for public consumption, and a great many saints' lives and religious biographies. One book, called *Three Phases of Christian Love*, typifies her work. It consists of the life of St Monica, of a Sister of Charity called Mère Devos and of Mademoiselle Victorine de Galard Terraube. All these little biographies are translated from French originals but the two not-so-well-known lives have been freely translated and added to briefly. The choice tells a lot about Lady Herbert. St Monica would clearly interest her. Like Lady Georgiana Fullerton she greatly admired the Sisters of Charity and Mademoiselle Victorine, like herself, was a society lady, at a slightly earlier date, who strove to lead a strictly prayerful life in the midst of society's demands and distractions. The tone is unremittingly pious, lending some colour to the unkind remark of a twentieth century writer on the Earls of Pembroke that 'Liz Herbert since her widowhood had been received into the Roman Catholic Church, and, as is so often the case with converts, was more Catholic than the Pope.'[7] In the life of Mademoiselle Victorine there is a passage that harks back to earlier times (carrying an echo of the thinking of the quartet at Baddesley Clinton): 'sometimes, on looking round our drawing rooms, we are tempted to ask, "What have become of the modest, gentle, pious English girls, who in olden times, distinguished us from other nations?"'[8] The reference to England marks this out as a comment by Lady Herbert. She ends the passage, 'May they return to the good old paths of loving, dutiful submission, modesty and reserve.' This is a curious addition from someone who was a friend to Florence Nightingale who would have achieved very little if she had kept to paths of dutiful submission.

Lady Herbert herself, undoubtedly sincere, devout and striving for Christian humility, could take the peremptory tone of an aristocrat. She wrote to Newman in June 1874 about a Mrs Morritt who wished to be received into the Church. 'May I venture to implore of you to come and receive her *as soon* as you can?'[9] All was to be done in Lady Herbert's chapel and Newman could stay at her house. The words 'venture' and 'implore' betoken the consciousness that she was addressing an eminent priest but it was not usual to send for him in this way. He was ready to comply but as usual cried off from being entertained in London longer than necessary – and in the event Mrs Morritt put off her reception.

As a benefactress, Lady Herbert was splendid and when she had adopted a scheme she was decisive so that she was nicknamed 'Lady Lightning'. She lived in Wilton and looked for what she could do for the Catholics of Salisbury, the nearest city. In 1865 she immediately undertook the maintenance of the Salisbury Mission which meant in the first place that she paid for the upkeep of a priest by covenanting with the Bishop of Clifton to give £100 per annum for that purpose. Seventeen years before a generous local Catholic, Sir John Lambert, had given money for a church and it was built by Pugin. Lady Herbert found it dilapidated and she extended the building, renewed its furniture and vestments, gave church plate, statues and finally a new organ. Pugin's son was then asked to design a building in the same style, to be put up near the church to provide a Parochial School. Then, to staff it, she arranged that three Sisters of Charity should come to Salisbury, two to teach and one to do parish visiting: they were housed and maintained at her expense. Lastly, urged by the Sisters, she set up an Industrial School which was a boarding school for poor children where they could be trained in skills by which they could earn a living. Herbert Vaughan warned her to count the cost of this venture and she duly made prudent assessment and then launched her scheme. There were as many as one hundred and twenty five girls housed and trained in the Industrial School at one time in the 1870's.

Just as Mrs Bowden became 'a positive mother' to the London Oratory, Lady Herbert became 'the mother of the Mill', that is to Father Vaughan's college for missionary priests at Mill Hill in London. The chapel there has a chalice, a missal, vestments, paintings and a Gothic censer, all bought by Lady Herbert. And in a grander style than that of the lady who fed the tired priest she loaded gifts onto Herbert Vaughan so that he once said, 'You are like a Providence that never fails.'[10] She would have liked to provide Newman with fine dinners when he was in London but generally he hurried to the railway station the moment his business in London was done. Once, however, he kept a gaudy day, lunching with Mrs Fitzgerald and her family (this was the time that he charmed them with his affability) and dined at Lady Herbert's in the evening.

When Newman set up the Congregation of the Oratory in Birmingham he had it clearly in mind that in time his Oratorians should do more than parish work, should take up tasks, such as establishing a school or a university college, that the secular priests could not do. All the same, parochial work was very important and this was demonstrated unequivocally when he took his community to Alcester Street, right in the middle of the city amongst the small factories for press-work, for which Birmingham was famous. Little back-to-back houses surrounded the converted gin distillery which he leased in Alcester Street, Deritend. It was not an idyllic spot, set amongst dirt and smoke, traffic on the canals, a shifting population of poor operatives and their families. Ambrose St John, more in the spirit of one who faced a challenge than that of a grumbler said that they had been given the hardest town in England for their work. The Alcester Street chapel never wanted for a congregation – hundreds crammed in for services and children 'flowed in for instructions as herrings in season'.[11] The youngest, employed in the press shops could only have schooling in the evenings so that the Oratorians had work crammed between seven and ten, with schools, lectures and confessions. Newman wrote to Miss Giberne in the Spring of 1849 to tell her how they were faring, about the people they were ministering to and the anti-Catholic prejudice that balked them.

> This is a dreadful trial on poor girls, who are looking out
> for service – it quite distresses one to convert them for
> this reason – it is throwing all kind of obstacles in their
> way – they don't get married – it is a dreadful problem,
> how best to provide for them. It obliges one to consent
> to their marrying Protestants. The poor factory boys
> seem to have no prejudice against us – many of them
> literally profess no religion, and numbers of them have
> not been baptized. We have a good many Irish come to
> us, very few indeed in our district, but they have found
> us out, and come to us though we cannot go to them.[12]

The phrases show what a thin line there was between
providing sacraments, religious services and instructions,
and carrying out what would now be called social work.
Newman's mind must have gone back to his Anglican
parish days, to his earliest time at St Clement's and work at
Littlemore when his sisters taught the children and ministered to the sick and poor. Alcester Street was a bigger
challenge than that parochial work had been and women
would be immeasurably useful especially in working
amongst the children, young women and girls. The idea
was developed in another letter to Miss Giberne three
months later.

> We are hoping to set up a girls' school here – and intro-
> duce if possible, some, not nuns, but nunnish ladies ...
> to be a sort of female oratory or missionaries. We want a
> house of refuge for Catholic girls out of a place – and a
> general centre of instruction for women. Ladies would
> not only instruct etc much better than we could, but
> would relieve us of a vast deal of work.[13]

He wondered whether she would be interested in such a
venture and wrote by the same post to Miss Munro to suggest
that she should come to Birmingham, set up as a
schoolmistress or find other useful occupations. Needless to
say, Miss Giberne was all for setting out for Birmingham at

once but Newman put her off for the time being: he still had nunnish ladies in mind but prospects were uncertain. Just at this time some munificent donations came in for the Birmingham Oratory and a house (Newman called it their Lady House) was acquired in Warwick Street, near the Oratory in Alcester Street. The first ladies to be considered were Miss Munro, Miss Giberne herself and Miss Moore, the sister of John Moore, the President of Oscott. Miss Bathurst was already on the scene and Newman had hopes of the sister of Father John Cooke who had just joined the Oratory. The Woodmasons, converts from Littlemore, had daughters who might join but that would mean financial worry for the Oratory for they had no money to support themselves and their father would be only too pleased to ship them off to Birmingham so that he did not have to pay for them. There should be young women at the Warwick Street house too who would be trained as servants by the ladies.

There are really two schemes wrapped together here. The first was a simple one, to have devout, competent women who would come into the parish and help the Oratorians in parochial work, living near enough to the Alcester Street chapel and house for their work and for direction from the centre. The second was more complex and more controversial – to band these women together into some sort of organisation. Newman read the religious rule of the Filippine, Italian nuns attached to the Oratorian way of life and he asked Miss Giberne, when he was still in Italy to find out what she could, presumably of their mode of living. He not only held the existing Congregations of Religious women in high esteem, he took if for granted that the demands on obedience were of the strictest kind, as witness his severe rebuke to Miss Giberne when she was about to enter the Visitation convent. His own Oratory followed a different way of life, bound together by a respect and love for the Community so that they would endeavour to act together as one, but not bound by a vow. Friendship, getting on together, was essential to the Oratory's life. He said of St Philip, in a verse, 'Love is his bond, he knows no other fetter.' Could there not be an organisation for women, more flexible, more on an Oratorian pattern? This idea was never thought through and finally abandoned, Newman saying that he thought after all that it was better for women to be under vows.

There is an interesting document which names the nunnish ladies gathered together in May 1857. The first part is a short note to Newman in Miss Giberne's handwriting and in her flowery style:

> We the undersigned in all humility entreat our kind and indulgent father not to deprive our thirsting souls of the conclusion of his most attractive sermon on the comparison of the saints of different nations – but to continue it for our instruction, from where the bell interrupted it, viz: The Seraphic St Francis –[14]

Six ladies then signed, leaving a good space to the right of their signatures which Newman filled in with gentle personal allusions, which are not all clear to a reader now because in-jokes need careful annotation. Was Elinor French particularly ignorant or distrustful of Irish saints, and was Miss St John a new convert and shy?

The document reads:

Olivia Acheson	if she will contrive to hear me, sitting at home in her easy chair.
Elinor French	as soon as she can go through all the Saints of the name of Colman, Finian, Kieran, Kentigern and Kebby.
C A Bathurst	when her school can show a Saint younger than St Rose and wiser than St Theresa.
M Georgina St John	must learn first to chirp, and must have a little down on her wings.
Elizabeth Moore	when she has made and illuminated vestments of the Spanish, Italian, cockney and every other cut.
M R Giberne	if she will be good enough to canonise half a dozen on occasion, and give me their measure.

J H N[15]

This devout band eventually dispersed. Elinor French, with Mrs Wootten who was also in Birmingham were employed in the boys' school when it opened. Miss Bathurst and Miss Moore became Dominican nuns. Miss Giberne also entered Religion. Miss St John, a vicar's daughter and a cousin of Father Ambrose St John, has disappeared into obscurity.

Lady Olivia Acheson who was required to sit at home in her easy chair was told she should do so because she was a sick woman. She was a delicate, sweet, generous person who did not have much time to work in the Oratory parish since she died young. She and her sister, Lady Annabella Acheson, were the daughters of the second Earl of Gosford who had been Governor General of Canada and they lived with their father at Gosford Castle in Ireland. At his death they inherited a fortune of £15,000 apiece. This was in 1849, in the spring. Four years earlier they had become Catholics and had earnestly discussed the stewardship of the money they knew they would inherit some day; each sister made the other her heir and they promised they would give their wealth to charitable causes. They thought they might become nuns in some active Congregation and their great hope was to finance a hospital. Lady Annabella died four months after her father, in London. It seems likely that both sisters were tubercular.

Lady Olivia had known Newman for some time and was friend enough to advise him on the composition of his shirts and underclothes when he was setting off for Rome to prepare for the Catholic priesthood: she said that they were 'knit cotton' whereas he had believed they were wool. This explained why he had been cold in the winter – this was of course before Jane Todd the seamstress took his clothes in hand. She knew his good friend William Monsell and was intimate with Lady Georgiana Fullerton. Alexander Fullerton, adept at money matters, was her financial adviser and the executor of her father's will.

A priest who had been helpful to the Achesons in Ireland and who became their spiritual director when they became Catholics had settled in England. Dr Whitty was a talented man who had known Newman in his Anglican days, was deeply atached to him and was considering founding an Oratory in London. He was slow in making up his mind so that he was too late in entering Newman's little Congregation to be sent with the first batch of Oratorians to London. In any case Father Faber disliked him. Still he could not make up his mind: Newman noted with amusement and some exasperation that he was torn between England and Ireland, between serving the poor and cultivating the spirituality of Lord This and Lady That. He did not have an Oratorian vocation and remained a secular priest in London for some years and then became a Jesuit, eventually holding high offices in that Religious Institute.

Lady Olivia Acheson illustrates the difficulties of being a benefactor. She was of a most sensitive conscience (not for nothing was she a friend of Miss Bathurst's with whom she at one time shared the house in Warwick Street) and confided to Newman that she was not sure of the facts about her pledging of money. She had accepted her sister's money on the understanding that it would go in charitable works – but did this mean the expenditure of capital or income? She had made some promises to Dr Whitty, either to fund some charitable work he had in prospect or to pay him a pension as an Oratorian – but his place was not to be at the Oratory. Newman took the matter of promises seriously and wrote out fine-drawn arguments on what she could do to sort out past intentions and present justice. She could be assured that she owed the Oratory nothing. The matter was sorted to the satisfaction of all parties.

She cannot have done much work in the parish because of her poor health. What she did accomplish was the conversion of a female cousin who was so impressed by the way she bore her illness and faced her death. She died in March 1852. Newman, who witnessed her death, spoke the next day of her pain but also he recorded her steady desire to be as little trouble to others as she could. She seems to have been like Marianne Bowden, but somewhat weighed down by the responsibilities of wealth. Her will revealed that she had left a good sum to the Oratory.

When that Oratory moved from Alcester Street to

Edgbaston the parish layout and responsibilities were
different. The Hagley Road was not in the thick of a smoky
industrial complex, nor did the area have the stench of
poverty but this did not mean that their contact with the
poor ceased. Newman is sometimes compared favourably
with Manning who was concerned with social reforms but
Newman, working on a more personal and small-scale
plan, was not unmindful of the plight of the poor. He was
personably charitable, known in Birmingham for paying
bills at the doctor's on behalf of those who could not pay
and for paying fuel bills. And his Oratory worked amongst
the poor as well as amongst the wealthier class who popu-
lated Edgbaston. Birmingham had little provision for its
Catholic population, swelled by immigrant Irish: there was
Pugin's cathedral dedicatd to St Chad, right in the centre,
the small church of St Peter hidden away in Broad Street,
not far from the centre, and now there was the Oratory
Church and the Oratory House, with a small band of
priests. In general it was only the secular priests not living
in community who were responsible for missions, outposts
from the parishes, but the Oratorians were gladly admitted
to the work. There is a touching story of parish affection,
shown at an early stage of their coming to Birmingham:
when Newman and another priest set off to Bilston in
Staffordshire to help the local priest in the midst of an
epidemic of cholera, the parishioners were griefstricken,
thinking they were going straight into infection and
certain death. They returned soon, unscathed, to local
rejoicing. The same local affection soon flourished in
Edgbaston and in their other territories.

   Some details of the work, though no clear and complete
account of what went on, are written down in notes
prepared by Father Edward Caswall. In 1855 he listed the
works they had in hand: the Mission at Harborne (a suburb
next to Edgbaston), the care of the Workhouse, the Gaol,
the Lunatic Asylum, the Mission at Smethwick, Schools at
Smethwick and Edgbaston.[16] Smethwick lies between
Birmingham and the Black Country, described by Father
Caswall as 'the dismal abode of flames and desolation.' He
also described Smethwick itself: 'in Smethwick was

constructed the first of those wonderful engines of modern times which are fast revolutionizing the world – I mean the steam engines.' There were forging and foundry works there with many poor workmen, and there were reckoned to be three hundred Catholics.

In 1859 he gave details of the schools. 'Our day Schools both of boys and girls have shown a steady increase. In the Report now preparing for the Education Commission at the request of the Bishop, the number of boys belonging to the Day School is given as 81 – of the girls and infants as 120. In the same Report the girls and young women in the evening school are given as 50.' It is not clear whether this account is of the schools in Edgbaston or also of the provision in Smethwick. There had been an evening school for boys but it had petered out. In the Sunday Schools there were eighty-five boys and sixty-five girls. The management of the girls' Sunday School was under the same person who ran the weekday school, that is Miss Bathurst, surely the most useful of the nunnish ladies. She is described as 'the heart and soul of nearly every good work' connected with the Oratory.

Other ladies gave their aid. A Mrs Poncia is often mentioned as a person who was zealous in the Oratory parish and there were many more, some whose names are not recorded. When reporting on the Workhouse, Father Caswall wrote: 'Our grateful thanks are due to a Lady who with extreme punctuality and to the great edification of the poor inmates attends every Sunday afternoon and with her little harmonious choir leads the Litany and Hymns, besides devoting a previous hour to the instruction and entertainment of the children.' A Miss Farrant, a parishioner who died in 1869, was described in a tribute to her as 'a Lady who endeared herself to hundreds of the Catholic poor.'[17] 'She not only sacrificed money and position in life,' the writer of the leaflet goes on, 'but devoted her time for years seeking out the most destitute children from the streets; through her charity numbers of poor little outcasts were rescued from crime and taken care of.... She took the greatest pleasure in gathering at her home the poor from the Workhouse, the Asylum and Prison.'

There was an organisation for lay men called the Little Oratory which provided three Sunday Schools and two night schools and visited at the hospital. There was no parallel organisation for women but for a time there was established for them the Pious Union (a name calculated to deter some). They set up a Guild for Young Women which in 1857 had 150 members. They were to give aid to one another in sickness, give mutual good example and meet for 'occasional recreation.'[18] Very usefully, the Pious Union established St Philip's Home where poor girls could lodge and have some training and twenty two who had been there were recorded as having obtained positions 'in noblemen's or gentlemen's families.' The ladies of the Pious Union also removed four Catholic orphan children from the Workhouse and provided for them with funds collected by a Mrs Phillips. However, an orphanage proper was set up and it was the indefatigable Miss Bathurst who put it on its feet.

Besides all this, women gave money, in lump sums or by means of legacies, and these too were recorded. Miss Ann Partridge of Harborne left a legacy for the schools, Mrs Nettleford gave £1000, Miss Roberts £500, the Farrants £200. Mrs Poncia contributed £11,500, a vast sum then. Friends of Newman who were in Birmingham temporarily also made their contributions: Miss Giberne, Miss Bowles, Miss Bathurst, one of Henry Bowden's daughters. Mrs Wootten gave more than £10,000 to the Oratory and Lady Olivia Acheson gave £8,225. They were extraordinarily generous with time, with money, with their talents for organsation. It is impossible not to smile at the account of the Lady who went to the Workhouse every Sunday afternoon to edify the inhabitants but she deserves recognition for turning out week after week to do something for those caught in a parsimonious and hard hearted system. Some poor person wrote some verses to commemorate the charitable Miss Frances Farrant and the wrestling with syntax, rhyme and pious sentiment together produced a triteness that is almost comic – but here too a smile is checked by the genuine feeling for genuine warm-heartedness.

> She fell asleep in Jesus,
> Calm and peaceful passed away
> And the little orphans missed her
> Who had been their earthly stay
> And they mourned her death like
> Children bereft of a mother's love;
> Day by day for her repose will
> They plead to God above,
> That she who toiled so nobly here
> For the poor and the oppressed,
> May for her loving labours now
> Obtain eternal rest.

Newman himself, in an address to his Oratorians, paid tribute to 'the pious women who are disposed to co-operate in our missionary labours'. 'The large sums bestowed upon our Oratory have come nearly entirely from women. The schools, our sick, our poor, our popular musci, owe a special debt to the services of women in various ranks of life'.[19] He proposed setting up a Little Oratory for women but nothing came of this idea.

It would be interesting to know of the lives of the Oratory parishioners in Newman's time, particularly to have the details of the circumstances and the opinions of those at the receiving end, the poor who thronged the church and whose children attended the parish schools. Inevitably such lives were unrecorded, though anecdotal fragments remain. When Newman had been through one of his suffering times an old woman observed of his preaching that Father always knew how to speak of the Cross. A less solemn story is told of an expedition to Rednal which was used as a country house for the Oratorians, for festivities for schoolboys and also for outings for poor parishioners. A girl on one of these outings tumbled down a hill and knocked out some teeth. She then told Father Ambrose it was the best time she had had in her life.

৵৩৬৩

There is just one parishioner whose story can be told in some detail. It is not, at least in its beginnings, a tale of poverty and need, but of a middle class, devout Catholic family, not laying claim to grandeur or great refinement of manners but leading a comfortable life and having some standing in Catholic circles. Peter Bretherton kept a repository for horses and carriages in Birmingham. He knew the Oratorians from their first coming to Alcester Street and both he and his wife were on very friendly terms with Father Newman. Bretherton's active involvement with Catholic affairs is shown from his being at one time the Vice-Chairman of the Birmingham Catholic Association. He had three sons: Edward, John who was to attend Newman's Catholic University in Dublin and William who was to lead a rugged life as a settler in New Zealand. There were several daughters and it is the eldest, Eleanor, who was in a special way in Newman's care.

She was sickly from babyhood, with weak lungs and when, as a young child, she was gravely ill Newman gave her a relic of St Philip and she recovered. This *grazia*, as he called it, made her an object of interest and care from then on. When she was old enough to make her first confession it was to Father Newman that she went and she was his penitent throughout her childhood. There was real affection between them: she thought the world of him and she seems to have been an attractive child with an artless, playful manner. Her health remained precarious; a letter to Mrs Bretherton when Eleanor was thirteen has the sentence. 'I have just heard that you have some cause for anxiety about dear Eleanor'[1] and that is typical of many exchanges.

In that year, 1859, Mr and Mrs Bretherton were both unwell too, particularly Peter Bretherton, and they were wealthy enough to travel, to see what a change of air and scene would do. Eleanor was not best pleased to be sent off to boarding school with the Dominicans at Stone. She hoped to see Father Newman before she went but he was at Rednal and the weather was too bad for her to make the trip. He sympathised with her dismay at being sent off to a strange place and promised he would not fail in saying Hail Marys for her.

The headmistress of the convent school was Sister Frances Raphael Drane, who had just published an Introduction to English History for use in schools. Eleanor was to thank her for the copy sent to the Oratory when she arrived. She also encountered Sister Mary Gabriel du Boulay, Newman's friend, and he obviously felt that Eleanor could not be in better hands. Away from home, she wrote regularly to Father Newman and to the other priests she knew, Father Ambrose and Father Nicholas Darnell. Once she put the wrong letter into Newman's envelope and he teased her that perhaps he now knew the secrets she was sending to Father Nicholas and perhaps he did not. The Oratory to her was a point of stability, a place of caring and comfort and she had this conviction throughout her life.

At Christmas Eleanor, with her little sisters, stayed at school – their father was still ill. On Holy Innocents day the convent school kept a festival where one girl was made Abbess and held sway, no doubt having strictly limited power over the nuns and the other children. In 1859 the Abbess was Eleanor Bretherton and she received a letter from Father Newman, the most charming of all his letters to children.

My dear Lady Abbess,

I wish your Venerableness as many returns of the duties and honors of this day as is good for your said V's soul and body, for honors sometimes turn the head, and duties sometimes distract the brain.

Also I hope you have grown well into your monastic habit, and that it fits you, and that you move easily in it.

I hope too you can give a good account of two young nuns or novices, who belong to your community, and who, I have reason to hope, do not give you much trouble, but on the contrary by their gravity and exactness are a consolation to your Venerableness. Especially take care that they are very tidy. And in consequence of the great austerity of life which you commonly practise, allow yourself in some indulgence in this festive season and do not scruple to eat a small piece of Christmas

pudding, or other good things which come in your way –
for Christmas comes but once a year –

Accept the assurance of my distinguished considerations,

Yours most politely, John H. Newman.[2]

The young novices are not, as one might think, the little
Brethertons but Sister Frances Raphael Drane and Sister
Mary Gabriel du Boulay, stately ladies both of them and
not in need of being kept tidy. Eleanor must have enjoyed
the joke: the splendid ironies of this letter would be clear
even to a young girl.

The letters continued and, since the Oratory church was
then going up and since she was interested in all that was
going on, Newman gave her details of all the tiresome
procedures of building. In December 1860 painters, brick-
layers and carpenters were all at it and the water pipes,
instead of giving warmth, occasioned the attentions of a
number of workmen who hammered in three places
throughout the services. The parishioners to their credit
attended Mass as though nothing was going on. Church
building does not seem a topic to thrill a fifteen year old
but Eleanor gloried in every letter. She emulated Mother
Margaret Hallahan in nagging him to come to Stone to
visit her but he refused with a joke first saying that he was
not a locomotive and then reminding her that St Philip
remained quietly in Rome for sixty years. He, Newman,
had been in Birmingham for fourteen years so he would
come and visit her when he was a hundred and eight and
she was an elderly schoolgirl of about sixty two. 'Well, I
promise you, I will not stop in Birmingham more years
than St Philip did in Rome.'[3]

She stayed at the convent until she was eighteen and
then went home to Birmingham. Before she was twenty she
met a young man called Francis Watt and fell in love with
him. He was a solicitor's clerk, working and lodging in
Oxford, and rumour had it that there 'his amusements had
not been innocent'. Also, supiciously, he was slow to
consult his parents about his possible engagement to
Eleanor Bretherton. Newman was alarmed – was Eleanor,

his pet, so innocent and well brought up, so devout, so much in need of care because of her fragile health to enter upon what might be a disastrous marriage? Peter Bretherton had died the year before so it was Eleanor's Mamma who must settle the matter. Newman put the case before her. He knew what the temptations of Oxford might be: the division between town and gown was absolute and Francis Watt could not enter on the social life of the undergraduates and, if he did not spend every dreary evening in his lodgings, he had little left but the low public houses and brothels for his amusement. Could he bear a long engagement, if there must be a long engagement because of his own poor prospects and Eleanor's youth? He was not reassured when Eleanor went to see him. 'All her playfulness was gone; she was very serious; and her manner, though she was not conscious of it, was nervous, and had the appearance of a mind anxious and uneasy ... I seemed to myself to see the day, (thought please God it may be only the despondency of old age in me) when dear Eleanor's face was pale, and her manner habitually subdued and sad.'[4]

There was something Micawber-like in Eleanor herself and in Mrs Bretherton: they hoped that something would turn up and at this time their hope was that Newman's rich and influential connections, perhaps Mr Hope-Scott, could find the young man a better job. Newman did try to oblige but as he said, it was not easy to obtain a position by favour: 'nothing can be got without money or high testimonials or without competitive examination.'[5] Mrs Bretherton replied speedily that she had reasons for rejecting the aspersions that had been cast on the young man and his parents had sanctioned the engagement. He was not a Catholic but he was prepared to take instruction and in due time he was instructed and then received into the Church by Father Caswall at the Oratory.

The question of what the pair were to live on was never satisfactorily settled. The Watts had little money, the lucrative post never materialised and Mrs Bretherton was widowed. Newman's vision of the time when Eleanor would forever be pale and careworn was only too accurate but,

wisely, he never said 'I told you so.' He married Eleanor
Bretherton to Francis Watt in St Chad's Cathedral in April
1866. There was nothing else he could do though he would
gladly have relinquished the task. He said civilly to the
young man that he had a great good will towards him and,
when he was about to meet him 'it would rejoice me to
perceive that you are worthy of such a young lady as Miss
Bretherton.'[6] The truth was that he did not reach such a
perception. However, he sent wishes for Eleanor's happiness, offered many Masses for that end, sent her money 'to
lay out upon yourself in any way you please',[7] gave her a
watch and performed the ceremony. A piece of the bride
cake went to the Oratory, and Eleanor wanted to give her
dog, Brenda, to Father Ambrose. She was a fine dog but he
could not take such a charge and declined with thanks.

Mrs Bretherton sold up and went to live with the young
couple. They were optimistic at first, Eleanor was well and
had hopes that her Frank would succeed and prosper. A
joyful letter came to the Oratory about Baby, who was then
brought to Birmingham and baptised by Father Newman,
being given the name Margaret – a name she did not hear
much in her childhood since she was always called Daisy.
Mrs Bretherton said that she was just as Eleanor had been
at the same age. Other children came in quick succession,
twelve in all. It is not known what the composition of the
family was but it seems there were few girls and many boys.
One was called William, after his emigrant uncle, another,
inevitably, was Philip, (Pippo) and one was called John
Henry Newman Watt.

They moved about, living first in Manchester, which was
cold, and then in Bolton, which was also cold and where
the people seemed rough, and Eleanor's health deteriorated. Then they came south, to Christchurch in
Hampshire and Eleanor tried bravely to augment the
family income by growing vegetables and keeping hens and
pigs. There is no evidence that Frank Watt (who was always
sent kind remembrances from the Oratory) was a bad
husband, despite his early dissipations, but he never prospered and life was a struggle for them.

Ten years after the wedding Eleanor became gravely ill

with consumption and it was thought most unlikely that she would survive. At that time she had four small children. Newman informed the nuns at Stone and Miss Giberne who had met Eleanor as a child, and journeyed down to Christchurch himself to visit her. In all his contacts with Eleanor he seems to have been abnormally conscious of age, of the discrepancy between her fragile youth and his own age, of the passing of time. In this year, when he was seventy five, he felt a strange bond with her. After the visit to Christchurch (a trying one) he went to stay briefly with the Froudes and wrote afterwards to Mrs Froude:

In proportion as you love me, you will pray for me that I may make a good end. When a man gets to my age, the awful future comes before him vividly and is ever haunting his thoughts. I am quite well according to all my sensations, but I was quite surprised at Christchurch to find what a unity of thought and feeling there was between the poor girl who was dying and myself who had no illness about me. We seemed both to be going beyond that dark curtain together.[8]

Eleanor did not die then but resumed her toiling, anxious life, often relapsing into illness in the winter. Her correspondence with Newman continued and she had as good a recollection of anniversaries as he had, always remembering his birthday, the date of his reception into the Church, St Philip's Day. This particular correspondence can be seen as trivial and negative: there are no analyses of Christian doctrine, literary criticism, comment on the times, no interesting revelations of his inner thoughts (as in some letters to Emily Bowles) in his letters to Eleanor Watt. There are simply greetings, words of encouragement, assurance of prayers and concern. Sometimes he sent her interesting stamps, as he did when she was a child. He felt himself that he had not much to say: 'I wish my letters were worth more to you than they are – but they cannot do more than thank you for the love you show, especially on the annual February 21'.[9] They were simply messages of real affection, as hers were and in that sense mightily positive and valuable.

The children grew bigger and the education of the boys had to be considered. Eleanor hoped that the Oratory would give her a free place at the school for the eldest but Newman pointed out that the cost of extras ('cricket, football and other games and sports-clothes – cricketing clothes etc etc., then pocket money, washing and extra washing which swell a boy's bill')[10] would mount up. He did not point out that a poor boy would not be happy amongst the richer ones. The young Watts were in fact able to go to Mount St Mary's, a good Jesuit school near Chesterfield. Newman on one occasion sent money for the children's clothes, having the boys particularly in mind for, though he did not want Daisy to be excluded, he knew that jackets cost more than frocks.

There was one hope still for Mrs Bretherton and the Watts. There was a rich relation, a Mrs Stapleton-Bretherton who had promised (but how seriously and in what terms is not known and probably was not known then) that she would leave money to the Bretherton girls. When she died in 1883 the newspapers reported that she had left a fortune to the Holy See for she had no heir, was a devout Catholic and had been made a Marchesa by the Pope. Newman wrote to console Eleanor for the disappointment and to tell her that the Pope really had need of funds ('the need of Peter's pence is no matter of words')[11] He also said that one couldn't go by what papers said and in this he was right for Mrs Stapleton-Bretherton had not bequeathed money to the Holy See though she had given large sums in her life-time. There were various bequests but none to the Brethertons. Newman wrote to Sister Maria Pia Giberne to tell her how Eleanor's health had been affected by her serious disappointment. 'Eleanor Bretherton is, I fear, in a serious way at last. She has winter after winter been confined to her bed – and has not been to Mass for many months together. At last she seemed getting better, and the wounds in her lungs healed. Lately came the news that old Mrs Stapleton had left the family nothing. The shock has opened the wounds'.[12]

Again, Eleanor Watt survived. The 'grazia' she had received was an extraordinarily tenacious hold on life and she approached the dark curtain several times and then came back to her difficult life with its piety, worry, struggle, joy and pride in her children and then the facing of another weary winter. It was truly a great sorrow to her to be kept from Mass and, in those days of a strict keeping of the Eucharist fast she was often unable to receive Communion. Newman was able to help in that respect: when writing to the Pope on other matters, in Latin, he asked for a special relaxation of the rule for her, explaining that often she was not ill enough to receive Communion as Viaticum (or Communion for the dying, when no preceding fast was required) but so weak that a fast from midnight was impossible.

When Newman was a Cardinal and his sight was poor and his fingers feeble he had a priest, William Neville, as his amanuensis. Eleanor Watt made use similarly of her daughter Margaret who wrote to the Cardinal sometimes on her mother's behalf. Newman's letters at the end of his life were necessarily brief and sometimes the phrasing was touchingly simple, as though the lack of time and strength meant that only basic things could be said. When he was eighty six he wrote, 'I am always thinking and praying about you.'[13]

The Watts moved to Bournemouth where a Jesuit priest, Father Henry Schomberg Kerr, was stationed. He knew or was related to friends of Newman, so felt free to write to him to express concern for the family when he had met them. The last 'Eleanor' letter is to this priest. 'Your concern for the poor Watt family is very kind. I take advantage of it by sending you a cheque for £50 herein enclosed, to be disposed of as you think best in their behalf.'[14] This was written the year before his death. Eleanor outlived him by five years – that she lived to be fifty is amazing.

One of her sons, F. P. Watt (Philip or Pippo) became a Jesuit and John Henry Watt emigrated to New Zealand, as his uncle had done. He lived until 1964 and the Bishop of Auckland wrote to the Birmingham Oratory in that year to tell of the reputation for sanctity that this man had had. He remembered Newman well, had kept some of his cards and greetings and had inherited the watch that his mother was given as a wedding gift. This son of Eleanor's was gentle, wise and prayerful. The Bishop did not say what profession he had taken up, nor whether he was reasonably prosperous in his adopted country. One hopes that he was, for the J. H. Watts had eleven children – and after the tale of his sick and struggling mother a second tale of a large, poor family would be harrowing. Poor Eleanor Bretherton! She had, as Newman said privately to a priest who knew the family, made a foolish match, but as he also said on another occasion when young people fall in love there is litle that can be done about it.

⌒⌒⌒

One very useful lady in the Oratory parish was the widow called Mrs Wootten. She was a very old friend of Newman's. She had been married to a medical doctor, John Wootten, who had lived in Broad Street, Oxford from the late eighteen twenties and who in time became a Tractarian. He was a friend of Pusey, in sympathy with Newman too, and he treated many Tractarians so that they had a physician who was in tune with their philosophy and aspirations.

Dr Wootten died in 1847 and his house was bought by Dr H. W. Acland. Frances Wootten became a Catholic three years later, helped and advised by Newman, and came to Birmingham, anxious to assist the Birmingham Oratory in any way she could. Many small tasks fell to her lot on occasions when a sympathetic woman was needed: it was she who saw Miss Giberne off to her travels to search out the Italian witnesses and it was she who met Lavinia Wilson when she came to Birmingham to be received into the Church. She was not short of money and was generous with it, pressing cheques on Newman when he needed a holiday and could not afford to pay for it as well as giving sums to the Oratory.

She came into prominence in the Oratory's affairs when it was decided to open a school for boys. Newman considered this possibility for some time and he was urged on by many converts who did not wish to send their sons to the existing schools run by Religious Orders or by secular priests such as those at Oscott. This was the school recommended to the Fullertons by Newman, with the one caveat that it was certainly rough. This was a mild judgement compared with the expressed opinion of a Mrs William Henry Charlton who wrote to a friend in 1858, 'Our own colleges and convents are so undeniably behind the times, in all things relating to education, it would distress me, to have my boys put under the care, of well-meaning, but, untutored "ecclesiastical" plough boys. A good manner is a sweet ingredient of religion! – in respect to which, we can only look to the aid of converts, for the prosperity of the old faith'.[1] Perhaps the converts, the men having received their own education at the traditional public schools, saw these schools through the rose-tinted spectacles of nostalgia for their own youth, and certainly the Protestant establishment viewed the Catholic schools with prejudice.

However the intellectual standards of the Catholic boys' schools were low and their regimes in general were both rough and spartan. Newman, who was so much concerned to obtain university education for Catholic youths, knew that there must be good schools as feeders and he had discovered in Ireland that there were too few Catholic boys ready for a university education. Many educated laymen supported him in this view, as did Sir John Symeon in 1857: 'It is to my mind axiomatic that, unless something can be done to improve the Education of our boys, it is impossible for the Catholic body in England to elevate themselves into intellectual equality with their fellow citizens....'[2]

A few boys had lodged at the Oratory to have their teaching from the Fathers but this was too small an enterprise to help the converts' sons sufficiently. A plan was forming in January 1857: Newman thought lay trustees could form themselves into a body that would promote 'a Catholic Eton' and Mrs Wootten should be appointed as 'Guardian of the Children'.[3] This is the first reference to the starting of what was to be the Oratory School and it is clear from this letter that Mrs Wootten was part of the scheme from the very beginning. There were two areas that

Newman intended to concentrate on: firstly the curriculum and the teaching, and secondly the care of the boys, their health, the catering, the provision for small boys and delicate boys. In this second area he was thinking not only of certain defects in the Catholic boys' schools but of the worries of Catholic mothers. The Headmaster would be one of the Oratorians, Father Nicholas Darnell, who had been educated at Winchester and Exeter College, Oxford, and had been a Fellow of New College and a lawyer before his conversion and ordination as a Catholic priest. There would be lay masters who would introduce a homely spirit with their wives and families, if they had them, and who would bring the standards of the public schools and universities where they had been educated, since they would probably be converts. Thoughts of Eton reminded Newman that there was a system of having 'Dames' there who attended to the domestic affairs of the school houses. Mrs Wootten, ladylike, sensible, used to running a home, would be excellent as Chief Dame, and this was the title she had, rather than Guardian. However, Newman saw her and the other Dames as more important than mere housekeepers. Women would inculcate gentle manners and this refinement would aid the religious ethos of the school, the Catholic spirit that should distinguish the Oratory School from Eton. Mrs Wootten was to be, to some extent, *in loco parentis*, seeing to it that small boys said their prayers and writing to their mothers on matters of health and about any personal difficulties that she could settle.

An old friend of Newman's, a lawyer called Edward Bellasis, was active with other laymen to promote these schemes for he was anxious not only for the whole Catholic lay body but for his own son, Richard, who was then eight years old. Newman was willing to take small boys who would grow into public school boys in time – in other words, the new school would be both a preparatory school and an embryo public school. He was able to assure Bellasis by October 1857 that 'Mrs Wootten was kind enough to say she would make herself Dame, if she were wanted and take the boys under her charge – Father Darnell would take the charge of their schooling'.[4] By February in the next year he was able to send Bellasis details of the Oratory's plans for building. There was to be a new building at the end furthest from the Oratory house containing the Dame's rooms, school rooms and an infirmary and the second storey of the Oratory was to be given over to dormitories. Mrs Wootten as Dame would have access to the boys from one end of the property and the Father Prefect (Darnell) from the other.

There were difficulties to be overcome. Bishop Ullathorne favoured the plan but Cardinal Wiseman was grudging and the London Oratory at first claimed that the whole idea of running a school was against the Oratorian Rule. Money was a problem. However, the school duly opened on 2 May 1859, with nine pupils, Richard Bellasis being the first boy to be entered. All augured well. Newman had very clear ideas of the nature of the school: it was to be an English public school, albeit a small one, but all was to be consistent with 'Catholic habits and thoughts'.[5] It is not to be imagined that all was to be soft and easy, even though provision had been made for good physical and pastoral care. The curriculum was classical and rigorous and defaulters were caned. Newman had no theories agaisnt corporal punishment and he maintained that 'the good old punishment of flogging, is, in due moderation as to severity and frequency, the most efficacious of all punishments, while it is the most prompt and summary, and the least irritating and annoying to the subjects of it. It is done and over – there is nothing to brood over, nothing to create a grudge'.[6]

With Father Darnell established at one end of the buildings punishing recalcitrant boys and Mrs Wootten cossetting them at the other end, there might be friction between them but Newman was aware that they were friends, Darnell having a warm regard for Frances Wootten who had been a kind of mother to him. Newman really valued her, his only doubts about her being on the score of her delicate health: he told Henry Wilberforce in the summer of 1859 that his 'dear boys' would be looked after by Mrs Wootten who took good care of her charges, but did more than her strength might allow.[7] He wrote to one of the mothers a little later, 'I only do hope that Mrs Wootten will not knock herself up – she is more like a Saint than most people you come across.'[8]

Also he valued her opinion. He said in a letter to Elizabeth Bowden that Willie Bowden, her nephew, was 'an exceedingly good boy'.[9] He had heard Mrs Wootten say to Father Ambrose that he was one of the best boys in the school. In discussing the choice of a junior seminary or a school for a boy who might become a priest he came down strongly on the side of an ordinary school, feeling that a true vocation would show itself in time and that an early segregation from the world of ordinary life and ordinary boys might engender a false vocation or a 'spirit of formalism, affectation, and preciseness.'[10] This interesting opinion, far in advance of its time, was endorsed by Mrs Wootten. Newman spoke as though his finding that she had the same view acted as a good reinforcement.

Splendid as she was, Frances Wootten could be tiresome at times. When there had been a minor scandal in the Oratory in the early fifties, a lay brother making advances to her under the guise of feeling great spiritual love, Newman gave the impression that he would have liked to knock many heads together. Miss Giberne had doubtless talked of her spiritual love for the Father, so fanning the flames. The Oratorians grew very excited about the whole matter. Brother Bernard could be forgiven for his offence but it was more serious that he gossiped outside the Oratory and Mrs Wootten did not help in that she mentioned the incident to Father Darnell in the confessional and gave him leave to speak to Brother Bernard. Why did not Nicholas Darnell ask to speak to Newman, Bernard's Religious superior? Indeed, further back, why did not Frances Wootten speak to Newman? A small matter grew confused and destructive and Mrs Wootten was unwise. At a much later date she drove Newman to distraction when she was to move from one Dame's house to another and would not come clean about which one she preferred. He said to Ambrose that he did not care a button whether she moved to Number 67 or Number 22 but he could not bear whispers about secret meanings and

wishes which she could not bring out. There was at times a
ladylike, niminy-piminy lack of directness about her.

However, in a major matter, a great row about the future
of the Oratory School, Frances Wootten conducted herself
very well, after a shaky start, and came out of the situation
vindicated and more valued that ever as the senior Dame at
the school. The trouble began with a small incident which
is slightly comic. A boy called Cholmeley developed very
bad chilblains and the doctor recommended that he
should rest in the sickroom until they were healed.
Cholmeley's mother, one of those fussy parents who are
the bane of schoolteachers, feared that he would become
depressed and Mrs Wootten promised that she would give
him outings in the afternoons. A group of boys, including
the school's most aristocratic pupil, the young Duke of
Norfolk, met Cholmeley with Mrs Wootten at the Dog
Show in Birmingham. The Duke said, 'Won't Father
Darnell be in a wax?'

Now in this matter sensible school matrons and level-
headed mothers would give judgement against Mrs
Wootten and think that Father Darnell could be excused if
he were in a wax when he heard about Cholmeley's outing
for it has always been a rule that a school child who is not
well enough to attend lessons is not well enough to go out
to amusements. However, Darnell's reaction was out of all
proportion to Mrs Wootten's offence. Not only were boys
on the sick list forbidden to leave the premises without the
Headmaster's permission but boys were forbidden to go to
the Dame's rooms without leave from a tutor. Mrs Wootten
told Newman that she simply could not do her work under
such a rule. Newman, seeing that dissension had broken
out between Headmaster and Dame, suggested a new
arrangement whereby Mrs Wootten would look after the
younger boys and her second-in-command, Miss French,
would look after the older ones, directly under Darnell's
command. At first it seemed that the compromise would
work, but then Darnell intensified his charges against Mrs
Wootten, maintaining that she undermined his authority
by making complaints to Ambrose St John who reported
them to Newman. If she had a juniors' House she would be

'a German princess regnant with a back way to the Emperors of Russia and Austria when she falls out with Prussia'.[11]

Newman was beginning to see that the root of the matter was that Darnell saw himself as Headmaster independently of Newman and the Oratory, though he did not see at that point how far Darnell was prepared to go. Next came an ultimatum: 'I have written to Mrs W. to say that as far as I am concerned,' wrote Darnell, 'the *status quo* cannot continue, that one or other of us must go.'[12] All had to be done at once. Again, Newman worked for compromise but Darnell would have none of it. He said that he would resign and threatened that the staff would go with him. Those responsible for the school were now in two camps. Darnell was supported by the four lay masters especially by two called Oxenham and Moody, the latter in his turn supported by his wife who disliked Newman and who together with her husband spread gossip and slander. Some of the Oratorians were also on his side and so was Miss French. Newman's lay friends, Bellasis, who had been a prime mover in setting up the school, and Hope-Scott were clear that this was not a personal dispute with Newman supporting his friend Mrs Wootten but a dispute about authority and they maintained that Darnell must understand that the school was not his but the Oratory's and Newman's in particular. It became clear amid the debates that Darnell's view of what the school should be and Newman's were diverging and matters which had worried Newman throughout the year 1861 came into sharper focus. Darnell wanted the Oratory School to be more like Eton and Winchester. He emphasised academic attainment, took matters very much into his own hands and gave severe floggings even for minor offences. Religious instruction was low on his list of priorities, he saw no great value in the pastoral care of the Dame and he played down the role of the boys' confessors, priests who according to the custom of the time were responsibile for fixing the dates of a boy's First Communion and Confirmation. Newman set out his own views thus:

I consider the mode of conducting the great schools of Eton, Winchester, etc., necessarily end in subordinating religion to secular interests and principles: and this consequence would ensue in ours but for the presence of Matrons of a high class and spiritual directors.[13]

Newman wondered at the start of the trouble whether Mrs Wootten might be assuming too much power and whether she might have to go at some later date, but he never intended to accede to Darnell's peremptory demand for her instant dismissal. Both his feeling for justice and his chivalry came into play and he wrote to a woman parishioner:

Every woman's heart would have cried shame on me, if I had been the coward to banish, or permit to be banished a lady and a benefactress, at a minute's warning, (whatever maybe her alleged faults) at the dictation of a lot of men.[14]

Darnell departed, taking the staff with him and Newman was left in the December of 1861 with the task of finding fresh teachers in time for the new term in January. He felt bowed down by trouble but he was in no mood to give in. He wrote to Mother Margaret Hallahan, who had sent greetings for St John's day, to say that it was on that very day that there had fallen 'the heaviest blow we have had as a Congregation and we need some consolation under it'.[15] He then applied himself to sending out letters to likely candidates for the vacant posts at the school.

It was only with Darnell's departure that the full tale emerged. The row had not been about the wretched Cholmeley and his chilblains or about any faults of Frances Wootten. Darnell had had a scheme, together with Oxenham and Moody, to move the school from Edgbaston and had been inspecting possible sites. Mrs Wootten had found out what was going on and, with the seriousness that she felt about Darnell's breach of loyalty intensified because she was so ill that winter that she thought she might not have long to live, she had lectured Darnell and begged him to pull back. Hence his determination to get rid of her. She did not report his plans to Newman from a feeling that Darnell was owed silence because of his old friendship with her and, since she was accused of backstairs talebearing, perhaps it was as well that she kept quiet. Newman found new masters, two of the old ones returned and Darnell himself left the Oratory for good. Father Ambrose St John took over the headship, bearing the title of Prefect of Studies, and the parents backed Newman to the hilt. Matters improved in the school for, with Darnell's keeping matters in his own hands and flogging boys unmercifully, disorder rather than order had been prevailing. Newman wrote a lengthy account of the events of that December and January to Mother Margaret saying that, in the words of the psalm, 'the net is broken and we are delivered'. Mrs Wootten's only fault, he told her, 'was that of up-holding the rights of the Oratory against what was very like a conspiracy'.[16]

She had been very ill during that dreadful winter, actually spitting blood, but she soldiered on as Dame. A replacement was needed for Miss French and Mrs Froude recommended a sensible woman who had been governess to her own children. This was Miss Mitchell, who looked younger than her years and wore curls. When Newman told her she was too young for the post she said she was forty four and would in future hide her curls and so, duly capped, she took her place. As for Miss French, Newman noted with mild malice that Protestant gossip had it that she had in fact run off with Father Darnell. She was all of fifty.

Inevitably the great row had done harm that could not be instantly removed; there had been much talk, scandal, harm to the relationships in the Oratory. However, all fell into place in time and the school prospered, from that time onward. Both Newman and Frances Wootten were deeply grieved by Nicholas Darnell's actions and attitude and by his departure because they were fond of him and they were to have their confidence restored three years later when he wrote to the Oratory with a full admission of his fault: he said he had been 'insufferably violent and headstrong and conceited, generally to the Congregation, and still more insufferably insolent and ungrateful to the Father'.[17] Newman wrote to restore full peace between them. Mrs Wootten was referred to with marked favour and esteem after the dispute. Bellasis wrote to Newman, 'Your name and, in a degree, Mrs Wootten's have brought the school together, not Father Darnell's'[18] and Newman himself, writing to another lay supporter, said of her, 'if she had gone, there was a chance of all the school going – for her care of the young boys and popularity with the mothers have been the making of the school – as I know full well, if I did not know it before, by what the mothers have said to me since the row'.[19] Boys' schools have not always been noted for taking the views of mothers very seriously but Newman certainly did.

One of the tasks he took to himself in the school was to write to parents giving end of term reports and these letters are very human documents, giving details of a boy's health, his behaviour and his general progress. They show his concern for the welfare of the whole person, his concept of education as an integral process, not a shovelling in of facts or an arid working towards examinations without proper attention to the whole development of a pupil. Given Newman's own intellectual stature, they show remarkable patience with immature minds. He wrote, for instance, to one mother, the widowed Duchess of Norfolk, about her son.

> The Oratory Brn April 16/62
>
> My Dear Duchess
>
> I suppose Henry has already shown you his prizes. They were well won. And they show what he *can* do. He said Wordsworth's Happy Warrior, right off, very frequently. Another boy did so also. They both got a prize. No other boy came near them. His other prize was for writing out passages of Shakespeare on dictation. There was no one came near him; but what made a doubt for a moment, was his spelling 'Thou' several times, 'Thow', and another false spelling.
>
> I hope we shall rouse him to exert himself in other

things, and these prizes may encourage him. He has fits of negligence when every thing goes wrong, and then we are perplexed with the number of impositions which fall upon him, from every quarter and we have to release him from the weight of them, as best we may.

There are boys who do him harm by encouraging him to make game of these magisterial corrections – and he sometimes comes up for the imposition, as if it were good fun. (Pray, do not hint this to him). He will become more manly in a little time. I think of the whole he is better in getting up – but here too he has fits of dawdling.

In spite of all this, he is exact and methodical in his habits – and it is amusing to see how well he keeps his books and clothes.

He has a great deal to do in arithmetic and grammar.

As to ourselves, the only fear is, that, from extreme anxiety about him, we should meddle with him too much, and make too much of little things....[20]

Mrs Wootten continued to write to mothers too and managed her work satisfactorily, despite continuing ill health. Newman told his sister Jemima in 1869, 'Mrs Wootten keeps up, fragile as she has been for thirty years.'[21]

Chapter Six

The Later Years

Jemima Mozley, Magdalene Helbert, Louisa Deane,
The death of Mrs Wootten, The young friends – Helen
and Mary Church, Mary Monica Hope-Scott, Louisa
Simeon; Lady Coleridge, Emmeline Deane, Elinor Hallé
(portraitists), Emily Fortey, The deaths of Catherine
Froude, Mary Holmes, Jemima Mozley, Maria Rosina
Giberne, Recognition with Anne Mozley, The death of
Maria Ruscombe Poole, The marriage of Isy Froude;
Grace Langford née Mozley, Newman's death

After the publication of the *Apologia* in 1864 Newman not
only came back into the public eye but was able to renew
old acquaintances. This was a time of reconciliation and
one such renewal was with Jemima, though it did not
happen without an exceedingly frank letter from him first.
Jemima had never broken off the relationship completely,
as Harriett did, but she had distanced herself and caused a
great deal of hurt over the years. An earlier remonstrance
had come from her eldest brother when he was at Maryvale
in 1846: she travelled and he did not know, he heard
nothing of the birth of his nephew, Frank, until the child
was two months old, he suggested coming to Derby to visit
old Aunt Betsey but there was no encouragement to do so
from Jemima. Now, nearly twenty years later, when their
brother Frank was visiting the Mozleys in Derby, Jemima
wrote (in rather cool terms) to suggest that John should
join the family party for a day.

His reply was a kind of blood-letting. The irritations of

years came out in the letter. John Mozley, the head of the
household, had never issued any invitation and was not
doing so, even now. The children had grown up but it
was only now, when Jemima's boys could visit their uncle
themselves that he had sight of them. She had visited him
in Birmingham in 1853, evaded the question of why she
had not brought any of the children with her and point-
edly refused to see Ambrose St John or Mrs Wootten,
though she knew both of them. 'You said, as plainly as
possible, "I come to see you because you are my brother,
but I will have none of your belongings" '.[1] He could claim
that he had not tried to force his own religious convictions
on her but she and John Mozley had behaved consistently
as if recognition of his religious position would act as a
kind of contamination. Apparently there was now some
change in her attitude but 'you cannot bring back past
years'.[2]

The letter had the desired effect on her and Newman
himself was far more kindly disposed to his sister once he
had spoken his mind. Thereafter they softened towards
each other. Newman did not go to Derby in response to
that first invitation but he did make visits there. Jemima
came to Birmingham in June 1867, bringing her husband
with her and her one daughter, Jane. There was a musical
interlude on this occasion, Newman playing Beethoven on
his violin with his niece; she, no doubt, accompanied on
the piano. Jemima played too, much admired by Mrs
Wootten and one of the Oratory priests who were listening
in: 'they never heard anything like your handling of the
piano'.[3]

The old friends kept up with him so that he had to have
elaborate notes and markings of calendars to be sure of
remembering his 'faithful women' in his Masses. There were
new converts too and new enquirers. Geraldine Fitzgerald,
for one, belongs to this later period: she was first in touch
with Newman in 1867 and, eight years later, when she
scolded him for not calling on her and her family when he
was in London, he remonstrated that he was an old man,
'like an owl in the daylight when I go abroad' and he signed
himself, 'though I am so old, Yours affectionately'.[4]

In 1869 he had a short but intense and important correspondence with an earnest woman called Magdalene
Helbert. She was a High Anglican, very devout, a married
woman with four small children. She was drawn to the
Roman Church but had grave doubts and she had
consulted Archbishop Manning whose books she had been
reading. He recommended that she should write to
Newman and her husband had made no objection to this,
though he had not approved her contact with Manning. In
his first letter to her Newman began to answer her questions but sought first to reassure her, using the same kind
of phraseology that he used in his own written devotions
and meditations. 'You can do your duty whether you are in
perplexity or in clearness of mind, look up to your Lord
and Saviour in confidence, being resolved with His grace
to do His will under all circumstances – and then no harm
can happen to you'.[5] When she recognised the Roman
Catholic Church as the Church, she was then called to join
it – but not before. His letters continued in the same way,
answering questions fully but also seeking to bring her
some peace.

She had particular difficulties about papal infallibility
and about the Marian doctrines concerning the
Immaculate Conception and the Assumption of the
Blessed Virgin. She found her arguments in history and
went through a course of hard reading. Her husband told
her she was like a Post Office, 'a receptacle of letters and
arguments'[6] and she grew more and more confused by
studying the arguments on either side. At the end of the
year Mrs Helbert wrote from an Anglican convent in
Clewer where she was staying; she had reached an impasse,
fearing to receive Anglican sacraments since she now
distrusted Anglican authority and yet feeling that her soul
was starved for want of Communion. She felt she was in
danger of drifting nowhere, and she intended to yield to
her Anglican friends and seek afresh a spiritual home in
the Anglican fold. So she would not come to Birmingham
to see Newman, as she had intended.

What she thought and felt in the next few years is not
known since the correspondence died. Perhaps Newman's

words continued to echo in her mind, not so much the detailed answers to her questions as the general outline of his own thinking about Catholicism, for he put down the reasons for his own conversion, 'because the present Roman Catholic Church is *the only church* which is like, and it is very like, the primitive Church'.[7] He followed this statement with an interesting and vivid reference to the comparatively new art of photography, describing the Church as a kind of photograph of the primitive Church, 'or at least it does not differ from the primitive Church near so much as the photograph of a man of forty differs from his photograph when twenty. *You know that it is the same man*'.[8]

Five years later the news came that Mrs Helbert, then thirty six years old, was gravely ill. A telegram came to the Oratory on 9 March to say that she had died the day before. She had been received into the Church before her death and her husband followed up the telegram with a letter sent a few days later to thank Newman for the masses said for her and to add, 'I am very grateful that she was permitted to join the Roman Communion ... I am sure that her mind was more at ease and her last moments more peaceful in consequence of the step she took'.[9]

When Mrs Helbert had been reporting her difficulties and on the books she had been reading, Newman wrote, 'you must recollect you have chosen a man's part – you have chosen to go by antiquity, by the Fathers, by history, and to ask answers to questions arising thence. In consequence you must not wonder that you are tried with the wearisome suspense which arises out of this course'.[10] He did not recommend that she should lay aside her studies, abandon the high and hard road for something intellectually easier, but encouraged her to battle through to the end. This is a very good illustration of the ambiguity of his attitude to the intellectual development of women; he had respect for the intelligence of such as Mrs Helbert and yet he saw her choice of the study of history as that of a man. His own experience had been of education in an all-male environment and there must still have been vivid memories of arguments about antiquity in the Oriel commonroom. His vision was not entirely of the past but when he thought hopefully of the future he saw the young Catholic men with university education opening up to them, saw them developing into a thinking, articulate laity, well instructed in their faith and a powerful force in public life. The women should be an active and well instructed body too (he said to Miss Bowles that he did not approve of those 'who wish Catholic women, not nuns, to have no higher pursuit than that of dress'[11]) but their higher pursuits were to be within defined limits.

Newman's role as a counsellor became more important when he was nearing his seventies, more strictly defined. He had to deal with the effect that the First Vatican Council, with its definition of the infallibility of the Pope, had on enquirers and on many who had been devout Catholics for years. The question had early been raised by Mrs Helbert in 1869, just before the Council, and Newman had made his own position clear then; he had no quarrel with the doctrine. 'I believe in the infallibility of the Pope myself – that is as an opinion. I think there are very strong reasons for holding it – but I quite recognize the right of others not to hold it. I think it could be made an article of faith by a General or Ecumenical Council; and if such a Council should so determine, I should formally *believe as certain*, what I now believe in my own private judgement *as an opinion*, viz that our Lord and Saviour so determined, and gave the privilege of infallibility to St Peter and his successors'.[12]

He said in another letter that if a definition were made it would be well hedged about by conditions and limitations. This is exactly what was done at the First Vatican Council in 1870 so that Newman could be said to have had little trouble with the Council and its major enactment. The Council and the question of infallibility worried him considerably, however, for the sake of others. A powerful party were agitating for a much more extreme definition, so that, in Newman's phrase, papal decreees would henceforth be as plentiful as blackberries. These Ultramontanes, as they were known, set up much agitation before the Council met; Manning was one of this party and hence no doubt the preference Mr Helbert had for Newman as his wife's adviser. While the Council was in session rumours flew about and it was not known for some time in what terms the definition would be made so that all in all there was plenty of scope for confusion. Earnest Catholic women in England were scandalised by the statements and the pressures put on by the Ultramontanes and some were in deep distress.

Even Miss Bowles, devout, faithful and knowledgeable, was very shaken. She visited Newman in the autumn of 1869 to tell him her fears and he told her 'God *cannot* leave His Church'.[13] She then said that she might cease to believe and leave the Church. 'You will not', he answered calmly, 'We all must go through that gate of obedience, simply as obedience. And mind, if the dogma *is* declared, you will find that it will not make the slightest difference to you'.[14]

Others wrote agitated letters. The question of papal infallibility (allied to the feverish campaign for a definition in extreme terms) was one of the matters that worried poor Lady Chatterton. Mrs Froude needed some reassurance. A convert called Mrs Perceval wrote in deep distress and so did a Mrs Beckwich and the wife of a prominent Liverpool Catholic, a Mrs Whitty. These ladies were not Newman's friends or his converts, but it seemed that he was the best person to turn to. A Mrs Margaret Wilson, a convert, had great difficulty with the matter and was harried about it when she went to confession. Newman urged her not to set herself against the definition but he also said how deeply he lamented the violence which had been used in the matter. 'I think there are some Bishops and Priests, who act as if they did not care at all whether souls were lost or not – and only wish to save souls on their own measure.'[15]

Needless to say, Miss Bowles urged Newman to make a public statement at the start of the Council to support the minority view, which was that the definition was inopportune. He did not, but chance made his views clear because a private letter which he had sent to Bishop Ullathorne was copied and leaked to the press (by someone unknown). For fear of inaccurate versions, Newman sent his letter to the *Standard* where it was published on 6 April 1870. He described it as a letter that was 'one of the most passionate and confidential that I ever wrote'.[16] The phrases in it are famous, especially his reference to an 'aggressive and insolent faction'[17] which was causing distress. Later on he wished he had included the text about little ones being scandalised and the perpetrators having a stone bound round their necks and being cast into the sea. 'Slowness in decision, tenderness for weaker brethren, are first principles in the exercise of Ecclesiastical authority', he wrote to a sympathetic Dominican priest. 'Of course I should not have written so abrupt a letter to my Bishop except confidentially – but if you saw a railway train at full speed bowling over some unhappy workmen on the line, what could you do but cry out and gesticulate?'[18] Despite the masculinity of the workmen in this robust metaphor, it can be said that many of the unfortunates bowled over by the aggressive faction were women. Also, as so often, it was they who called forth so much of what Newman thought on the matter, more than once bringing out the serene prophecy that one day there would be a second Council that would restore balance.

Before the Council began, Newman had been invited, via his bishop, Ullathorne, to go to Rome as a Consultor on the Commission that was preparing for the Council. He declined and wrote in a memorandum, 'there are things I *can* do – others that I *can't*'.[19] He preferred to stay in his own place and get on with the work he had in hand. This was his book, *The Grammar of Assent* which he judged to be one of the most important books he had undertaken, and which proved to be a most difficult enterprise.

It was published in March 1870. Although it has been a quarry for scholars, it was meant to be a book that would be helpful to intelligent questioners who sought to know how assent could be given to religious doctrines when the proofs in such matters are not of the same kind as those of mathematics or those drawn from direct experience. Newman asked Miss Holmes for her opinion on the last section of the book and his letter makes his intentions very clear. These last hundred pages were written 'especially for those who can't go into questions of the inspiration of Scripture, authenticity of books, passages in the Father etc. etc. – especially for such ladies as are bullied by infidels and do not know how to answer them – a misfortune which I fear is not rare in this day. I wanted to show that, keeping to broad facts of history, which every one knows and no-one can doubt, there is evidence and reason enough for an honest enquirer to believe in revelation'.[20]

Copies went out to the ladies, sometimes buttressed by the author's modest warnings and disclaimers. A letter to Henry Wilberforce commended the book to his clever daughter, Agnes: she was not to begin at the end nor to skip, 'but to get it up from the first page on. And she will have a profitable Lent exercise of mortification'.[21] Miss Holmes was told she would be disappointed in the *Grammar:* 'it is what it is, and it is not what it isn't – and what it isn't most people will expect that it is'.[22] These readers, however, were enthusiastic and Lady Chatterton wrote to say that she was pleased with the book.

Newman had said of the *Grammar* that it would be his last work of significance and that old men like himself could only fiddle-faddle. However, five years afterwards he produced another important piece, not a stout book, certainly, but a significant and influential piece of writing, an answer to a pamphlet of Gladstone's against the papacy. It was brought out as a *Letter to the Duke of Norfolk*, dedicated to the chief representative of the Catholic laity, the pupil at the Oratory School now grown to responsible manhood. The *Letter* sorted out the confusion in many English minds brought about by those who exaggerated the Pope's prerogatives. Newman had been urged to write an answer to Gladstone by many friends, including Lady Georgiana Fullerton, on this occasion taking on Miss Bowles' usual task of persuasion. His reply, she said, would command an attention 'which no other pen could obtain from the English nation' and he alone could 'meet the sophistry of Gladstone's genius with superior genius to his and the calm reasoning which the task requires'.[23] When the pamphlet was published she wrote to say that she had read it with a kind of breathless admiration. Her husband had joined in her first letter urging the reply and Newman was grateful to them both. The Duke of Norfolk himself, who had been shy at first at the idea of his own name in use on the title-page in case he should be accused of 'swagger', wrote to say how moved he was at the ascription which he interpreted as a mark of Newman's affection, and his mother followed this with her own words of approbation. Emily Bowles put into greater relief an important aspect of the pamphlet; it was not simply an answer to Gladstone, a defence of Catholics, but a clear and comforting exposition of traditional and moderate views on infallibility for Catholics themselves. It had lifted a burden from her mind and doubtless helped others who had suffered at times in the confusions and rumours at the time of the first Vatican Council.

It is not to be supposed, however, that Newman's life was wholly devoted to the high matters of the elucidation of doctrines, reasoning out the nature of religious assent, strengthening the faith of the perplexed. He was busy bringing out his Anglican writings afresh. He was also busy with the constant round of parochial duties at the Oratory. He had his lighter hours, renewing old friendships and yielding occasionally to invitations to issue forth from his home.

In that year of stress, 1870, he travelled to Whatley, near Frome in Somerset to visit his old Anglican friend R W Church, later the Dean of St Paul's. He made a visit to Longleat with the Churches and was reported to be well and happy, walking and even running in very hot weather and making himself at home with Mrs Church and the children, Helen, Mary and Edith. Thence he went to Bath to have lunch with his cousin, Louisa Deane (her maiden name was Fourdrinier), and thence to Henry Wilberforce's house at Woodchester and home via Cheltenham where he lunched with a Catholic friend, George Copeland and his brother, William, an old friend from Anglican days and still an Anglican. Thus relatives he had not seen for years, dear friends from his Anglican past, seasoned friends like Henry Wilberforce, young new acquaintances like the Church girls and visitors who joined the celebratory meals all made up a pattern of friendship, reconciling past and present.

The short visits had a continuance in letters and presents. Louisa Deane sent a plant, a young mulberry tree for Rednal. Church's daughters, who had discussed children's books with the guest, sent him *Alice in Wonderland*, which he found 'a very original, clever book' and one which took off better than any other 'the wayward meaningless sudden changes which take place in dreams'.[29] He did not know the verses that are parodied by Lewis Carroll so a further package came from Whatley Rectory to equip him with copies.

He was generally well in the decade of the seventies, with an elasticity of mind and a tranquillity of spirit that was often noted by those who met him. It was, however, a time which included that repeated sorrow that comes to the elderly, the death of friends. His brother-in-law, John Mozley, died in the autumn of 1872 and Newman, anxious to support Jemima, wrote frequently to Derby, offering advice on business and financial matters that his sister and niece, Janie, could not manage on their own. Some letters went to John Mozley's sister, Anne, ('I can ask you questions, which might tease her'[25]); Anne Mozley was intelligent and level-headed and had been steady in her friendship over the years. He wrote to Louisa Deane, telling her that John Mozley's death was 'mercifully circumstanced, neither sudden nor painful',[26] and that Jemima was bearing up well. The mulberry tree that had come from Louisa had died, indeed had never come to leaf. It was a kind of symbol: the month, November 1872, was mournful and two friends were likely to die soon, Henry Wilberforce and James Hope-Scott. 1873 was a bad year: Newman's two old friends died within six days of each other, in April. At the end of the year there was a less personal loss, the death of one of the most active and faithful parishioners of the Oratory, Mrs Poncia, who nursed her husband through erysipelas and caught the disease herself. There were many mourners, especially among the poor of Birmingham. Newman wrote to Sister Mary Gabriel du Boulay on St John's Day, 'What a year this has been of deaths! The shafts have been flying incessantly and unexpectedly on all sides of us, and strewing the ground with friends. It makes one understand St John's dreary penance of living till ninety'.[27]

The deaths of James Hope-Scott and Henry Wilberforce were very grievous to Newman but, as with John Mozley, these deaths were expected for both had been in poor health for some time. The death which shocked was that of Ambrose St John in 1875, a loss which Newman called the greatest affliction that had ever befallen him. The marvel is that his letters in answer to messages of condolence always contained some sentence of thanksgiving: 'I thank God for having given him to me for so long',[28] he wrote to Sister Mary Gabriel at Stone, and the phrase occurred again and again. Mrs Wootten resolutely made her words of comfort to him as positive as they could be; she maintained that the death of Father Ambrose had been a cause of blessings. 'She feels a grace, and as if a light, had come upon the whole house, on the Oratory and on the school, since God has taken him away'.[29]

Newman reported this at the end of the year and also told his close friends that Mrs Wootten herself had not long to live. She continued her work, interviewing boys from her bed or her sofa when she needed to, and was so bright and alert in manner that the boys did not guess how ill she was. The end came in January 1876 and Newman wrote to Miss Holmes: 'Mrs Wootten died on Sunday night.... She suddenly fell off in the afternoon and slept herself to death by 11. All along she had no fear of death, but was cheerful and joyful, and we could not tell the moment when she went'.[30]

Another Dame had to be found at once and Emily Bowles immediately volunteered, as she had suggested coming earlier in order to help the ailing Mrs Wootten. The funeral was the 14th of January and Frances Wootten was buried in the Oratorian's grave plot at Rednal, the only woman to be so honoured. How Miss Bowles must have envied her her last resting place and also Sister Maria Pia Giberne! The day after the funeral a grateful letter suggested that Miss Bowles should come, but as a stop gap until half term. Newman thought she would find the company of boys hard to tolerate, after years of the company of educated ladies, and she might not get on with Father Norris, the new Headmaster. Moreover, he did not wish her to undertake a work which she would not have considered if she had not been motivated by her personal loyalty to Newman. To accept her offer out of hand would be to 'wantonly misuse'[31] her feelings towards him. However, Miss Bowles came and she stayed. The boys found her a dubious substitute for the motherly Mrs Wootten, stern and tough by comparison.

Many Oratory boys were now grown men and girls that Newman had known as babies were sending news of their weddings. Mamo Hope-Scott, the heir to Scott's house, Abbotsford, had been presented at court, enjoyed a London season and then came home to be with her sick father. She accompanied him abroad, stayed with him as he weakened, wrote faithfully to Newman to report the ups and downs of his illness. After a mourning period for him she married the Hon. Joseph Maxwell and became Mrs Maxwell-Scott. She joined the band of writing ladies with some Catholic biographies and two books about Abbotsford and kept in touch with Newman at all times.

Since faith cannot be handed on as a material inheritance can (such as a house) the children of Catholic converts sometimes had their own spiritual crisis as they came to adult life. One of Newman's friends, Sir John Simeon, had a daughter called Louisa, sometimes called Louy. She had been at school with the Sacred Heart nuns at Roehampton and, on leaving school, had tried her vocation with the Benedictine nuns at Atherstone. Despite a childhood and early youth full of religious practices, she went through a period of doubt, caused, according to Miss Bowles, by attending the brilliant evening parties at her father's house where unbelievers came as well as literary lions. Miss Bowles herself attended such a party and met Tennyson there, 'whom I was very glad to see and know. Otherwise it was painful'.[32] She conversed with young intellectuals who had no religious beliefs and concluded with strictures on her host who invited such people and subjected his daughter to their company. 'And poor Louy –

looking so bright and noble – in the midst of all this throng of half-unbelieving protestants half unCatholic Catholics'.[33] Newman tactfully offered his services to Louisa and entered into her difficulties, knowing, as he said, that it was one thing to battle through theological arguments and doubts as his own generation of Tractarians had done and another thing to face the world as a young person not grounded in the facts of religious truth. By this he did not mean that she had lacked religious instruction but that she needed to 'ascertain the starting points for arriving at religious truth'.[34] He wrote for her a kind of summary of his main arguments that had been explored in the *Grammar*. To gain the starting points, he said, we must interrogate our hearts 'and (since it is a personal, individual matter), our own hearts, – interrogate our own consciences, interrogate, I will say, the God who dwells there'.[35] She should, in this frame of mind, meditate on the Gospels and on St Paul's second Epistle to the Corinthians, earnestly seeking to find the truth and follow it. Every letter to her left it open to her to respond or not, as she chose, and he succeeded in finding her precise need. This was wise counselling of a high order and Louisa Simeon seems to have discovered an adult faith as a result.

Three years later, Richard Ward, who had been at the Oratory School wrote to Newman in confidence to tell him that he and Louisa were engaged. The pair wanted him to marry them but he politely refused ('Ain't I cruel?' he said, in a letter to Ambrose St John). Louisa wrote, 'Your "No" was so much more beautiful than anyone else's "Yes" could have been that we can only thank you from our heart for your letter....'[36]

✤

Late in 1877 Newman received a great and unexpected honour – his first college, Trinity, wished to make him an honorary Fellow. He said to Ullathorne: 'Trinity College has been the one and only seat of my affections at Oxford, and to see once more, before I am taken away, what I never thought I should see again, the place where I began the

battle of my life, with my good angel by my side, is a
prospect almost too much for me to bear.'[1] Ullathorne was
all in favour of Newman's accepting the fellowship and he
duly went to Oxford to be fêted, called on Pusey, saw Keble
College, newly built, and saw his old tutor, Mr Short. It is
clear from the letter to Ullathorne that the occasion
touched him dearly but he was not a man to talk at length
about the episode or his deep feelings that the reminder of
the past and the honour of the present had called forth. So
he disappointed Sister Maria Pia who, from her convent,
asked for a full account of his reception at Trinity, his feelings and his thoughts. He reminded her of a phrase from a
story by George Canning in the eighteenth century. 'Your
letter just received made me both sigh and smile. I can
only say with the "Needy knife grinder", "Story, heaven
bless you, I have none to tell you –" I assure you I made no
record of my feelings when I went to Oxford, and recollect
nothing. I know it was a trial to me and a pleasure – but I
could not say more, if you put me on the rack.'[2] He told
her that the Trinity Fellows were pleasing and kind and
listed the places that he had visited. Also he reported on
Pusey, who looked much older. And with that she had to
be content.

A much greater honour was in store, and one that was
quite unexpected. It was signalled by a little incident that
involved the new Pope and a woman from the Oratory
parish in Birmingham. Pius IX died in February, 1878, and
was succeeded by Cardinal Pecci, Leo XIII, a thin, shrewd
man who was more prepared to meet the difficulties and
the challenges of the modern world by positive action than
his predecessor had been. He admired Newman and
showed it during an audience. Margaret Dunn lived near
the Oratory and went to confession to Newman. She hoped
to be a nun but had to look after her parents and so abandoned all thought of the Religious life. She worked as a
governess and kept in touch with Newman who realised
she was lonely and wrote her notes of encouragement.
Eventually she took a post as governess at the French
Embassy in Rome and met Father Rossi of the Roman
Oratory. He gave her an introduction to Monsignor

Macchi at the Vatican who arranged for her to have an audience with Pope Leo and was particularly interested that she was Newman's penitent. The Pope, on hearing this, took a little picture from his breviary, autographed it and gave it to Margaret Dunn to send on. This she did with care and Newman kept it as a token of affection from the Pope. It was a great feature of Catholic life to collect religious pictures, little cards with prayers, notification of the death of friends or of a priest's jubilee. Prayer books could bristle with cards or send forth a shower of large confetti, and such cards were popular tender among girls in convent schools. It is an intriguing thought that there should be this exchange from one intellectual and eminent man to another – and it was a presage. Probably it was in the Pope's mind then that he would make Newman a cardinal. He said later, 'My Cardinal, it was not easy ... they said he was being too liberal, but I had determined to honour the Church in honouring Newman. I had always had a cult for him.'[3]

The little picture (of Our Lady of Lourdes) went out in December 1878. In the summer of that year the young Duke of Norfolk and a noble convert, the Marquis of Ripon had taken an important initiative and had asked Cardinal Manning to make known to the Pope the wish of many in England that Newman should be made a cardinal, not simply because of his personal qualities but as a sign of approval of his work and a recognition that his account of the teaching of the Catholic Church was both orthodox and valuable. A letter from Manning conveying their request went to Rome borne by Cardinal Howard but that messenger travelled slowly, staying here and there, so that by December he still had not reached Rome. So the Duke of Norfolk himself, who was in Rome, made his own approach to the Pope at a private audience. The Duke was taking on himself responsibility for the matter but he had no idea then what complications would ensue. He continued, however, and showed pertinacity and diplomatic skills: the young boy who had not been in the top flight at the Oratory School and who had been slow at getting up in the morning had matured to be a good leader of the lay Catholics of England.

The story of the events between the end of January 1879 and the middle of March has often been told. Cardinal Nina, the Cardinal Secretary of State, wrote to Manning asking whether Newman would accept a cardinal's hat. This question was relayed to Newman via Ullathorne. He was both moved and grateful but stated a difficulty – He did not feel, at his age and with his responsibility for the Oratory that he could go and live in Rome, which would be customary for a cardinal who was not also the bishop of a diocese. Yet he did not feel that he could strike bargains with the Pope. Ullathorne understood his position very well and wrote a letter himself which was a model of clarity: he said that nothing stood in the way of Newman's accepting the dignity except the distress at leaving the Oratory in Birmingham and he, Ullathorne, did not think it was the Pope's intention to transfer him to Rome, rather considering his presence in England to be important 'where he is in communication with those who are in search of the truth'.[4] Manning sent on a letter from Newman which, in its desire not to hint at terms and bargains, could, just possibly, be construed as a refusal. But he did not send on Ullathorne's covering letter.

Newman meanwhile sent a short letter directly to Manning, who was about to depart for Rome, saying 'I could not be so ungracious whether to the Holy Father or to the friends at home who have interested themselves in this matter, as to decline what was so kindly proposed, providing that it did not involve unfaithfulness to St. Philip.'[5] Manning then let it be known that Newman had refused the cardinal's hat and this was given out in the English newspapers. Pusey and also Frank Newman thought he was right to refuse and his Catholic friends were dismayed.

On 20 February Newman told the Duke of Norfolk that he must not believe the newspapers: 'if so high an honour was offered me, I should not answer it by a blunt refusal.'[6] The Duke sent a copy of this letter to Manning in Rome with this clear directive, 'I think the Pope ought to know that Father Newman did not mean in his letter what the papers say he did.'[7] Manning then saw the Pope, ascertained that there would be no requirement for Newman to leave the Oratory and sent the news both to the Duke and to Ullathorne. Just as Ullathorne was writing to Manning in reply to this good news and signalling Newman's glad acceptance Lady Herbert wrote to Newman to express her hope that he would not persist in his refusal. Alarm bells rang. Lady Herbert was a friend of Manning and of Vaughan, and it was still possible that the tale of his refusal would get out again. Copies of parts of her letter went at once to Ullathorne and to the Duke, and Newman wrote to Manning, 'wishing to guard against all possible mistake.'[8]

All was well, however. Newman set out for Mother Mary Imelda Poole, amongst other friends, exactly why he was happy to accept the cardinal's hat. 'It was hard to receive letters to the effect that I was under a cloud... Now, the Pope in his generosity has taken this reproach simply away...'[9] Both among Protestants and among Catholics there had been those who had said Newman was only half a Catholic but the elevation to the cardinalate was a triumphant justification of his views. She and some of Newman's other friends at the convent at Stone thought of Mother Margaret Hallahan and how she would have rejoiced.

Newman went to Rome in April, accompanied by Father William Neville. He did not have to worry about expenses (which were considerable, a cardinal's clothes, at that date, being of a quantity and cost that pained him to think about) for a group of Catholic gentlemen, led by the Duke of Norfolk, had set up a fund for him. One of the committee was the Hon. Joseph Maxwell Scott, the husband of Mamo. This state visit to receive the cardinal's hat was part triumph and part misery for he caught cold and was ill enough to cause considerable alarm. He lamented afterwards that he had been weeks in Rome and had had to live like a pagan, shut up on his doctor's orders and not allowed to say Mass. On the other hand, he was able to see the Pope, who was extraordinarily kind and interested in the affairs of the Birmingham Oratory and he carried off the necessary ceremonies with aplomb. Luckily his cold did not become very severe until the main

functions were done. He received the *biglietto*, the official
summons to the consistory, at a reception in Cardinal
Howard's apartments and the occasion and his speech
were noted and received with interest in the English
papers. Rome too was impressed and a group of Italian
ladies at the reception (more vocal in public than their
English counterparts) sighed and exclaimed audibly that
he was '*bellissimo.*'[9] The next day he received his biretta
from the Pope and there was a further ceremony, the
consistory at which the new cardinals' hats were presented.
There was also the reception at the English College where
he received an address from the English residents in Rome
and many gifts, vestments and church plate. His cardinalatial motto was '*Cor ad cor loquitur*', '*Heart speaks to heart*'.
The Oratorians with him, William Neville, Thomas Pope
and Thomas Eaglesim were proud of him: he was old and
frail but impressive, relaxed and gracious. Then fever and
congestionof the lungs set in and when they left Rome for
Leghorn he was still weak, though recovered, and was laid
low again, with diarrhoea.

An English lady, Mrs Sconce, whose son had been at the
Oratory School, was then in Florence and she was most
anxious to help. Doubtless she felt that a parcel of men,
however clerical, attentive and devout, would not make
such good nurses as women would. She came over from
Florence to Leghorn and found a good Italian doctor for
Newman, pending the arrival of an English doctor from
Rome.

He meant to go across to Autun on the way back to
England to visit Sister Maria Pia. They had not seen one
another for nearly twenty years. However, when the party
reached the north of France Newman was tired, rain was
incessant and the doctor forbade the extra journey.
Newman wrote to his old friend, 'We must subject
outselves to the Will of God. What is our religion, if we
can't?'[10] There is no word from her on her feelings as she
waited in her convent, expecting to see him and to harry
him to get an account of all the grand functions in Rome,
no outpouring of her terrible disappointment. He had said
'we must subject ourselves' and they were justly yoked

together in those powerful little sentences for he was disappointed too – but her grief must have been greater than his.

England was thrilled to see him back and Birmingham – unused to having a cardinal in its midst – was immensely proud. Once back he took up many of his old tasks and he lived as simply as he could. There were, however, some scenes of grandeur and a great deal of fatigue. All that summer delegations came to present addresses to the new cardinal: replies had to be made each time and William Neville, who took on the functions of helper, nurse and guardian, worried that the Father did not get any rest. Every reply to an address emphasised that the honour done to Newman himself was also an honour intended for the Catholics and the converts in England. In 1880 it was arranged that he would stay in London, at Norfolk House, for a few days in May. He gave Benediction at the London Oratory, preached to their Little Oratory, and returned later for a reception attended by two hundred clergy. At Norfolk House there were receptions, one after another, luncheon and dinner parties, a constant stream of visitors. The Dowager Duchess of Norfolk came to lunch and Lady Georgiana Fullerton with her husband – in other words, amongst that great press of people he could have some brief enjoyment of friends.

More quietly, he took lunch with Mrs Bowden at her house and on Wednesday 12th May there was a quiet dinner at his host's, the only guest being Emily Bowden. Her cousin Fanny (one of Henry Bowden's daughters) heard about it and wrote in a letter that Emily, 'really had an opportunity of conversation with him – and he talked much of his friendship with her father.'[11]

Later in the same month he spent three days in Oxford. This visit was a much grander affair than his previous one. He arrived at Trinity College late in the afternoon of Saturday 22 May and that evening a conversazione was held in his honour; the hall was made into a flower-decked drawing room and the lime walk was illuminated. Twice on the Sunday, Newman preached to a large congregation in St Aloysius Church (now the Oxford Oratory). On Monday he breakfasted with the Fellows of Oriel and attended a Trinity Gaudy: there were many guests at the Gaudy dinner and a reception was held for the ladies.

During this visit he went to see his old rooms at Trinity, inhabited by a young man called Douglas Sladen, who later became a writer, and looking very different from the way they were in the young Newman's day because there were photos of actresses on the mantelpiece. Sladen wrote of the occasion:

> It was one of the great moments of my life. The Cardinal, a wan little old man with a shrivelled face and a large nose, and one of the most beautiful expressions which ever appeared on a human being, talked to me for a couple of hours, prostrating me with his exquisite modesty. He wanted to know if the snapdragons, to which he had written a poem, still grew on the wall between Trinity and Balliol; he wanted to compare the undergraduate life of his day with the undergraduate life of mine... He told me the marks by which he knew that my rooms were his rooms; asked me about my studies, and hobbies, and aims in life: I don't think I have ever felt any honour of the kind so much....[12]

Newman must have enjoyed this encounter and the whole time was gratifying – but he was glad to return to the simplicities of home. As cardinal he had two rooms, not one, a bedroom and a room which was partitioned to make a little chapel as well as a study and a sitting area. In the chapel Sister Maria Pia came into her own. St Francis de Sales was her saint, as the co-founder of the Visitation Order and he was a fitting patron for Newman as the patron saint of writers. She drew a series of pictures illustrating his life and they were put up on one side of the little chapel, where they are still to be seen. She was busy completing the series at the beginning of 1880 and Newman warned her not to increase any picture's size by so much as an inch, else it would not fit. The set taxed her drawing skills – the many figures are not all on the same scale.

Photographers and portrait painters had an interesting subject to hand with Newman. One of Newman's friends, Lord Coleridge, Lord Chief Justice and son of the Coleridge who was judge at the Achilli trial, had in his wife Jane a sensitive artist who frequently exhibited portraits at the Royal Academy. She too was Newman's friend and asked him to sit for portraits in 1874. She made three portraits in all and one of them (probably the first one she did), a drawing in black and white chalk that shows Newman resting his head on his hands, is singularly beautiful.

When he became Cardinal Newman the call for portraits was more insistent. The best known one is by Millais, the painter having hs subject dressed in all the splendour of cardinalatial robes so that the fine old head emerges from an expanse of scarlet watered silk and the gnarled hands rest on the lace of his rochet. Millais treated his sitter with facetious good humour, asking His Eminence to mount the eminence (the model's dais) and encouraging him with the words, 'Come, jump up, you dear old boy.'[13] Sister Maria Pia Giberne, hearing of this projected portrait, sent some painter's queries, but Millais was not very helpful. Another portrait, by Ouless, was done for Oriel and Newman wrote amusingly to his niece, Jane Mozley: 'I am to be painted for Oriel. It is a wonderful change of feeling – and wonderful that I should live to see it – but I could not have been painted unless I had lived.'[14] This was in 1878, marking the change in feeling towards him that came about first in Oxford and then in Rome, but the painting was not done until 1880 when he was a cardinal. A second version was presented to Newman by his Birmingham parishioners.

Women played their part in this matter of pictures. Louisa Deane had artistic daughters and one of them, also Louisa, sent Newman a painting of San Giorgio in Velabro, his titular church in Rome, a gift that pleased him very much. Her sister Emmeline took on a much greater task. She came to the Oratory, made sketches and painted two portraits in oils, one of which now hangs in the National Portrait Gallery. It brings to mind Douglas Sladen's description of the Cardinal as 'a wan little old man' – it is a late picture, showing him in extreme old age. Two women designed medals showing the Cardinal's head; one Elinor Hallé, was much praised for this work and won a prize as a medallist. She had studied at the Slade and was working professionally, a detail which shows a shift in attitude to women's talents from the earlier part of the century to this later date.

Newman grudged the time spent as a sitter for portraits. He wrote to Emmeline Deane, 'What chance have I of doing my small work, however much I try? And you lightly ask me, my dear child to give up the long days, which are in fact the only days I have!'[15] He was still responsible for the Birmingham Oratory, still concerned for the parish (where two of "Mrs Connelly's nuns" had come to look after the school), still alive to what was happening in the world and to theological thought and development. For instance in 1889 he wrote an article *On the Inspiration of Scripture*, which looked forward to the views laid down on the subject at the Second Vatican Council.

Converts still consulted him. One of these was a sixteen year old girl called Emily Fortey who lived at Clifton. She maintained that she had been thinking of becoming a Catholic for about four years and did not know where to turn: she had a stepmother and her father spent much time in India so that she did not know him well. She had read extracts of Newman's writings and *Loss and Gain*, and felt herself to be a Catholic at heart. Newman sent her a careful letter: what she had said had led him 'to entertain great hopes that God is calling you by His grace into His Church'[16] but she was very young, dependent on her father, and should realise the seriousness of the step she was taking. It would be best to consult the Jesuit Fathers in Bristol.

Emily Fortey had a schoolfriend at Clifton High School called Marion Tucker who also wrote to Newman to say she wanted to be a Catholic. The reply was in much the same terms as the one he wrote to Emily Fortey but more distant and even more cautious, and written in the third person. Marion Tucker had taken a copy of her friend's letter (no doubt, serious as these two sixteen year olds were, they had a delicious and excited tête-à-tête over the Cardinal's kind reply) and it got into the hands of John K. Tucker (presumably Marion's father) who sent it to *The Times* for publication. Emily's father, Henry Fortey, was extremely vexed. He disliked the idea of publicity for himself and his daughter and he also disliked the fact that Cardinal Newman had been so scurvily treated by someone's publishing a private letter. He wrote to say that his daughter had not been responsible. 'I am strongly opposed to your creed,' wrote Henry Fortey, 'and will continue to do all I can to dissuade my daughter from joining your Church; but fair play is a jewel and I therefore write to apologise for my daughter's indiscretion in giving a copy of your letter to Miss Tucker....'[17]

Henry Fortey was a decent man who cherished that jewel, fair play. He made his daughter wait two years and then allowed her to become a Catholic. Newman wrote to Emily as he had once done to Isy Froude, to say that joy and delight might die down in the heart of a young convert but prayer and trust would carry her along. He also said, 'I think your Father has been very good to you. It was right you should have a trial, but he has not opposed your convictions, as some parents have in their dealings with their children.'[18] He never said, as he might have done, that the letters from Clifton, two years earlier, had caused him trouble. There had been the publication in *The Times* and letters to papers in Bath, complaining that Cardinal Newman had been writing to Protestant schoolgirls.

In 1887, when Emily Fortey was twenty one she wrote again asking to come to Birmingham to see Newman. 'I want to see your own face instead of pictures and to hear your own voice instead of reading your books.'[19] The visit was duly made on 8 August. Nothing more was heard, however, of Marion Tucker.

The encounter between the young woman and the very aged Cardinal is an image of a person at the end of a long life seeing new life and growth. The very old must of necessity turn their gaze towards the future in another sense, thinking of their approaching end, and such thoughts are often prompted by the news of the death of their contemporaries. In Newman's little cluttered room a wall (the one opposite the pictures of St Francis de Sales) was turned into a little picture gallery, the photographs of friends. Between the two walls was the altar of the tiny chapel and Newman used the photographs to prompt prayers for those he loved who had died. Also he had a book (the entries went back years) where the names and dates of departed friends were carefully written.

In 1877 news came of the death of a young woman who had married young Hurrell Froude. This was Beatrice, the daughter of George Ryder, who was known as Bice, pronounced in the Italian way, which Newman acknowledged by sometimes spelling it Biche. She was in India with her husband and, to add to the sorrow of it all, Hurrell was away from home when she died. She left a small daughter, Mary, and a baby called William Hurrell. It was like history repeating itself in a sad pattern for George Ryder's wife died young and Newman remembered going to preach at her funeral and seeing the baby, Beatrice, in her nurse's arms. Isy Froude went out to India to be with her brother, probably debating where her first loyalty was because her mother was not well. Newman wrote to urge this ailing friend not to go to church fasting. He was right to be anxious: Catherine Froude died in the summer of 1878. William did not survive her long. In the hope of better health and as a diversion from his grief he went on a cruise to South Africa and sent Newman a very long letter written during the leisure hours of his trip abroad, an exposition of his views on religion and his inability to accept dogma. Newman replied. They were both going over old ground. William Froude never returned for he caught dysentery and died in South Africa in May 1879.

Isy, who had been her mother's prop and, like Daisy Watt, was the person to write the letters when her mother was too weak, made a late marriage. When she was forty she married Baron Anatole von Hügel, the younger brother of Friedrich. He was appointed Curator of the University Museum of Archaeology and Ethnology in Cambridge and they moved there in 1883. The next year the pair visited Birmingham to find Newman sitting for his first portrait to Emmeline Deane and since he was so anchored they could talk at length. Isy was anxious that Newman should like her husband and that her husband should like and admire him – it was the bringing together of the two people most dear to her. She need not have worried: her husband was so impressed that he said that the meeting made him feel how it is worthwhile to be a saint. As for her brother Hurrell, he married again, this time to Agnes Wilberforce. She had three children but was desperately ill at the birth of the first one and died after nine years of marriage.

The year of the death of Mrs Froude also saw the death of Miss Holmes. At the end of her life she wrote Newman a poem, sentimental, unmistakably Victorian and also sincere: he had, after all, been a loyal friend for years, a fixed point in her wandering life. This effusion was written in 1878.

> The years in onward course have brought to me
> Old age, made dreary by infirmity.
> My singing days are past, but still I long
> To hail the day I love with song.
> Again it comes, like to a cheering gleam
> Of sunshine on a winter's day, a theme
> That cuts upon the mem'ry like a spell,
> Leading the thought upon the Past to dwell,
> And in it find bright pictures, which can lend
> Light to the gloomy Present, and can blend
> With the dim unknown Future, bringing Hope
> To whisper comfort, when we blindly grope
> Along that shore where darkness ever dwells,
> The unknown Future! Like a chime of bells
> Heard on a morn when snow is falling fast,
> The voice of Hope keeps ringing 'In the Past
> Seek earnest of the Future' and I feel
> That heaven doth not its best gifts idly deal,
> Like fabled Fortune with her rolling wheel,
> But that past blessings are a pledge and deal
> Of others still to come; and I may dare
> To hold that even Death itself will ne'er

Dissolve the tie that binds me to my Friend,
That best of gifts that Heaven vouchsafed to send
When wandering in a world that seemed to me,
At first, made bright with such sweet liberty
As one on lonely mountain path doth taste
At sunrise; but when day is done and haste
Will not suffice to gain the vale below,
Before night comes, unless a guide doth show
The one safe path to take; then doth despair
Threaten the lonely traveller: all his care
Is now for guidance through the deepening gloom
Where spectres, hid by dazzling day, now loom:-
So did I seek, and my darkest hour
The help I needed came:- Storms yet may lower
But I will hope that when my life will end
I shall not be divided from my Friend.[20]

Jemima Mozley, widowed but surrounded by affectionate children and by her many sisters-in-law who lived in houses in or around Derby, was ailing for months before her death. Newman was worried about her and did not trust her doctor. He could hardly write of his fears to his sister, but he had the reassurance of the sensible and sympathetic Anne Mozley. She had always been friendly and he placed reliance on her judgement. Miss Anne Mozley was a convinced and steadfast Anglican but she had no difficulty in communicating freely with this Roman priest and their letters went to and fro just as easily and readily when he became a cardinal. She was much easier to deal with than the John Mozleys. When Jemima died, in 1879, Jane was reserved with her uncle and the family as a whole took exception to the fact that he wrote to say he had said Mass for Jemima (which he considered the most loving act he could perform) but did not write effusively. The misunderstanding called forth some magnificent phrases from him: 'I believe that I shall never die; this awful prospect would crush me, were it not that I trusted and prayed that it would be an eternity in God's Presence. How is eternity a boon, unless He goes with it? And for others dear to me, my one prayer is that they may see God.'[21] He said Mass for his sister that all distance between her and God should be removed.

Old age made the memories of the past more vivid and more dear. He wished his mother had talked more of her own youth and her family but he thought sorrows had made her disinclined to turn to the past and happier days. The revived links with the Deane family (who were related to the Fourdriniers) were a pleasure. And in losing Jemima he had lost one who had shared childhood and youth and who was someone with a talent for dates and accurate memories. 'I knew quite well, as anniversaries of all kinds came round, she was recollecting them, as well as I – eg. my getting into Oriel – now I am the only one in the world who knows a hundred things most interesting to me. Eg. yesterday was the anniversary of Mary's death – my mind turned at once to Jemima, but she was away.'[22]

The one left in the world who would share the memory of Mary's death was old Sister Maria Pia, writing down some reminiscences in her French convent. They shared too some of the afflictions of old age and, since she had never been good at eating sensibly and looking after herself, and since she was a very old friend who could take some plain speaking, he was direct with his advice. He was worried that she was not taking care enough about a hernia and said he would obtain a truss for her in England if she would send details of her girth. Also she should be careful with her diet. 'If you have not teeth, you *cannot* eat hard substances without danger. Unchewed meat is as dangerous to the stomach as brick or stone, or a bunch of keys. You are not an ostrich.'[23]

Sister Maria Pia died suddenly in December 1885. She had been in retreat and renewed her vows and then seemed very happy. She went and wrote a letter to Mr Fullerton, a letter that showed no confusion or deterioration in her handwriting and went then to her own room where she had a stroke, remained unconscious and died the next morning. The letter to Alexander Fullerton told him of some pictures she was busy with and she had just sent Newman a critique of the Emmeline Deane portrait. At eighty three, she was still a busy artist. The Oratory was informed of her death by telegram and Newman wrote to the Visitation Convent at Autun to send condolences and to thank the nuns for the promptitude in sending news of the death of one 'for whom I had so true and deep an interest'.[24]

A descendant of Maria Rosina Giberne (she was Lance Sieveking's grandfather's sister) published *The Eye of the Beholder* in 1957, in which he celebrated Gerard Manley Hopkins and more briefly, this other relative who amused him and who was a source of pride as one who was 'certainly dynamic and not a little eccentric'. He described her in these terms:

> She was a very beautiful woman with a wild, passionate nature... Many men fell in love with her, and so did women. She seems to have responded with embarrassing violence, irrespective of their sex, and with an entirely naive innocence. The passionate friendship with John Henry Newman lasted all her life[25]

Lance Sieveking also spoke of her conversion to Rome in one brief sentence: 'She had fallen in love with John Henry Newman (later Cardinal), and this led to her conversion'.[26] All this is a little simplistic. There is plenty of evidence that men fell in love with her but, with the possible exception of Selina Bacchus, little evidence that women did. Miss Giberne felt a strong attraction to some women even if her feelings were not reciprocated. Lance Sieveking is nearer the mark with the observation that 'in sexual matters, she remained in a state of ingenuous innocence, hardly understanding the significance of her own impulses'.[27] Newman was certainly instrumental in her conversion to Rome but her commitment was genuine and she was devout and persevering enough to enter a convent (against the odds, because religious houses did not want her) and she lived out her life in far-off Autun where she did not see Newman again. As for the 'passionate friendship', time and his resolute curbs on her 'spiritual love' made her settle for something calmer. The letters between the two old people, exchanging news, reminiscences, discussing spiritual matters and also such concerns as soft food, trusses and elastic stockings are far from romantic.

She sent Newman a self-portrait in the habit of a Visitation nun. She looks resolute under the stiff headdress and still has some resemblance to Napoleon.

రుల

There was still the question of Newman's biography to be settled. Years before he had known that he must authorise an account that would represent him fairly: he had had plenty of experience of being misrepresented by the careless or ignorant or traduced by his enemies and he dreaded an over enthusiastic account given by some friend and supporter like Miss Giberne. Ambrose St John would have been a good chronicler if he had lived but who could fulfil the task now when the cardinalate made the matter more pressing?

In 1876 Newman wrote a memorandum about his wishes for a biography. He saw his life clearly divided into two parts, the Anglican years and the Catholic years. As to the second, it would be better to be silent, for an account would incur the risk of 'great scandal, controversy, partisanship.'[1] All his papers were to be kept so that the facts could be ascertained but he did not wish anything written about the period after 1845 until time had put many matters in perspective and the participants had departed from the scene. As to his time as an Anglican, 'I don't want a panegyric written of me, which would be sickening, but a real fair downright account of me according to the best ability and judgement of the writer.'[2] Who that writer would be was not the question that he was considering at that moment but it should be 'some Anglican friend or well-wisher.'

A great letter writer and a keeper of letters, Newman had placed reliance on letters as a day-by-day chronicle of events, reactions and feelings. He outlined his theory in a letter to Jemima in 1863:

It has ever been a hobby of mine (unless it be a truism, not a hobby) that a man's life lies in his letters. This is

why Hurrell Froude published St Thomas à Beckett's
Letters, with nothing of his own except what was necessary for illustration or connecftion of parts...

A much higher desideratum than interest in
Biography is met by the method, (as it may be called,) of
Correspondence. Biographers varnish; they assign
motives; they interpret Lord Burleigh's nods, they
palliate or defend. For myself, I sincerely wish to seem
neither better nor worse than I am.[3]

He went on to meditate on the difficulties facing an editor of
letters. A collection of letters would be prolix and 'there
must be a selection of passages; sometimes one half sentence
alone is valuable in a whole letter.' The task would be further
complicated in that the letters of any man of affairs would
involve many people and touch on party interests yet the
editor, in making his selection, should not hurt people,
make mischief or enter into controversy. Newman himself,
prompted to this exchange with Jemima by their passing on
family letters to each other, told her in effect that he was
seeing to it that he had the material ready for someone to
edit his letters one day. 'When I have a little leisure I recur to
my pigeon-holes of letters, where they stand year by year
from 1836 down to this date. I have digested them up to the
former year. Thus from time to time I do a little work in the
way of sifting, sorting, preserving or burning.'[4]

The 'downright account' that he hoped for was not
simply for himself, a justification and a setting of the
record straight. What he had said and done had had effects
on many others and Anglican church history and indeed
Roman church history had been altered because of his life.
He pondered on the need for that partial but authorised
biography by means of letters and, at the end of his life,
chose the editor with care. It was a woman, Anne Mozley,
who was an Anglican and a true friend and well-wisher.

Correspondence in those later years was particularly
cordial between the pair. Miss Mozley was a valuable link
between Jemima, Jemima's family and himself and her
memories reached back to early days when she first met his
family and some of his friends. His mood of elderly reminis-

cence was matched by hers. Jane Mozley, sorting papers after her mother's death found a letter from Mary Newman. Jane's aunt read it and reported her impressions. 'She put self into a letter.' 'It seemed to make one know the writer, and so fresh, like a bird's song on a breath of spring.'[5] Such a sensitive phrasing, such a response to a letter that dated back to the years when they were all young, were treasured by Newman. Miss Mozley was a very thoughtful, sensible correspondent. When he returned to England as a cardinal she wrote, 'I feel that you will take indulgently a few words of welcome home needing no answer.'[6] After Jemima's death she wrote for his birthday, knowing that he would miss his sister's usual remembrance of the day.

On re-reading some of his sermons she wrote, 'I felt with renewed force that while the English language lasts these sermons will last,'[7] and her letter to greet the new cardinal expressed her ecumenical spirit and her regard for him. 'to have inspired a universal feeling of personal affection and reverence does so much to soften the bitterness of religious party differences.'[8]

She made a visit to Littlemore in 1875 and took the trouble to give him all the details. He had re-visited the place himself, seen some of his old parishioners, wept at seeing the memorial to his mother. Anne Mozley could give a more complete picture since she stood a little to one side, the observer with a keen eye for the present who yet remembered the past. She could say more because she had not been the chief person in that significant little parish.

She visited several elderly people who had been Newman's parishioners. Their reminiscences were clear – Miss Mozley said they all seemed to 'talk pictures'. Several still had 'Mr Newman's' portrait over the fireplace, like Mrs Stroud who remembered the 'young ladies' who looked after the school and that the children were as quiet as mice when Mr Newman called. Martha King remembered a golden time in her youth when she was being prepared for confirmation and was told to read the thirteenth chapter of the First Epistle to the Corinthians. Meditating on the theme of charity, she said, 'I think there was more Christianity than there is now.' Martha Phipps and her husband ('a very primitive old couple') were pleased to think back to Mr Newman's day. It was old Mrs Phipps who did most of the talking, telling Miss Mozley that Mr Newman had read the funeral service over her baby and sending a careful message: 'you must tell him we be old but we be still alive and hopes Mr Newman will enjoy himself in the condition he is in and pray for we.'

Anne Mozley remembered very clearly how she had helped in adorning the new church at Littlemore all those years before. She was a keen needlewoman and had helped to embroider the famous altar cloth which had been made to celebrate Easter. It had been done 'under Mr John Mozley's auspices' – presumably he had paid for it – and sewn by Jemima and her sisters-in-law. John Rouse Bloxam, who had been Newman's curate at Littlemore and who continued to be his friend and admirer, sent Miss Mozley his recollections of the altar cloth: it was of crimson velvet, hanging in copious folds with a border round it of embroidered heraldic shields and, in the front, the text 'The Lord hath risen indeed and hath appeared to Simon.' Although this was in 1885, she too remembered it very clearly.

Dear Dr Bloxam,

Your letter throws one's memory into the far past when we sisters and Mr Mozley were all exercising our untrained powers on the Littlemore altar-cloth. I feel sure it *was* the beginning of the fashion – or shall I say *passion* for Church needlework that filled High Church female bosoms in those bright ignorant days. The Littlemore altar-cloth was as you describe, not fitted to the Altar as it ought to have been, but falling in folds, which had a beauty and dignity of its own nevertheless.

It had a border round it some twelve inches deep of the two colours alternatively. Emblems embroidered in the centre, and (small) the Arms of the Archbishop and the Oxford Diocese, I think. The text you quote in the centre, I remember working at it. If you were here I could show you sketches, specimens, but they won't go into a letter....

Very truly yours,
Anne Mozley[9]

She used some apologetic phrases when talking of the cloth (whose two colours may have been red and yellow or gold, since Bloxam remembered that the text was sewn in yellow silk), pleading that zeal and ignorance went together in its making. The embroiderers were blazing a trail. Certainly the descriptions betoken zeal rather than careful taste but no one can judge – the cloth was 'banished to the colonies' when a new order of things took over in Littlemore.

Anne Mozley used the pen as well as the needle. She was of literary and scholarly tastes and wrote many reviews of poetry. It was another writing Mozley, however, who published reminiscences of the days of the Oxford Movement: Tom Mozley's *Reminiscences of Oriel College and the Oxford Movement* came out in 1882. His sister Anne deplored its inaccuracies and was sorry to think of the effect it would have on those who had been present at those events which he had described in so slapdash a way: 'I doubt if he can put himself into other people's frame of mind or guess what they will feel.'[10] Newman felt the inaccuracies so strongly that he politely refused to discuss the book with her in detail.

She herself took on a literary work of some magnitude after the death of her brother James. He had been first at Oriel and then a Fellow of Magdalen College and at one time he had been a theologian of the High Church party. Eventually he became Regius Professor of Divinity at Oxford. His sister edited his essays and then his letters. Newman followed the progress of this work and read the books with interest. In October 1884 he commented that the edition of the letters was 'well done as a sample of clear and careful putting together and of good judgment in literary work'.[11] He told Miss Mozley of his plans for a biography, sent her a brief memoir of his early life that he had written in 1874 and asked for her judgment on it. He was leading up to a request that she should edit the memoir with the considerable number of letters that covered the Anglican period.

There followed an extraordinary episode in Newman's life and in hers. Anne Mozley, after some hesitations, took on the task, though she was then seventy six and her eyesight gave trouble. The scheme was to be a secret one though she was allowed two people to be consultors, Dean Church and an old friend of Newman's, Lord Blachford. Newman himself supplied the necessary papers but left the editing to her, keeping himself apart and in the dark about what she said, what she included or omitted. Bulky packages arrived at Barrow sent by post and sometimes, and discreetly, Father William Neville came by train with a portmanteau of letters, took lunch and travelled back to Birmingham. Her book was not to come out until after Newman's death. She gave as her aim the making of a book where all should be 'as true and simple as I can make it'.[12] The work was done, despite her difficulties, by the time he died and appeared in 1891, entitled *Letters and Correspondence of John Henry Newman during his Life in the English Church with a Brief Autobiography*, with the additional phrase 'edited at Cardinal Newman's request'. She herself died a few months after its publication, in her eighty-second year.

He had placed great trust in this old lady's abilities, her industry and her literary tact. She justified this trust in the main, though there were some gaps in the narrative. A modern commentator notes that she left out passages that bore directly against the Church of England and, like most of her contemporaries, she was inclined 'to consider some details of everyday life not sufficiently dignified'.[13] The account of Newman's Sicilian journey gave her real trouble; there was an intensity about it, a sense that the illness and the recovery were a kind of battle between supernatural powers, and a frankness about the details of the illness that she could not make public. 'Anne deleted all references to the devil and to Newman's bowels'.[14] A photograph of Anne Mozley shows a solid lady, with a pleasant, sensible face. She had a good mind, with great seriousness, and served Newman and Newman scholars very well. Indeed, her work could be described as the opposite of that of her brother Tom – careful where he was wild, having its focus on the subject rather than on her own opinions whereas he had issued his own thoughts and memories with no check on their authenticity.

When she was busy and William Neville toiling with portanteaux the Cardinal at home was becoming increasingly frail. His mind was still clear but his eyesight was poor, he grew deaf, he stumbled and fell many times and his fingers had grown clumsy. His friends had given him a splendid violin some years before but his playing days were done and he had given the instrument to Mary Church, as a consolation when her twin sister went off to be married. After visiting the convent at Stone in November 1881 (earlier than the years when he had been employing Anne Mozley) he apologised to Sister Mary Gabriel du Boulay, a frequent recipient of letters, for his rough behaviour in quoting a poem with reference to himself. This was *The Three Warnings* by Mrs Piozzi, a story in verse which tells of Death's promise to give three warnings to a young man. When the man is eighty, Death comes, saying, 'If you are lame and deaf and blind, you've had your three sufficient warnings'.[15]

This visit to his dearest convent was to say Mass for Mother Imelda Poole who had died very suddenly. The nuns wrote an account of the day:

> After his breakfast, he came to the Community Room and spoke to us in the most beautiful and touching way, of the joy we ought to have in the midst of our bereavement.... After dinner the Cardinal asked to be taken to the Choir that he might pray by Mother Margaret's and Mother Imelda's graves – he knelt by them for some time in silent prayer, evidently deeply moved. There was a most wonderful hush and silence all the time; no sound indoors or out, but a profound stillness. It was a dull grey morning; but as we knelt there one clear bright ray of sunshine suddenly darted thro' the casement and fell directly on the grave of our dearest Mother Imelda. The effect of *that silence*, and that sudden *ray of light* was something impossible to describe.[16]

He told the Prioress that he would not have missed this visit for the world. She was Mother Frances Raphael Drane, who succeeded Mother Mary Imelda as Provincial. Later still another visit was chronicled when Ullathorne (who had been given a titular Archbishopric) was staying at the convent. He was the stronger of the two venerable guests, supporting Newman with an arm, and pouring tea for him and holding the cup to his lips. The Archbishop, however, was to die first, in the spring of the next year, 1889, uttering on his deathbed the robust words, 'The devil is a jackass'.

In November Newman set about a pastoral task which concerned the chocolate factory at Bournville. Old and frail as he was, he went to talk to the Quaker employers, the Cadburys, about the Catholic girls who worked there. They were obliged to attend Bible Study every day but after Newman's intervention (described by George Cadbury as offered in a 'loving Christian spirit') they were allowed to pray apart. The anecdote illustrates how things have changed in a century, both on the industrial and on the ecclesiastical scene. Employers today, however, devout, could not demand Bible study from the workforce and Catholics would pray with others. Set in the world of 1889, however, the story says much of Newman in extreme old age. He was pastoral to the end, the old charm had not gone and he was alert in mind and concerned about affairs. When he visited the Cadbury works, snow lay on the ground but he was not deterred.

One more act of reconciliation was to be done, a personal and family one and in unexpected circumstances. Newman in these last years was on friendly terms with Jemima's family and had a special care for the only daughter, Jane, persuading her to draw on a small annuity of his own. It was to her that he commented on the better conditions for employing the talents of women – but the job she was offered was not one to stretch her capabilities since it was to keep house for a schoolmaster brother. Frank Newman had been in touch for years, despite the deep divisions of opinion between them. He outlived his brother the Cardinal and wrote a somewhat bitter account in 1891, *The Early History of Cardinal Newman*. Charles had died in 1884, as eccentric as ever. Two years earlier

Newman went alone to Tenby where Charles lodged, hoping to find him turning back to God in his old age but he died an atheist. With Harriett's little family Newman had had no contact for years.

Grace, now Mrs William Langford, was visiting England from Australia and staying with John Rickards Mozley, Jemima's son, and his wife Edith. On 1 August, 1880, Edith wrote to say that Grace would like to visit her uncle before she returned home in the autumn, but was shy of proposing it. A prompt reply came, written by William Neville. 'Thank you for your wish to see me. I embrace it readily....'[17] This was Newman's last letter and Grace was his last visitor. They sat for some time in a cold parlour, holding hands, and she said afterwards she wished she had removed her gloves. The old Cardinal was full of memories, of seeing Grace when she was three, of hearing about her son Willie. She told him that she had once met Maria Giberne in Rome, who had been very good to her and nursed her through an illness. Grace received his blessing and William Neville concluded the visit, handing on 'a small volume nicely bound of the Cardinal's earlier poems',[18] with his initials and her own inscribed in it. He told her how touched her uncle had been by her way of speaking of Miss Giberne. This was Saturday, 9 August, in the afternoon. Newman caught cold, and became ill with pneumonia in the early hours of the next morning. When he went to his bed for the last time, William Neville was amazed at his soldierly bearing, his firm step. He stood upright and unsupported and the careworn look had gone from his face. He looked resolute, calm, years younger. He died on Monday 11 August and his body was laid out in state in the Oratory church.

Thousands of people lined the streets to watch the funeral cortège pass from the Oratory to Rednal, where he was laid to rest in the same simple grave as Ambrose St John. Some reactions to his death could have been expected. English Catholics mourned him, Birmingham was proud of him, Oxford honoured him and the President of Trinity College was quick to accept his ticket to gain admittance to the funeral. Frank Newman refused to attend but Jemima's family came and were proud to be his relations. The number and the warmth of the tributes, however, must have surprised even his friends. Every newspaper in England wrote of him – the papers that were the organs of the Jewish community, the sporting fraternities, the local papers of unimportant towns. Messages came from abroad, the Oratory was deluged with telegrams and letters.

There were tributes from Anglicans describing what he had done for their Church and what he had done in England to break down hatred for Catholicism; there were many accounts of his books, his preaching, his intellectual stature. The women who had known him confined themselves to simple phrases, all adding up to statements that they thought him pre-eminently a man of saintly life. Emily Fortey ingenuously said that when she heard of his death she said the *Te Deum*, thanking God for him and also giving thanks that he had gone to his reward. She then said the *De Profundis*, the psalm usually recited for the repose of departed souls, not because she thought it necessary to pray him into heaven but because she thought she ought to do the customary thing. 'I do love him with all my heart', she added.[19] Elizabeth Bowden rejoined that he had gone 'to his immense reward'. Jane Todd, the seamstress in Scarborough used some perceptive phrases; he was 'carried through labours and fatigues of mind and body by the vision of the unseen'. Emily Bowles, who had retired from her post at the Oratory School and who lived with her brother Frederick spoke of Newman as 'our lost Saint'. Eleanor Watt said, 'Please God my prayers may be answered that I shall live to see his canonization begin before I die. He has certainly been canonized by the voice of the people'.

The nuns, especially the Sisters at Stone, added their loving tributes. Mother Frances Raphael was delighted to have the news that in Oxford the great bell of St Mary's was tolled for an hour to mark Newman's passing. She wrote several times, kindly remembering poor William Neville who was at once bereft of his great charge and inundated with business. Sister Mary Gabriel said that now there would be no more letters from Newman there was indeed a blank. One of the Sisters of Mercy at Hunter's Road, Birmingham (who remembered Newman's bringing Lavinia Wilson to the convent) used the same word. 'Birmingham without the dear, precious old Cardinal! What a blank!' She piously added the word '*Fiat*'.

Remembering Newman was something that went on and on, far beyond the months that followed his death. One little picture comes down to us from Cambridge where Isy von Hügel, in her later years, gathered some students from Newnham College at her house, Croft Cottage, and read to them regularly from Newman's works. These clever young women, going out to live their lives amongst the uncertainties of the twentieth century, had the privilege and the challenge of a university education, something which neither Newman nor his women friends had envisaged but which was implicitly desirable in his plan for an active, educated laity.

Once he thought of writing an account of the ladies he had known, putting them together in what he called a 'galaxy'. The idea was dropped – but the notion itself shows his regard for his faithful women. They did not shine as identical stars and some of them were small luminaries but his word, galaxy describes them very well.

Notes

(for details of books quoted, see Bibliography)

Introduction

1   LD XXI p.456
2   LD XIII p.419

Chapter 1

Section 1

1   DM, p.96
2   *Apologia,* p.96
3   LD XIX, p.415
4   S O'Faolain, *Newman's Way,* p.18
5   ibid., p.19
6   letter unpublished in LD
7   *Apologia,* p.96
8   LD XV, p.397
9   LD I, p.24
10 S O'Faolain, op.cit., p.80
11 *Apologia,* p.97
12 LD I, p.115
13 ibid., p.114
14 ibid., p.182
15 ibid.
16 ibid.
17 AW, p.176
18 ibid., p.175
19 ibid., p.63
20 LD I, p.157
21 AW, p.11

22　DM, p.7
23　LD I, p.298
24　LD II, p.7
25　AD, p.171
26　LD I, p.291
27　MT, vol.1, p.52
28　LD I, p.190
29　AW, p.207
30　ibid., p.196
31　LD II, p.55
32　ibid.
33　MT, op.cit., p.60
34　LD I, p.187
35　AW, p.79
36　ibid., p.206
37　DM, p.16
38　MT, op. cit., p.69
39　ibid., p.72
40　ibid.
41　LD II, p.49
42　LD II, p.62
43　LDV, p.314
44　MT, op. cit., p.155

Section 2

1　A Trollope, *Barchester Towers*, p.505
2　T. Mozley, *Reminiscences of Oriel & Oxford*, vol.2, p.44
3　LD V, p.82
4　ibid., p.25
5　ibid., p.314
6　LD IV, p.330
7　LD V, p.106
8　ibid., p.314
9　ibid.
10　ibid.
11　DM, p.66
12　*Apologia*, p.100
13　ibid., p.113
14　LD III, p.43
15　*Loss and Gain*, p.110
16　LD III, p.70
17　*Loss and Gain*, p.198
18　LD V, p.263
19　LD VII, p.285
20　MT, vol.1, p.237
21　ibid.

22   E Bowles' Memoir
23   ibid.
24   ibid.
25   MT, op. cit., p.277
26   DM, p.121
27   ibid., p.129
28   ibid., p.133
29   ibid.
30   ibid., p.135
31   ibid.
32   *Loss and Gain*, p.185
33   DM, p.141
34   ibid., p.142
35   unpublished letter
36   ibid.
37   MT, op.cit., p.350
38   LD XI, p.8
39   DM, p.165
40   ibid., p.16
41   MT, op.cit., p.606
42   DM, p.199

Chapter 2

Section 1

1   AW, p.137
2   *Apologia*, p.310
3   DM, p.111
4   MT, vol.1, p.330
5   ibid., p.331
6   ibid., pp.341–342
7   LD XI, p.131
8   ibid., p.187
9   DM, p.174
10   ibid., p.170
11   LD XI, p.255
12   ibid., pp.272–273
13   LD XII, p.45

Section 2

1   R Flaxman, *A Woman Styled Bold*, p.111
2   MT, vol.1, p.383
3   E Bowles' Memoir

4   R Flaxman, op.cit., p.113
5   E Bowles' Memoir
6   R Flaxman, op.cit., p.222
7   ibid., p.219
8   ibid., p.222
9   E Bowles' Memoir
10   LD XII, p.433
11   J. Pope-Hennessy, *Anthony Trollope*, p.366
12   ibid., p.314
13   LD XV, p.16
14   ibid.
15   ibid., p.33
16   LD XXII, p.4
17   LD XVI, p.228
18   ibid., p.480

Section 3

1   MT, vol.1, p.209
2   LD XI, p.96
3   ibid.
4   ibid., p.108
5   unpublished letter
6   LD XI, p.102
7   Unpublished letter
8   T Mozley, *Reminiscences of Oriel & Oxford*, vol.2, p.43
9   LD XIII, p.414
10   ibid., p.103
11   MT, op.cit., p.536
12   Unless otherwise indicated all quotations in this part of the narra-
     tive are from M R Giberne's unpublished account.
13   LD XIV, p.460
14   LD XV, p.14
15   ibid., p.24
16   ibid., p.233
17   ibid., p.425
18   ibid., p.504
19   MT, vol 2, p.133
20   ibid. pp.133–134
21   LD XVI, p.336

Section 4

1   LD XVI, p.365
2   LD XIX, p.392
3   LD III, p.7. 'Rowings' means cramming

4   LD XVI, p.251
5   MT, vol.1, p.321
6   LD XX, p.101
7   LD XIV, p.201
8   LD XVI, p.103
9   ibid.
10 LD XVI, p.66
11 LD XIX, pp.268–272
12 ibid., p.273
13 LD XXI, p.44
14 ibid.
15 ibid., p.111
16 LD XVI, p.503
17 LD XIX, p.189
18 ibid., p.467
19 LD XX, p.452
20 unpublished letter
21 LD XXIV, p.61
22 unpublished letter
23 unpublished letter

Section 5

1   LD XIV, p.211
2   ibid., p.469
3   LD XX, pp.209–210
4   LD XII, p.217
5   ibid.
6   unpublished letter
7   LD XXI, p.57
8   LD XII, p.265–268
9   ibid., p.273
10 ibid., p.377
11 LD XXI, p.331
12 ibid., p.387

Chapter 3

Section 1

1   DM, p.109
2   K Tillotson, *Novels of the 1840's*, p.5
3   ibid.
4   DM, p.120
5   H J Coleridge, *Lady Georgiana Fullerton*, p.28
6   ibid.

7   Quoted in R L Wolff, *Gains and Losses*, p.78
8   LD XV, p.141
9   ibid.
10   ibid., p.237
11   ibid.
12   LD XI, p.149
13   DM, p.170
14   Quoted in R L Wolff, op.cit., p.83
15   ibid., p.85
16   ibid.
17   LD XIII, pp.345–346
18   LD XVI, pp.475–476
19   H J Coleridge, op.cit., p.407
20   ibid., p.387
21   ibid., p.366
22   LD XXI, p.96

Section 2

1   K Tillotson, *Novels of the 1840's*, p.134. Quoted from an essay of
     Newman's, 1843.
2   *Loss and Gain*, p.199
3   K Tillotson, op.cit., p.130
4   E Bowles, *In the Carmargue*, p.233
5   LD XXVII, p.77
6   ibid., p.8
7   LD XXI, p.440
8   ibid.
9   ibid., p.457
10   LD XX, pp.445–448
11   ibid., pp.453–454
12   unpublished letter
13   ibid.
14   ibid.
15   LD XXVI, p.146
16   ibid., p.141
17   unpublished letter
18   ibid.
19   ibid.
20   LD XXVI, pp.5–6
21   LD XIX, p.479
22   LD XXVII, p.207
23   LD XXX, p.111
24   ibid., p.113
25   ibid.
26   *Saturday Review*, 28 Nov. 1885, pp.719–720
27   V Glendinning, *Anthony Trollope*, p.395

28 LD XXI, p.409
29 LD XXVI, p.87
30 LD XXVII, p.393
31 LD XXIII, p.110
32 LD XXI, p.74
33 ibid., p.75
34 ibid., p.76
35 ibid., p.156
36 LD XXII, p.86
37 LD XX, p.453
38 LD XXX, p.316
39 unpublished letter
40 ibid.

Section 3

1 LD XX, p.471
2 ibid., p.465
3 National Trust handbook for Baddesley Clinton written by Geoffrey Haworth, p.37. It is quoting from a memorandum book in Rebecca Dering's handwriting – Baddesley Library ref. OFF 45.
4 ibid. The quotation cannot be traced to its source.
5 Quotation from appendix to E H Dering's novel *The Ban of Maplethorpe*.
6 LD XXI, p.381
7 LD XXVI, p.122
8 LD XXV, p.209
9 LD XXII, pp.193–195
10 LD XXVI, p.275
11 ibid., p.281
12 LD XXVII, p.358
13 ibid.
14 LD XXVIII, p.361
15 ibid., p.22
16 ibid., p.23

Chapter 5

Section 1

1 LD VI, pp.84–85
2 LD XII, p.215
3 MT vol.1, p.485
4 LD XVIII, p.37
5 S Leslie, *Letters of H Vaughan & Lady Herbert*, p.20
6 LD XXIX, p.181

7   T Lever, *The Herberts of Wilton*, p.230
8   E Herbert, *Three Phases of Christian Love*, p.169
9   unpublished letter
10 S Leslie, op.cit., p.451
11 MT op.cit., p.458
12 LD XIII, p.103
13 ibid., p.239
14 LD XIV, p.291
15 ibid.
16 Quotations from Father Caswall's notes come from papers at the Birmingham Oratory.
17 This leaflet is also in the Oratory.
18 This is also from Father Caswall's notes.
19 P. Murray, *Newman the Oratorian*, p.311

Section 2

1   LD XIX, p.12
2   ibid., pp.260–261
3   LD XX, p.438
4   LD XXI, pp.468–469
5   ibid.
6   LD XXII, p.20
7   ibid., p.186
8   LD XXVIII, p.86
9   LD XXVII, p.228
10 LD XXIX, p.332
11 LD XXX, p.301
12 ibid., p.398
13 LD XXXI, p.188
14 ibid., p.273

Section 3

1   LD XVIII, p.444
2   ibid., p.17
3   LD XVII, p.510
4   LD XVIII, p.153
5   ibid., p.253
6   LD XXIV, p.216
7   LD XIX, p.179
8   ibid., p.188
9   ibid., p.474
10 LD XX, pp.21–22
11 MT vol.2, pp.252–253
12 ibid.

13   LD XX, p.91
14   ibid., p.119
15   ibid., p.96
16   ibid., p.146
17   MT op.cit., p.271
18   letter quoted by A Nash, *Newman's Idea of a School* (no paging)
19   LD XX, p.143
20   ibid., p.187
21   LD XXIV, p.221

Chapter 6

Section 1

1   LD XXII, pp.87–88
2   ibid.
3   LD XXIII, p.255
4   LD XXVII, p.247
5   LD XXIV, p.323
6   ibid., p.338
7   ibid., p.325
8   ibid.
9   ibid., p.417
10   ibid., pp.337–338
11   LD XXV, pp.326–327
12   LD XXIV, p.324
13   ibid., p.341
14   ibid.
15   LD XXV, p.216
16   ibid., quoted in introductory note
17   ibid., p.62
18   ibid., p.101
19   LD XXIV, p.162
20   LD XXV, p.68
21   ibid., p.39
22   ibid., p.43
23   LD XXVII, p.197
24   LD XXV, p.183
25   LD XXVI, p.206
26   ibid., p.197
27   ibid., p.400
28   LD XXVII, p.314
29   ibid., p.395
30   LD XXVIII, p.11
31   ibid., p.13
32   LD XXIV, p.280

33   ibid.
34   ibid., pp.274–276
35   ibid.
36   LD XXVI, p.156

Section 2

1   LD XXVIII, pp.283–284
2   ibid.
3   LD XXIX, quoted in Introduction, p.xiii
4   LD XXIX, p.20
5   ibid., p.22
6   ibid., p.32
7   ibid., p.47
8   ibid., p.60
9   ibid., p.63
10   ibid., p.148
11   ibid., pp.429–430
12   ibid., p.430
13   quoted in S Foister, *Cardinal Newman 1801–90*, p.75
14   LD XXVIII, p.334
15   LD XXXI, p.194
16   LD XXX, pp.109–110
17   ibid., p.183
18   ibid., p.404
19   LD XXI, p.225
20   from papers at the Birmingham Oratory
21   LD XXIX, p.241
22   ibid., p.226
23   LD XXX, p.49
24   LD XXXI, p.102
25   L Sieveking, *The Eye of the Beholder*, p.279
26   ibid., p.278
27   ibid., p.279

Section 3

1   AW, p.24
2   ibid.
3   LD XX, p.443
4   ibid., p.444
5–8 unpublished letters. The account of her visit to Littlemore is from
     the same source.
9   R D Middleton, *Magdalen Studies*, pp.40–41
10   unpublished letter
11   LD XXX, pp.417–418

12 LD XXX, quoted in the Introduction, p.xiv
13 MT vol.2, p.618
14 ibid., p.617
15 LD XXX, p.27
16 ibid., p.17
17 LD XXXI, p.299
18 ibid.
19 The phrases quoted in this and the next paragraph are from the letters of condolence at the Birmingham Oratory.

Bibliography

Primary Sources

Dessain, Charles Stephen et al., ed: The *Letters and Diaries* of *John Henry Newman* Vols. I–VI (Oxford University Press, 1978–84) Vol. VII (Oxford University Press, 1995) Vols. XI–XXII (London, Nelson, 1961–72) Vols. XXIII–XXXI (Oxford University Press, 1973–7) LD in Notes.

Mozley, Anne, ed: *Letters and Correspondence of John Henry Newman during his life in the English Church*, 2 vols. (London, 1891)

Mozley, Dorothea: *Newman Family Letters* (London, SPCK, 1962) DM in notes

Murray, Placid, ed: *Newman the Oratorian: His Unpublished Oratory Papers* (Leominster, Fowler Wright Books 1980)

Newman, J.H. *Apologia pro Vita Sua* (Collins Fontana edition, 1959)

——*Loss and Gain* (Burns and Oates Universe Books edition, 1962)

——*Meditations and Devotions* (Longmans edition, 1953)

Tristram, Henry, ed: *John Henry Newman: Autobiographical Writings* (London and New York, Sheed and Ward, 1956). AW in notes

I have also made much use of unpublished letters at the Birmingham Oratory, particularly those of Newman's correspondents. The Oratory had also supplied a Memoir by Miss Bowles, Memoirs by Miss Giberne, including a detailed account of her mission to Italy to collect witnesses for the Achilli trial, and notes by Father Edward Caswall on work in the Oratory parish and beyond it.

Mother Margaret Hallahan's Dominican Sisters at Stone in Staffordshire allowed me to use their archive material, letters of the foundress and a Memoir of Mother Mary Imelda Poole, written by her sister, Elizabeth Anstice.

Secondary Sources

Agnew, Emily: *Geraldine: A Tale of Conscience*, 2 vol. (London, 1837) with a third published in 1839

Bowles, Emily: *St Martin's Home or Work for Women* (Dublin, 1864)

——*In the Carmargue* (London, 1873)

Coleridge, H.J.: *Life of Lady Georgiana Fullerton*, translation from the French life by Mrs. Augustus Craven (London, 1888)

Convent of the Good Shepherd, Finchley: *A Daughter of the Venerable Mother Pelletier* (published for private circulation, 1902)

Dering, Edward Heneage: *Memoirs of Lady Chatterton*, with some passages from her diary (London, 1878)

Dessain, Charles Stephen: 'Heart Speaks to Heart: Margaret Mary Hallahan and John Henry Newman,' sermon published in *The Month*, 1965

Devas, Francis: *The Life of Mother Magdalen Taylor of the Sacred Heart* (London, 1927)

Dictionary of National Biography to 1900

Drane, Mother Francis Raphael: *The Life of Mother Margaret Hallahan* (London, 1869)

Flaxman, Radegund: *A Woman Styled Bold*: The Life of Cornelia Connelly 1809–1879 (Darton, Longman & Todd, 1991)

Foister, Susan: *Cardinal Newman, A Centenary Exhibition* (National Portrait Gallery Publications, 1990)

Fullerton, Lady Georgiana: *Ellen Middleton: A Tale*, 3 vols. (London, 1844)

——*Grantley Manor: A Tale*, 3 vols. (London, 1847)

Gilley, Sheridan: *Newman and his Age* (London, Darton, Longman and Todd, 1990)

Gillow, Joseph: *Bibliographical Dictionary of the English Catholics* (London, 1885 and later)

Glendinning, Victoria: *Trollope* (London, Hutchinson, 1992)

Hardiman, Malcolm: *Six Victorian Thinkers* (London and New York, Manchester University Press, 1991)

Herbert, Lady Mary: *Three Phases of Christian Love* (London, 1867)

Ker, Ian: *John Henry Newman* (Oxford University Press, 1990)

Leslie, Shane ed: *Letters of Herbert Cardinal Vaughan and Lady Herbert of Lea* (London, Burns and Oates, 1942)

Lever, Fresham: *The Herberts of Wilton* (London, John Murray, 1967)

Middleton, R.D.: *Magdalen Studies* (London, 1936)

Mozley, Harriett: *Family Adventures* (London, 1852)

Mozley, Thomas: *Reminiscences Chiefly of Oriel College and the Oxford Movement*, 2 vols. (London, 1882)

Nash, Andrew: *Newman's Idea of a School* (published by the Oratory School Association, 1990)

Newsome, David: *The Convert Cardinals, J.H. Newman and H.E. Manning* (London, John Murray, 1903)

Norris, Henry: *Baddesley Clinton, Its Manor, Church and Hall* (London 1897)

O'Brian, Susan: 'Terra Incognita: The Nun in the Nineteenth Century,' *Past and Present*, November 1988.

O'Faolain, Sean: *Newman's Way* (London, Longmans, 1952)

Pope Hennessy, James: *Anthony Trollope* (London, Jonathan Cape, 1971)

S.M.C. *Steward of Souls* (London, Longmans, 1952)

Sieveking, Lance: *The Eye of the Beholder* (London, Hulton Press, 1957)

Tillotson, Kathleen: *Novels of the Eighteen-Forties* (Oxford University Press, 1954)

Trevor, Meriol: *Newman: The Pillar of the Cloud* (London, Macmillan, 1962)

——*Newman: Light in Winter* (London, Macmillan, 1962) MT in notes.

Trollope, Anthony: *Barchester Towers* (1857 World's Classics edition, Oxford University Press, 1990)

——*Lady Anna* (1874, World's Classics edition, Oxford University Press, 1990)

Wells, Ruth Gilpin: *A Woman of Her Time and Ours* (Charlotte, NC, USA, Laney-Smith Inc. 1988)

Wolff, Robert Lee: *Gains and Losses: Novels of Faith and Doubt in Victorian England* (London, John Murray, 1977)

Index